The Roots of War in the 21st Century

Geography, Hegemony, and Politics in Asia-Pacific

Randall Doyle

UNIVERSITY PRESS OF AMERICA,® INC.
Lanham • Boulder • New York • Toronto • Plymouth, UK

Copyright © 2009 by
University Press of America,® Inc.
4501 Forbes Boulevard
Suite 200
Lanham, Maryland 20706
UPA Acquisitions Department (301) 459-3366

Estover Road
Plymouth PL6 7PY
United Kingdom

Library of Congress Control Number: 2009928914
ISBN: 978-0-7618-4629-1 (clothbound : alk. paper)
ISBN: 978-0-7618-4630-7 (paperback : alk. paper)
eISBN: 978-0-7618-4731-4

Dedicated to

Howard Zinn and Noam Chomsky

Contents

Acknowledgments

This is the section where an author feels ethically and morally compelled to acknowledge the significant assistance and contributions of the many individuals who participated in the creation, development, support, and, eventually, the publication of an idea, or thesis, that the writer conjured up years ago. In this particular case, I have many people to thank in this section of the book. This book was written during my time at Central Michigan University (CMU). Therefore, as expected, many of the individuals mentioned are administrators, professors, or staff personnel at CMU.

To complete a book is often an exhausting experience and it is common that the memory of such a demanding ordeal is simply to be avoided—if possible. This is my fourth book. However, I have not fallen—yet—into this state of mind because I am presently in an academic environment that promotes quality scholarship and provides the proper clerical, financial and institutional mechanisms that are absolutely necessary for finishing any serious scholarly project. This constructive and supportive environment exists at CMU. Thus, the individuals listed below have played significant roles in the publication of this book.

My gratitude and my appreciation for the following is boundless.

President Michael Rao is an ardent believer in internationalizing education at Central Michigan University. His leadership and support for my speaking, teaching and writing on international topics and the global community are invaluable. Thus, Dr. Rao has provided the necessary leadership for the university's mission to expand its educational curriculum and vision for its student body.

The Dean of Humanities and the Social Behavioral Sciences, Dr. Gary Shapiro, has enthusiastically supported this particular project on Asia-Pacific. Again, a strong supporter of international education, Dr. Shapiro and I first met, in 2005, before I gave a talk on Japan and the atomic bombing of Hiroshima in 1945. I have found him to be a constant supporter of research *and* teaching on East Asia, Modern China and Asia-Pacific.

The Chair of the CMU History Department, Dr. Timothy Hall, has provided unstinting support for this project. His vision of creating a history department that offers courses focused upon *all* regions of the world has lifted the department's academic credibility to a new level of respectability and stature.

I also want to recognize the substantial efforts of the history department's executive secretary Annette Davis. Annette constructed the book's bibliography and she also agreed to read the entire manuscript. I wanted a fresh pair of eyes to read it, and to recognize any unintentional errors of prose or presentation. She did a great job on all accounts.

The Office of Research and Sponsored Programs (ORSP) at CMU has been an enormous help. The three primary individuals, who have been irreplaceable in terms assisting me in acquiring the necessary funding for my research trips are the following: Research and Program Officer Deborah Clark, Administrative Secretary Maria Bourdet McNeel and Executive Secretary Deborah Stanek. ALL of whom have played vital roles in helping me obtain the financial assistance necessary to travel to Australia, China, Japan, South Korea and Vietnam.

Professors Guilan Wang and Patrick Shan are two other individuals that I feel must be recognized for their contributions to my book. Dr Wang, the former Director of the Office of International Education at CMU, and now Assistant Dean at Roger Williams University, was a great help on two crucial matters: financial assistance and providing me contacts within China. Both of which are vital to the success of any project, particularly for a writer traveling throughout China. Dr. Shan, who teaches Chinese History at Grand Valley State University and is also a fine scholar and teacher in his own right, has been a wonderful colleague and friend. Over the years, Patrick has provided me with many insights concerning modern China, and he also introduced me to Professor Sun Ling Ling, a Research Associate at the Institute of Japanese Studies within the Chinese Academy of Social Sciences (CASS). CASS is recognized as the most prominent think-tank in China. Professor Sun has also provided me with additional contacts in Beijing, China. Altogether, these individuals have vastly improved and extended my reach and understanding of modern China.

I also want to recognize a number of individuals who graciously provided me assistance in writing this book. Their acts of cooperation, generosity and kindness greatly assisted me in completing this book project. Thus, I feel compelled to recognize these scholars and representatives of various research institutions. To all, I am deeply grateful. Please forgive me if I have forgotten to mention your name below. Your comments and observations will certainly be recognized within the footnotes and text of the book. The following individuals are noted in no particular order – alphabetically or in importance. Thus, *all* those mentioned below were important in the making of this book:

Noam Chomsky, Department of Modern Languages and Linguistics, MIT

Howard Zinn, Professor Emeritus, Boston University

Jenni Jeremy, Development Librarian, The Bob Hawke Prime Ministerial Library University of South Australia

Zhang Yuping, Associate Professor and Vice-Dean of College of Humanities and Law North China University of Technology (NCUT), Beijing, China

Guo Tao, Dean of the Division of International Cooperation and Exchanges North China University of Technology (NCUT), Beijing, China

Lifeng Jiang, Director of Institute of Japanese Studies, Chinese Academy of Social Sciences (CASS), Beijing, China

Sun Ling Ling, Research Associate, Institute of Japanese Studies, Chinese Academy of Social Sciences (CASS), Beijing, China

Norio Suzuki, Political Philosophy and International Studies, Aichi University, Nagoya, Japan

Goro Takahashi, Deputy Director, International Center for Chinese Studies (ICCS), Aichi University, Nagoya, Japan

Introduction

The 21st century represents a new historical epoch in which historians and other types of analysts and experts will evaluate, either immediately or in the future, its importance and significance to human history. Already a multitude of perspectives and earnest forecasts are being presented by a plethora of associations, forums and institutions with concern to the present century's potential—good and bad. In Asia-Pacific, many believe the 21st century potentially represents a new opportunity for the region to create a new beginning and identity for itself. This sense of potential optimism is important because history has clearly shown that the Asia-Pacific region has been bedeviled by various forms and sources of indigenous and foreign oppression (particularly by Western and Japanese colonialism and imperialism) which has resulted in a terrifying degree of death, destruction, exploitation and war.

In point of fact, for the past four centuries within the Asia-Pacific region, millions of people have perished and indigenous cultures have been humiliated, subjugated and brutally suppressed. Hence, a strong case can be made by historians and scholars that the region's present-day political volatility is really nothing more than the historical manifestation—represented by instability and turmoil—usually associated with a haunting and lingering dysfunctional and violent past.

Nevertheless, despite these destructive and divisive historical forces, an undeniable geopolitical epoch is now evolving upon the global stage—the 'Asia-Pacific Century'. What this means, or will mean, to world history remains speculative at best. Yet, today, most global analysts and observers agree that the world is indeed witnessing a new and significant degree of economic development and social evolution throughout Asia-Pacific. As a consequence, the region itself is increasingly seen as being one of the most important in the world. As expected, its future influence is just now beginning to be acknowledged and understood by regional scholars. Thus, their collective attention is now being re-directed and re-calibrated from the post-WWII U.S.-Atlantic paradigm toward the more dangerous, dynamic, undefined and unpredictable arena now represented by the U.S. and Asia-Pacific.

Many point to the fact that China and India, currently representing approximately one-third of humanity, are just now re-establishing themselves to their prior historic standing. Western intervention, along with domestic cultural factors and political decision-making within these Asian behemoths, had without a doubt interrupted and constricted their natural social development and economic growth—which, in turn, diminished their hegemonic status in Asia and Asia-Pacific.

However, in 2009, there is a growing consensus among regional and global observers concerning the rise of Asia-Pacific. They are absolutely convinced that the world community is presently witnessing a fundamental restructuring of the global hierarchical system itself. With regards to China, specifically, though it could be applied to Asia-Pacific as a whole, it is believed that Napoleon Bonaparte had once stated centuries ago, "Let China sleep, for when she wakes, she will shake the world."[1]

We are now approaching the end of the first decade of the twenty-first century, and it is widely acknowledged that China is, indeed, at the transitional stage of re-emerging from an extended hegemonic absence. Since the early 19th century, China has tragically experienced cultural humiliation, societal devastation and millions of deaths by their own hands and by those of foreigners—primarily American, European and Japanese. However, during the early years of the 21st century, the tide has now irrefutably taken a turn toward a more favorable outcome for the Middle Kingdom. This good fortune for the Chinese people has had a traumatic affect upon the Western industrialized world.

Thankfully, China and the Asia-Pacific region are not seen as 'evil' by most U.S. workers, even in my adopted home-state of Michigan. Yet, in 2009, the Asia-Pacific region is certainly perceived by millions of workers in the West as an emerging threat to their economic futures. As a result, the much proclaimed globalization of the world's economic activities and the Phoenix-like rise of the Asian juggernaut over the past quarter century, are increasingly viewed with a greater degree of fear and skepticism by American politicians, voters and workers, respectively. Instinctively, a majority of American workers acknowledge that their future economic status is now at the mercy of those unseen and undefined market forces that can literally destroy a productive and vibrant community almost overnight.

As expected, millions in the West have learned the hard way that their economic destinies are now tenuous, at best, due to the activities and decisions by powerful U.S.-based multinationals. These corporate entities are steadily moving their assembly production and research facilities and literally millions of good paying jobs to the Asia-Pacific region. Corporate bottom lines, as always, are increasingly reflecting an almost religious commitment toward reducing in-house administrative expenditures, labor costs in their manufacturing sector, and the demands of their stockholders who are continually clamoring for larger returns on their investments.

Thus, in short, continued profitability remains, of course, the primary driving force of these transnational economic giants. To be fair, the global competition within their respective realm of business has truly become Darwinian in the 'Age of Globalization'. Therefore, these multinationals constantly pursue new geographical venues that consist of ever-cheaper labor, less taxes and non-existing regulatory laws (especially with concern to labor unions and the environment) in which to produce their products and maintain their expected market shares and profitability. In truth, this form of predatory economics is the natural development and outcome within the cutthroat business world that has become increasingly amoral and cold-blooded in its entrepreneurial endeavors.

If this nightmarish economic situation is not enough to frighten most workers in the West, now they are discovering that their employment is not the only segment of their lives being affected by the emergence of the Pacific Century. Specifically, the U.S. consumer has also discovered, to its consternation that Asia-Pacific's rampant growth has now begun to substantially affect the availability and cost of much needed primary resources, such as oil, gas, food, metals, lumber and other valued materials.

It is now Asia-Pacific banks, primarily Chinese and Japanese, that are now financing America's reckless and irresponsible fiscal and trade policies, not to mention America's misguided wars in Iraq and Afghanistan, which have produced stunning national deficits and has placed the future fiscal health of the U.S. economy in a very dangerous and vulnerable position.

Put succinctly, America's global aspirations (read: empire) during the 21st century are increasingly dependent upon the economic conditions and realities emerging in Asia-Pacific. Specifically, the region's overall wealth accumulation and future development will play an absolutely key role in our own future capacity to function and remain a viable global force.

Paradoxically, Asia-Pacific's enhanced fiscal capabilities are now vital in assisting the U.S. in meeting its own burgeoning and frightening financial burdens: huge annual budgetary and trade deficits; a breath-taking overall national debt that has now topped 10 trillion dollars—and the financial hemorrhaging doesn't appear to be stopping anytime soon. Tragically, these monetary crises are indeed self-inflicted. Americans are now witnessing the steady decline of the U.S. dollar internationally, the steady erosion of our global influence and power, and the rising costs of commodities which is steadily undermining the standard of living for most Americans.

As a result, most regional observers now acknowledge that the destinies of both America and Asia-Pacific (particularly East Asia) are now irrevocably intertwined. If a negotiated understanding was to occur within this vast region, relating specifically toward creating a new economic and security framework, then quite possibly peace and prosperity could remain as the status quo. However, these potential foundational pillars upon which a new regional power-paradigm can be constructed in the Asia-Pacific region during the 21st century remains, at the present time, purely speculative.

If we accept the potential viability of such a geostrategic premise, which will certainly affect the lives of Americans and the people of Asia-Pacific, then, perhaps, such a common understanding can be arrived at without contrived rhetorical arrogance, hegemonic hubris or nationalistic rancor, because all parties understand intuitively what is at risk. Right now, all nations, but particularly the major powers, within Asia-Pacific are presently calculating, deliberating and deciding what issues or factors are considered to be vital to their own national interests. And, that is the focus of this book—to identify how potentially geography, hegemony, and politics could be the "roots of war" in the Asia-Pacific region, and to evaluate whether we can avoid conflict in the 21st century due to the existence of these factors. I believe the collective fates of both the U.S. and Asia-Pacific have converged and their future influence and relevance in global affairs is greatly dependent upon a mutual commitment toward the eradication of these potential 'roots of war'.

Put simply, the only way the Asia-Pacific region avoids a major catastrophe or conflagration, if not outright self-destruction, is too create a new future-oriented blueprint that establishes a new and understood economic and military coordinating structure for the entire region. Perhaps, it could be called the East Asia Security and Trade Organization (EASTO). It would provide a constructive venue for all the nations within the region to negotiate important economic and military issues, while respecting an understood hierarchy of power and, most importantly, the sovereignty of each nation would be acknowledged and respected by fellow members. However, the key factors within this confederation must be the belief that *every* nation can contribute and provide input toward achieving short and long-term economic growth and also be able to participate in the decision-making process in achieving security throughout the region.

Therefore, it is my belief that the key geopolitical issues confronting the Asia-Pacific region, at this juncture in the 21st century, are the following:

a) Recognizing a new hegemonic structure in Asia-Pacific based upon the realities of geography, hegemony and politics
b) The recognition that geopolitical relations amongst the primary powers in the Asia-Pacific region are currently being re-evaluated and transformed due to the re-emergence of China and the Asia-Pacific region as a whole
c) Will the Asia-Pacific region become the 'Pacific Century' in the 21st century, or will the Asia-Pacific region suffer the same fate as pre-WWI Europe?

It is these crucial realities, topics and questions that must be dealt with directly in a comprehensive and detailed manner amongst the nations of Asia-Pacific. The eventual agreed upon framework and language will no doubt demand a concentrated and substantial degree of energy and time. Simply put, Asia-Pacific is experiencing an historic epoch due to the irrepressible and transformative revolutions occurring with the areas of global communications, information and transportation systems, as well as the continued application and integration of technology in our daily lives. This wave of techno-modernity continues unabated throughout all corners of the world.

Therefore, the *real* challenges confronting present-day Asia-Pacific, which is constantly in a state of flux and unpredictability, is how does it develop a new regional super-structure peacefully? Can modernity with its increased capacity to enhance an individual's, and a nation's, ability to learn, travel, and develop, decrease the ever-present tensions and potential for destructiveness that is clearly associated with the region's recent past? Are the region's major powers willing to cooperate and work with the middle and minor powers toward developing a new regional language, methodology and an organization that will enhance and promote the collective and national securities of all Asia-Pacific nations? Finally, can the major powers also ensure the fair distribution of critical and vital resources that are essential for the continued growth of the economies within the region?

It should be noted that currently there are significant voices within the U.S. foreign policy establishment who strongly believe that in the relatively near future, due to the overall empowerment of Asia-Pacific, particularly China, that conflict will almost certainly occur somewhere within the region. The primary "root" cause for their concern is the belief that America and China are both driven and immersed in a non-stop pursuit to achieve "hegemonic" influence and power within Asia-Pacific. At the end of the first decade of the 21st century, these hawkish analysts see serious tensions developing between these two major powers, and the potential for regional conflict—similar to what happened between the U.S. and Japan during the first half of the 20th century.

Though, a Pearl Harbor-type event is not anticipated between the U.S. and China in the immediate future, nevertheless, there is always the possibility that regional tensions could erupt into a catastrophic war between these two Pacific powers due to issues relating to their hegemonic status within Asia-Pacific. Presently, it is primarily conservatives within the Washington establishment and like-minded think-tanks in the nation's capitol, who are the most vociferous believers of such a scenario developing in the region during the early decades of the 21st century. Yet, at the present time, there is no real substantive evidence, or overt indicators, to support such a gloomy and apocalyptic geopolitical analysis.

Nevertheless, there are others who strenuously believe that conflict will occur within Asia-Pacific, but not due to primarily a hegemonic struggle between these Asia-Pacific titans (America and China, or even China and Japan), but instead it will be due to the diminishing availability of the world's natural resources. In essence, 'resource wars' will become increasingly the "root" cause for conflict and instability within the region because all Asian nations will be pursuing the same shrinking pool of available resources in order to maintain the sustainability of their respective economies. And, already, there is emerging evidence that tensions are present amongst the nations of Asia-Pacific due to growing concerns related to the availability of commodities such as oil, gas, food and fresh water.

Finally, can 'history' prevent these potential apocalyptic scenarios from occurring? Due to the exponential growth and power of various communications and information systems throughout the world, especially for the wealthier nations in Asia-Pacific, widespread historical ignorance can not be used as a blanket excuse for any future conflict. I have learned quite well from my almost ten years in the region that every indigenous culture uses and exploits history to justify its existence and value as a people and society.

However, during my years of living in various Asian nations, studying Asian history, and traveling throughout the Asia continent, I have encountered examples of history being used to justify heinous and terrible crimes against humanity in several of these nations. Thus, the question must be asked: In the 21st century, can the revolutionary advancements in communications, information and technology neutralize the potentiality of history being used, again, as a "root" cause for death, destruction and war within the Asia-Pacific region?

In conclusion, my book will examine these potential "roots of war" that could quite possibly create, or represent, the future basis for conflict in the Asia-Pacific region during the 21st century. I am of the belief that these "roots of war", which lie deep within the psyche and soils of Asia-Pacific, can be mostly eradicated in order for this region to develop and reach its fullest potential. Yet, I am not naïve to the fact that the human factor remains the greatest unknown (and danger) for this region. The emergence of the 'Pacific Century' is neither an illusion nor a false creation by anxious geo-strategists or hopeful historians who have dedicated their professional careers to analyzing and writing about Asian history. Quite the contrary, it is indeed, from an historical standpoint, a real and substantive human and regional development of great consequence.

Yet, in the end, it will be these same geo-strategists and historians who will evaluate this period of global history (the first decades of the 21st century). They will determine whether this specific period of time had represented unprecedented economic growth, relative peace and widespread prosperity throughout Asia-Pacific, and that the world had also witnessed the dramatic re-emergence of this ancient, diversified and dynamic region. And, that literally hundreds of millions of human beings escaped abject poverty and/or became part of the global middle-class. In short, this era represented an historic epoch.

Or, will they determine it was the beginning of a period reflecting emerging economic, military, political and social strife, within Asia-Pacific, due to numerous disparities and injustices. As a consequence, another tragic and destructive war(s) ensued, like so many in the 19th and 20th centuries, because the people and the nations of Asia-Pacific were unable to overcome their lust for power, incapable of rectifying and resolving the sins of history and, finally, unable to formulate a proper distribution system of the world's valued resources. Thus, sadly, these human frailties and shortcomings led to the eventual demise of an era that represented the greatest economic development in world history.

Which historical scenario will prevail—peace and prosperity or war and destruction? No one knows. This book will make a modest attempt in identifying a number of the challenges, dangers ("roots of war") and prospects that lie ahead for the Asia-Pacific region in the 21st century.

NOTE

1. James Kynge, *China Shakes the World: A Titan's Rise and Troubled Future—and the Challenge for America* (Boston: Houghton Mifflin Company, 2006), p. xiv.

Overview

My book has been divided into (3) sections:

Part I: Hegemonic Power in Asia-Pacific
Part II: Significant Powers in Asia-Pacific
Part III: The Asia-Pacific Century

The first part will deal with the new geographical, historical and hegemonic power dynamics emerging throughout the East Asian Hemisphere. Never before in history, within this expansive region, has so many nations (America, Australia, China, Japan and South Korea) been powerful—economically and militarily—simultaneously. This irrefutable fact alone makes the Asia-Pacific region very complicated and dangerous. As expected, the future role of the U.S. within this vital region is presently being intensely debated within the corridors of the American government. Nevertheless, a geopolitical stratagem for Asia-Pacific remains elusive and undefined.

There is one indisputable point of fact, and it is often overlooked or unacknowledged by analysts or experts, it is that the U.S. has a different economic and military relationship with each one of these Asia-Pacific powers. This hard reality further complicates a process—already difficult—in creating an overall solution, or strategy, for the continued maintenance of peace and stability in this increasingly integrated but tense neighborhood.

Therefore, during the next few years it will indeed take an enormous effort and commitment by the American government, and its various foreign policy entities to create and implement an adaptable, comprehensive and flexible 'power-paradigm' strategy for this volatile region. Without question, trying to identify common interests and formulate policies that recognize and reflect the respective vital interests of each country (including the smaller and weaker nations as well) will be unquestionably difficult, if not impossible on some contentious and historic issues between these proud nations.

As expected, geography, hegemonic power and politics will be the major determinants within the enigmatic and evolving environment of Asia-Pacific. If a consensus can be negotiated by the significant powers, and acceptable to the smaller powers, on these (3) fundamental factors, perhaps, just maybe, the 21st century will be an era that represents hope and prosperity within a region that has often experienced war and destruction since the early 19th century.

The second part will examine the recent economic, military and political developments which are transforming the regional foreign policies of the major powers within the Asia-Pacific realm: America, Australia, China, Japan and South Korea. I decided not to include India in this work because it is simply not seen as a part of the Asia-Pacific region. Though, I do recognize the fact that India may indeed someday have a profound affect upon Asia-Pacific, but, for now, it is not viewed nor accepted as being a major force within Asia-Pacific.

And, I have also decided not to specifically focus upon the Association of Southeast Asian Nations (ASEAN) as a significant force because the major Asia-Pacific powers—identified in this section of the book—view this 10-member association as primarily an economic entity that provides valuable and voluminous amounts of natural resources to the major economic power-houses within Asia-Pacific. Though, once again, I do recognize that several members, such as Singapore and the Philippines, participate in regional security operations and planning. Nevertheless, ASEAN remains extremely vulnerable to the unpredictable ebb and flow of the hegemonic power dynamics existing within the region. Put simply, ASEAN is fundamentally viewed by the major Asia-Pacific powers as being essentially a trading organization.

Finally, the third part will examine selected topics that are of great interest to me and hopefully to the reader as well. First, the emerging competition for the natural resources needed by the major powers in Asia-Pacific. Secondly, the emerging environmental crisis that continues to envelope the region. Finally, the emergence of a new language that is indicative of the shift in influence and power within the Asia-Pacific region. It is my intention to bring the Asia-Pacific situation full circle by connecting geography, history and the pursuit of hegemonic power to the primary issues addressed in this section of the book: the absolute need for natural resources by the major economies, the terrifying specter of an environment crisis in the region and the recent evolution of a new strategic language that defines and describes what we are witnessing as the 21st century unfolds.

As expected, during the writing of this book, the geopolitical jockeying by the major, middle and minor powers continued non-stop in Asia-Pacific. The region's primary security alliances, trade associations and regional organizations also continued at a frenzied pace. Consequently, this energized daily process often consists of intense negotiations and strategic decision-making. Thus, the economic and security issues throughout Asia-Pacific are continually being reshaped and shifted toward the recognition of the ever-changing circumstances and environment existing within the Asia-Pacific region.

Yet, it is no surprise that despite all the public acknowledgements and proclamations that further interdependence and integration will continue to occur in Asia-Pacific. Yet, it is with caution and trepidation, the major, middle and minor powers within the region continue to position themselves into the best possible—economic and military—positions in case things go terribly wrong.

In the end, I hope my book will have addressed a number of the important challenges, dangers and prospects that will become evident and which will transform the Asia-Pacific region in the 21st century. I believe the region will indeed become the focal point of global affairs for the next several decades. However, if history is any judge, the short-term prospects for Asia-Pacific, nevertheless, can not be regarded in an overly optimistic manner. The elements of power, history and resources have created an unpredictable alchemy throughout the region—if not the world.

Also, the region, and the world, is currently experiencing an historic financial calamity which will have a profound affect upon Asia-Pacific's future, particularly the region's economic and security structures. If you also take into consideration the revolutionary changes involving the proliferation of global communications, information and technology systems, then it is easy to understand why experts, observers and scholars are extremely wary of making any predictions concerning the future direction or trends with regard to the Asia-Pacific region.

The global financial collapse, beginning in late-2008, will also undeniably affect the hegemonic, historic and political environment within Asia-Pacific as well. Thus, to competently convey the *ultimate* outcome from the convergence of *all* these factors to readers, will represent a monumental challenge for this author, and other writers and scholars, who have dedicated their working lives toward defining and understanding this dynamic and diversified region. Yet, Asia-Pacific geographical immensity and stature remain daunting and, at times intimidating, even for the best of us who have lived for years in this part of the world.

However, in closing, I would like to present one more caveat concerning the future of Asia-Pacific. If the world is further enveloped by the current economic dilemma, and it evolves into the worst economic situation since the 1930s, it is my opinion that human history will find itself riding the proverbial tiger of destiny. Unfortunately, though it sounds exciting and potentially transformative, in reality, there is a great deal of danger confronting the global community, particularly for the Asia-Pacific region. Thus, no matter what destiny has in store for us, I am dead certain that the journey that the Asia-Pacific region is about to embark upon during the 21st century will be one hellacious ride and the world, involuntarily, will also find itself a passenger on this trip as well—whether it wants to be or not.

(Note to the Reader: I will use interchangeably the terms Asia-Pacific and East Asia within this book. The primary reason for this 'geographical' literary occurrence is that I will at times note, or refer to, important historical events, prominent individuals or geopolitical situations that currently exist within the Asia-Pacific region, and are often identified as being East Asian—geographically. Nevertheless, the reader will understand quite clearly throughout the book that the collective destinies of the people and nations throughout the Asia-Pacific region are truly intertwined. It is an irrefutable fact that a global epoch of historic proportions is upon us, and that the world's economic and military axis is steadily shifting toward Asia-Pacific. This work is a reflection of that reality. It is my hope and intention to provide a modest, but informed, glimpse into this emerging reality at the beginning of the 21st century.)

Part I

HEGEMONIC POWER
IN ASIA-PACIFIC

Chapter One

Geography, Hegemony and Politics: Asia-Pacific in the 21st Century

Every generation of geopolitical analysts has it own jargon and terms for describing the current state of affairs for any particular area or region of the world. In fact, their literary flourishes are also often used to describe the world itself at any given point in time. For instance, today, the vast majority of geopolitical analysts and experts use such terms as "globalization", "transnational", "global hegemony", "full spectrum dominance", and other colorful and descriptive terminology to explain the recent developments that have occurred throughout the global community. I know this to be true, because I have used these terms myself within my own teachings and writings, and I have seen them used thousands of times within the works of others. Yet, when you look a bit closer to what they are really saying in their articles and books, and the topics that they are really attempting to address, then it becomes quite obvious, at least to this writer, that these myriad of talented authors are really confronting the hard-core fundamentals of geopolitical analytical work: *Geography*, *Hegemony* and *Politics*.

Thus, it is the primary goal of this chapter to analyze the emergence of Asia-Pacific which is one of the fastest evolving and growing regions in the world at the beginning of the 21st century. My analysis will be based upon the old fashion and fundamental factors mentioned above: Geography, Hegemony and Politics. It is my belief that colorful jargon and vacuous terminology often obfuscates or simply misdirects the readers' attention from the real issues that matter. Clever explanations are often implemented within a work in order to avoid the uncomfortable truths that exist and must, at some point in time, be addressed directly. And, the author, when pressed for further explanation, due to a readers' inability to comprehend what the writer is actually trying to convey, can always say that the quote or segment in question from his/her book was, of course, taken out of context or simply misunderstood. It is my hope and intention to address these fundamental factors related to Asia-Pacific in a straight forward fashion and with as much clarity as possible.

GEOGRAPHY, HEGEMONY AND POLITICS

One of my great regrets as a college student is that I did not take more geography courses. I took one geography course as an undergraduate at William Jewell College. I thoroughly enjoyed it and I did quite well academically. If my memory serves me correctly, students could not minor or major in geography at William Jewell College during my time there. I have often thought about this due to my continued and intense study, teaching and travel throughout the Asia-Pacific region during my academic career. In short, Asia-Pacific's geography clearly shows this diverse and dynamic region possesses a multitude of challenges and complexities.

Of which, the understanding of the regional geography is absolutely crucial to any expert or scholar who attempts to explain this vast area and the critical roles that hegemony and politics play within it. Harm de Blij, Distinguished Professor of Geography at Michigan State, writes in his excellent work, *Why Geography Matters,*

"Ten years ago it seemed that the world could not possibly change any faster than it had over the previous decade. The Soviet Union had disintegrated into 15 newly independent countries, China's Pacific Rim was transforming the economic geography of East Asia, South Africa was embarked on a new course under the guidance of Nelson Mandela...Yet, the pace of change during the decade straddling the turn of the century has not slowed down."[1]

Simply put, I believe comprehending the geography of Asia-Pacific will irrefutably sharpen one's ability to understand the historical contours and evolution of its economic, military and political decisions made by the indigenous nations existing within it. Within this chapter, I will briefly analyze the "geographical" situation of the following Asia-Pacific powers: America, Australia, China, Japan and South Korea. Each of these nations, due to its own geographical circumstances, looks upon the Asia-Pacific region through a different prism in terms of history and power. In short, their geographical realities can, to a large degree, explain their domestic and foreign policies. Thus, their specific actions, as nations, are often reflective of their 'real time' geographical positioning within Asia-Pacific.

America is seen as an Asian-Pacific power, but it is not considered an Asian power. The two territorial entities that are closest to Asia, representing direct U.S. interests, are Guam and Hawaii. In recent years, there has been an emerging dialogue concerning the development of a Asian Union, or an Asian IMF Bank, or, perhaps, even an Asian Free Trade Area (AFTA) that would exclude the United States and Europe. If AFTA ever developed into an actual entity, it would certainly rival the North American Free Trade Agreement (NAFTA) and the European Union (EU) in terms of economic prowess. And, without a doubt, would certainly eliminate the need for the continued existence of the Association of Southeast Asian Nations (ASEAN) and the Asia-Pacific Economic Cooperation (APEC).

Though, as of 2009, these developments have not occurred, nevertheless, these types of discussions and ideas are not simply idle chatter amongst various finance ministers or malcontent nations within the region. Yet, the U.S. should be concerned about the growing chorus of voices, within the Asia-Pacific region, who are increasingly willing to explore the idea of developing such institutions in the 21st century.

The key event that triggered this new dialogue within Asia-Pacific was the 1997–1998 financial meltdown in East Asia, which seriously affected all nations but was particularly painful to Indonesia, Thailand and South Korea. Also, the rough handling and insensitivity shown these nations by the Washington-based IMF had left an indelible mark and an extremely sour taste in the mouths of Asian governments throughout the region.

As a result, voices that were once ignored about Asia creating its own financial institutions—separate from the U.S. were no longer ignored or ridiculed. In fact, the Asian Summit held in Kuala Lumpur in December 2006 was interpreted by some regional observers as potentially representing the beginning of a new era for Asia-Pacific and its relations with the West, but especially with America. Geography matters.

Kishore Mahbubani, Dean and Professor in the Lee Kuan Yew School of Public Policy at the National University of Singapore, writes about the importance of the East Asian Summit in 2006,

"Many in the West treat these diplomatic gatherings as a big yawn. This is true of many summits. But sometimes, history is made at these meetings. With the center of the world's economic gravity shifting to East Asia, which is providing the rising new powers, it would have been quite natural to see increased political competition and tensions in the region. This is what American scholars expected. Instead, there has been growing cooperation."[2]

What is America's future role in the Asia-Pacific region? The vast majority of analysts and experts on this geopolitical subject believe that the U.S. will not leave, nor will it reduce its presence within this vital area. For now, the American plan for Asia-Pacific will remain the same. In fact, the region is an essential part of an even greater U.S. global strategy, according to Walter Russell Mead, the Henry A. Kissinger Fellow at The Council on Foreign Relations, who has described the American agenda as the following, to "protect our own domestic security while building a peaceful world order of democratic states linked by common values and sharing a common prosperity."[3]

In September 2006, U.S. Congressman James Leach (R-IA) gave a more definitive interpretation on how the U.S. should view its role in the Asia-Pacific region during the 21st century. In a statement made before the U.S. House of Representatives at a subcommittee hearing on Asia and the Pacific, grandly titled, *America and Asia in a Changing World*, Congressman Leach spoke directly to the issue concerning how important Asia will be for America in the near future. Leach, then Chair of the House Subcommittee on Asia and the Pacific, did not mince words, "It is Asia where the United States will face its largest geopolitical challenges in the years ahead."[4] He also stated that "maintaining a robust overseas military presence has historically been a key element of the United States national security policy in the Asia-Pacific."[5] Congressman Leach finished his statement before the Asia and the Pacific subcommittee by focusing upon the fact that regional harmony "has been maintained by successive U.S. administrations, all of which have emphasized the linkage between our network of alliances and friendships to a regional environment in Asia conducive to confidence in economic growth."[6]

Congressman Leach was not exaggerating about the massive U.S. presence in the Asia-Pacific region. The United States Pacific Command (US-PACOM) which has its headquarters situated in Hawaii, and its overall territorial responsibility is almost beyond comprehension. This specific military command extends from "Alaska to Madagascar and from India to the South Pacific."[7] There are 43 different nations and territorial entities within this command region. It encompasses about 50% of the earth's surface and 60% of the world's population. The USPACOM was originally designed in 1947, and it remains the oldest and longest unified command structure within the U.S. military.[8]

China has established a powerful presence within Asia-Pacific, but its regional neighbors, especially the other major powers within the region, remain skeptical and unconvinced that their real and ultimate intentions are only meant to be peaceful and harmonious. The primary reason for the growing unease throughout the region is China's continued rise, economically and militarily. Despite repeated denials from Beijing that they do not possess a secret geopolitical strategy to replace the U.S. and Japan from their post-WWII leadership positions in Asia-Pacific, mistrust continues to exist throughout the region. Recent history continues to loom large over this region and it has produced wary sentiments that accurately reflect Asian cynicism, especially toward those countries, like China, with the power to influence and shape events in the region.

As a consequence, I believe it is quite proper for analysts and observers of Asia-Pacific affairs to ask the following questions: 'What are China's future intentions for the Asia-Pacific region, and what role does it see itself playing for the next twenty-five years?' 'Will increased global competition, especially amongst the major economic powers, for the world's resources force China to become more assertive in its foreign policy?'

In May 2008, to get some fresh perspectives on these questions mentioned above, I visited the Chinese Academy of Social Sciences (CASS) in Beijing, China, which was founded in 1977. CASS is considered to be the top-rated think-tank in China and, perhaps, within Asia. It is heavily relied upon for advice and counseling by the Chinese leadership.

Dr. Wu Huaizhong, a senior research scholar in the Institute of Japanese Studies at the Chinese Academy of Social Sciences, believes that both "America and China should talk about important Pacific issues and that the U.S. should allow China to play a role on major international and regional issues."[9] Dr. Wu also noted that U.S. fears concerning China's military development are ill-founded because, "In truth, there are limits to China's military development due to huge domestic needs within China."[10]

Zhang Yong, a research scholar within the Institute of Japanese Studies at the Chinese Academy of Social Sciences, stated that China's relations with Japan are also crucial to future stability in Asia-Pacific. Mr. Zhang observed that "China is one of the biggest political countries in the world, and it is rising. Japan is already an established economic power. As a result, both nations are now beginning to see each other as equals in Asia."[11] Zhang finally mentioned that the "security dilemma in East Asia will greatly depend upon America's attitude during the 21st century, because the U.S. does not want a competitor in East Asia."[12]

Dr. Wu, unexpectedly, quickly responded to Mr. Zhang's belief concerning future U.S. behavior (I interviewed both scholars together) that "'Triangular Diplomacy' between America, China and Japan may be the key for the region's future, and it should be remembered that China has never threatened U.S. hegemony within the region. China desires to be a partner and not a competitor."[13]

Australia finds itself uncomfortably situated between these two Asia-Pacific giants (America and China) at the beginning of the 21st century. It has also discovered that its ability to maneuver is increasingly problematic as events and time exposed their geopolitical juxtaposition. Thus, the fundamental questions confronting the Australian foreign policy establishment is two-fold: 'How do we maintain our post-WWII security alliance with the most powerful nation in the world?' And, 'how do we maintain quality relations with the nation that is increasingly our most important trading partner in Asia-Pacific?'

In the November 2007 elections, Kevin Rudd, the Australian Labor Party leader, decisively defeated the incumbent Prime Minister John Howard. Journalist Laurie Oakes wrote in the Australian newsmagazine, *The Bulletin*, that "He (Rudd) believes he can achieve his aims through consensus and cooperation"[14] . . . Yet, Oakes also notes that "he is no saint. He is ruthless and calculating. As Machiavellian as any successful politician...you don't get to the top of the greasy pole in politics by being nice all the time."[15] These characteristics will serve Prime Minister Rudd well in the upcoming years as Asia-Pacific continues to evolve and transform itself economically and politically, and Australia's role in this dynamic region will hopefully reflect these changing circumstances as the 21st century unfolds.

Within Australian foreign policy circles the debate concerning Australia's future strategy has intensified. Allan Gyngell and Michael Wesley, both foreign policy experts associated with the Lowy Institute which is located in Sydney, wrote in an article published in *The Australian Financial Review*, that "China is central to his (Rudd) foreign policy experience. He studied Chinese history and language, was posted to the Australian embassy in Beijing and has worked in China as a business consultant . . . He (Rudd) considers China's rise as the first of three or four big challenges facing Australia."[16] They also extol the fact that "the Prime Minister can communicate an image of modern Australia directly to the Chinese public. He can converse at the highest level without the artificial barrier of interpreters . . . as the first Western leader to speak an Asian language fluently, Rudd in Beijing will be a world media event—a potent symbol that Australia stands at the forefront of the West's response to a rising Asia."[17]

Yet, it is Rudd's own Chinese language and business fluency and expertise that have unnerved many within the Australian business and political establishments. In terms of national policy, his critics want to know the endgame concerning Australia's relationship with China. Some have questioned whether Rudd possesses the capacity to walk away from the negotiating table if China's trade and geopolitical proposals were unacceptable to the Rudd government. John Mc Donnell, an Australian trade adviser who negotiated with the Chinese government, between 1986 and 1989, during the first years of the John Howard prime minister-ship, wrote an op-ed piece that reflected these concerns,

"Rudd has started moving Australia closer to China. He has represented himself as an expert on Chinese affairs and intimated that he wants to move China into a central role in the multilateral strategic and economic environment. China may well agree to be proactive in international affairs, but underlying any policy position it takes will be the core objective of extending the international commercial reach of the main (China) state-owned and supported conglomerates."[18]

Right now, Australia and China are immersed in intense and serious negotiations with concern to completing a Free Trade Agreement (FTA) between the two nations. McDonnell will continue to feel uncomfortable about this process until Prime Minister Rudd exhibits "clean hands" during these economic meetings.[19] He believes Rudd will experience greater success, and will receive stronger support within the Australian business community, during these negotiations if he does the following,

"First, he needs to consolidate the position that the free trade agreement is not the be-all and end-all of Australia's trade policy. Second, the (Rudd) government should make it clear that if Australia's does not get what it believes is a reasonable outcome from the FTA negotiations, then it will rely on the multilateral system to implement its policy objectives. As Henry Kissinger pointed out, with the Chinese you have to be prepared to walk away."[20]

Then there are others who are also concerned about the realistic prospects of Prime Minister Rudd achieving his visionary hopes in trying to create a new regional framework for Asia-Pacific. Paul Kelly, a longtime observer of Australian foreign policy and highly respected columnist for the newspaper, *The Australian*, which is Australia's only nationwide newspaper, spoke with "Australia's pre-eminent diplomat"[21], Richard Woolcott, about Rudd's ambitious plans for future Australian relations with Asia. Woolcott, ever the diplomat, described Prime Minister Rudd's new vision for Asia-Pacific as "important and forward looking."[22] However, Ambassador Woolcott also believes that the U.S. response to Rudd's new ideas will have to wait until the intense and unpredictable 2008 U.S. presidential has ended with a new American president elected.

Thus far, however, the response from the Asian community has been mixed at best. Plus, many in the region believe that the plethora of regional forums and meetings will have to be restructured and reduced in number. Woolcott properly points out the obvious to Paul Kelly during their (blog) interview, "The (U.S.) President has got to work out which meetings he goes to and which ones he doesn't. Also, (the leaders of) China, Japan, and I suppose, India and Indonesia, already have a lot of commitments. This issue needs to be worked out."[23]

Despite the significant challenges confronting Prime Minister Rudd's ambitious plans for creating a new Asia-Pacific security paradigm, his efforts are seen by many observers as, perhaps, prescient and timely. Yet, Professor Hugh White, a highly influential foreign policy analyst at Australian National University and at the Lowy Institute, represents the view that real danger exists within the region,

"The Taiwan and North Korean situations have clearly posed a threat of major conflict in Asia. But many have tended to see these flashpoints as residuals risks from an earlier age—throwbacks to the Cold War. The question I want to raise is whether they are not better seen as premonitions of a darker future in which Asia becomes more systemically dangerous, and if so what can we do about it.[24]

Professor White also perceives the current situation in Asia-Pacific as being deeply fragmented and fundamentally unstable,

"On the one hand, we saw the reality of a region characterized by cooperation, integration and growth, in which shared interests predominate, and in which there is real hope of close regional cooperation to address a range of newer security threats such . . . energy security, environmental challenges and the proliferation of WMD to 'rogue states'. In this reality, major war is indeed unthinkable. On the other hand . . . the reality of active and intensifying military and strategic competition fuelled by suspicion, distrust and even hostility, in which major war is clearly not unthinkable, for the simple reason that some of the major powers in Asia are clearly building their forces with exactly that possibility in mind."[25]

Japan is a nation experiencing a difficult and intense transition internally, and in its external interactions with the outside world as well. Christian Caryl and Akiko Kashiwagi, both writers for *Newsweek* magazine, have captured quite well the ambiguity and the almost absolute refusal by Japan to accept any foreign investment or financial involvement that may affect the sovereignty of their economy and Japan's stature in the world.

Caryl and Kashiwagi point to a recent incident that involved well-known hedge fund manager Christopher Hohn, an activist investor who presides over a London-based Children's Investment Fund, made a bid to double his organization's holdings in J-Power, Japan's most important electricity wholesaler. Hohn's bid was flatly turned down due to the Japanese government's concern with the "maintenance of public order."[26] Hohn, as expected, has made an appeal to the EU Trade Commissioner. He has requested that an investigation into Japan's current business practices be made—to find out if they are based upon accepted and recognized international law.[27]

The Newsweek writers, Caryl and Kashiwagi, believe that this recent incident merely reflects the historic attitude and perception that the Japanese have held toward foreigners—especially those who have attempted to penetrate their society. They write,

"The resistance toward not only Hohn, but many other foreign investors, encapsulates growing Japanese anxiety about their economy and place in an increasingly competitive world. Japan, of course, has always had an ambiguous relationship to the outside world. Throughout its history the country has oscillated between pathological suspicion of foreigners and eager imitation of alien ways. Recently, some of the buried legacy of isolationism—manifested in a stubborn resistance to foreign investment and a reluctance to capitalize on the opportunities of globalization—has been coming back to the surface."[28]

Though, its economic conservatism appears to be the current stratagem of the Japanese government with concern to globalization. Conversely, however, the nation's foreign policy within the Asia-Pacific region has shown signs of being much more aggressive and farsighted. An editorial in the Japanese newspaper, *The Asahi Shimbun*, congratulated the Japanese government for its activities involving the Association of Southeast Asian Nations (ASEAN) which might eventually lead to the creation of an East Asian Economic Community. The editorial stated,

"Japan and the Association of Southeast Asian Nations (ASEAN) took an important step Monday toward making the proposed East Asian Economic Community a reality. Long regarded as a pipe dream, there is now real hope that such a body will come into being. The economic partnership agreement (EPA) struck by Japan and the 10-member nations of ASEAN has huge implications for the future of this grand vision."[29]

Though, bold and visionary, this economic 'grand vision' reflects another geopolitical reality that is fast emerging upon Japan's regional radar—the stunning rise of China. I believe it is not a coincidence that Japan has strengthen its economic ties with ASEAN and has now embarked upon creating new relations with China and South Korea. Since WWII, Japanese relations with their immediate neighbors have often been quite frosty, if not downright hostile, due to the violent acts committed by the military of Imperial Japan during the first half of the 20th century.

However, short of a war or an economic meltdown globally (unfortunately, in 2009, this is occurring), China will soon surpass Japan in total GDP—though not in per capita terms—at the beginning of the 21st century. And, South Korea is now ranked the 13th largest economy in the world. Altogether, these regional economic developments have hit home within Japan who, since the 1980s, had become accustomed to being the second most powerful economy in the world and the number one economy throughout Asia. This traumatic turn of events has forced the Japanese to re-examine its relations with the key powers in northeast Asia—China and South Korea. In short, Japan has realized that the power dynamics of the region has been transformed irrefutably.

Professor Seiichiro Takagi, who teaches at the School of International Politics, Economics and Business at Aoyama Gakuin University in Tokyo, wrote in an article that he believes that a "strategic relationship of mutual benefit" has developed between China and Japan.[30] Professor Takagi, within the article, identifies the two types of "common strategic interests" between these powerful Asian nations: reciprocal and identical.[31] Takagi goes on to define these two concepts quite clearly,

"The former includes the two countries includes the two countries extending their support to each other's peaceful development, enhancing mutual trust and cultivating mutual understanding and friendship between their two peoples. The latter—although some may be identical only in principle and differ in details—includes common development, peace and stability in Northeast Asia, peaceful settlement of the nuclear issues on the Korean peninsula (especially its denuclearization), reform of the Security Council and the United Nations as a whole, support for ASEAN's larger role and promotion of regional cooperation in East Asia."[32]

Professor Takagi realizes that this is a rather large and challenging agenda between these two Asian powers, but, nevertheless, he states emphatically that "Japan and China must exercise wisdom and endeavor to manage differences, while attempting to realize and expand their common strategic interests."[33]

Tomohide Murai, Professor of International Relations and Director of the Library at the National Defense Academy in Japan, believes that the Japanese are simply facing up to a reality that has no alternative scenario for the near future. Professor Murai writes, "While Japan's international influence is diminishing, that of China is rapidly expanding on the back of its growing economic might. It is only a matter of time before our country is overtaken by our neighbor in economic size."[34] He provides an old Chinese proverb to describe China and Japan's current dilemma in Northeast Asia, "Two tigers cannot share the same mountain."[35]

Hiroyasu Akutsu, a senior Fellow of the Okazaki Institute in Tokyo, perceives a new spirit of cooperation between Japan and South Korea since the swearing-in of Lee Myung-bak as South Korea's new president on 25 February 2008. Professor Akutsu writes that "Japanese Prime Minister Yasuo Fukuda and Mr. Lee have already agreed to resume shuttle diplomacy, revive trilateral talks among Tokyo, Seoul and Washington, and promote negotiations on a free trade agreement (FTA). (Note: Though, Yasuo Fukuda was replaced by Taro Aso, in late-2008, there still appears to be a determination to improve and strengthen Japan-Korea relations). A major challenge ahead is how to steer this new momentum into efforts to build an effective security cooperation mechanism."[36]

South Korea, at the beginning of the 21st century, often finds itself uncomfortably caught in the middle of intense and serious geopolitical maneuverings between the major powers of Asia-Pacific. I always tell my students the two countries with the worst geography—geopolitically speaking—are Poland and South Korea. These nations find themselves situated in very dangerous neighborhoods—Poland flanked by Germany and Russia, and South Korea is wedged between China, Japan and Russia. And, the U.S. has approximately

30,000 troops in South Korea. As expected, South Korea's foreign policy is often a reflection of European-style 'realpolitik' and post-WWII Cold War 'realism', simultaneously. Again, geography matters.

South Korea is currently the 13th largest economy in the world, and its military is considered one of the strongest in Asia-Pacific. Yet, it finds itself continually vulnerable to the constant ebb and flow of regional events—economically and militarily—despite determined efforts to exhibit and possess greater autonomy for itself. The simple truth is that their powerful neighbors (China and Japan), and the presence of 30,000 U.S. troops on its soil, makes daily life for the South Korean government an exercise in caution and frustration.

Nevertheless, the South Korean government continues to establish its own identity amongst these powerful entities. This is an important fact to remember because many observers view northeastern Asia as increasingly smaller and more difficult to maneuver within economically, militarily and politically. Thus, in 2009, on a daily basis, the South Korean government's domestic political activities and decisions concerning itself and its standing in the immediate region are becoming more problematic. Point of fact, reaching a policy consensus on almost every issue within the South Korean government is increasingly difficult.

Hahm Chaibong, a professor of political science at Yonsei University in Seoul, writes, "South Korea today is a bitterly divided country. Clashes between conservatives and progressives over everything from the direction of economic and political reforms to the location of the nation's capital have created a deep domestic fissure."[37] Chaibong believes that it is a mistake to accept the casual explanations used to deflect the seriousness of the recent attitudes shown toward their post-Korean War guardian the United States, and toward their Korean brothers and sisters in communist North Korea.[38]

Thus, Professor Chaibong asserts that, "Some observers try to explain away anti-American and pro-North Korean views in South Korea as a largely harmless sign of the country's maturity, a manifestation of an effort to steer a more independent course in foreign policy vis-à-vis the United States. . . In reality, anti-American and pro-North Korean attitudes in South Korea are anything but passing trends or transitory reactions to a particular U.S. policy or administration, nor can one cheerfully dismiss them as signs of a maturing democracy. Rather, they are the logical extension of the current ruling coalition's "leftist-nationalist" ideology, which lies at the root of South Korea's deep division between conservatives and progressives."[39]

Professor Chaibong wrote this article, in 2005, during the progressive presidency of Roh Moo-hyun (2003–2008). However, it should be duly noted that the same divisions within South Korean politics, so aptly described by

Professor Chaibong, have become quite evident again during the first year of the conservative presidency of Lee Myung-bak (2008–2013). Korea is not only a nation divided geographically, but South Korea's political establishment appears to be as divided as the Korean peninsula itself.

The editors of the British-based weekly newsmagazine, *The Economist*, in 2005, wrote a special report titled, "The Cold War in Asia."[40] They strongly believe that a disturbing and growing degree of *real* danger exists throughout Northeast Asia due to the nature of the activities, events and relations evolving between the major powers, including the United States. They write, "Relations between the big powers of north Asia are notoriously bad. . . Balances of power and influence in north Asia are shifting in unpredictable ways."[41]

The report points to China's rising presence in the region, Japan's growing anxiety related to this fact, North Korea constant defiance concerning its nuclear program, South Korea steadily being drawn into China's geopolitical orbit despite being a military ally of the U.S., and the increased competition for the region's resources. At the end of this special report, the editors recognizing that there is a lot of history existing between these energetic and proud nations, and history itself could very well be the key determining factor for the future of Asia-Pacific, especially for northeast Asia. In fact, the last sentence of their report states, "There is no getting away from history."[42]

GEOGRAPHY, HEGEMONY AND POLITICS

These (3) fundamental pillars of human existence continue to exert and exist within the political and societal structures existing within the Asia-Pacific region. The major powers within the region—America, Australia, China, Japan and South Korea (even Russia)—are presently struggling with creating a comprehensive and coherent regional framework and stratagem that provides a geopolitical equilibrium. There are more than a few analysts, experts and observers who truly believe that this 'geopolitical equilibrium' is simply beyond the capabilities of those interacting and living in these historic and transformative times in Asia-Pacific. Their formidable arguments are founded upon the recognized and collective affect that geography, hegemony and politics possess in shaping and determining the course of human endeavors. Without a doubt, these are very powerful factors and forces, indeed.

Nevertheless, there are a couple of reasons, I believe, for remaining somewhat positive about the ultimate outcome of Asia-Pacific. First, the region's recent emergence and recognition, at the beginning of the 21st century, for being the new prism from which global affairs are viewed, is generally accepted by most geopolitical strategists. This new reality will have a very sobering affect upon the leaders within the region. They now realize that their decisions will not only be closely scrutinized by regional observers, but that their (potential) mistakes in judgment, especially concerning the environment, could have significant ramifications for the entire planet.

Second, my guarded optimism is also based upon the modern-day and unprecedented capacity to have access to related history, vital information and universal knowledge that exist throughout the world. This global capacity is, of course, a direct result of the present-day and brilliantly constructed information systems. These systems are presently transforming the lives of billions. And, this 'globalized' information phenomena truly represents a legitimate and significant hope for the leaders of the Asia-Pacific region. These knowledge providing revolutionary processes have now interconnected the world and its leaders to a degree never witnessed before in human history. Thus, isolation from human affairs is really no longer an option for ALL leaders and nations. Everyday, the world continues to develop and evolve technologically. Leaders, who consciously remain outside, or on the periphery, of global activities are truly putting their respective nations at risk.

That is the present situation for the major powers in the Asia-Pacific region. None can remove themselves from the quickening pace of regional and global events. In truth, these leaders representing Asia-Pacific, in the 21st century, are faced with significant challenges and dangers, and potentially hopeful prospects, simultaneously, in the near future. Without argument, the region is truly experiencing revolutionary times, economically, and (geo) politically. Presently, however, there is no established consensus on how to maintain the high rates of economic growth and regional stability which has been the reality for Asia-Pacific during the past 30 years.

Yet, in the end, I believe there are (3) fundamental factors that will ultimately decide the destiny of the Asia-Pacific region during the 21st century: Geography, Hegemony and Politics. Therefore, the real challenge for the leaders of this critical region will be their collective ability to handle these (3) crucial and volatile elements without destroying the region's historic and phenomenal economic progress and Asia-Pacific's new stature in world affairs—a standing it has not experienced since the early 19th century.

NOTES

1. Harm de Blij, *Why Geography Matters: Three Challenges Facing America* (New York: Oxford university Press, 2005), p. 3.
2. Kishore Mahbubani, *The New Asian Hemisphere: The Irresistible Shift of Global Power To The East* (New York: Public Affairs, 2008), p. 270.

3. Walter Russell Mead, *Power, Terror, Peace and War: America's Grand Strategy in a World at Risk* (New York: Vintage Books, 2004), p.7.

4. Bruce Vaughn, "U.S. Strategic and Defense Relationships in the Asia-Pacific Regions" (Washington, DC: Congressional Research Service Report for Congress, 22 January 2007), p. 1.

5. Ibid.

6. Ibid.

7. Ibid., p. 11.

8. Ibid., pp. 10-11.

9. Interview with Dr. Wu Huaizhong, 20 May 2008, Chinese Academy of Social Sciences, Beijing, China.

10. Ibid.

11. Interview with Zhang Yong, 20 May 2008, Chinese Academy of Social Sciences, Beijing, China.

12. Ibid.

13. Interview with Dr. Wu, 20 May 2008.

14. Laurie Oakes, "Election That Changes Everything", *The Bulletin*, 4 December 2007, p. 14.

15. Ibid.

16. Allan Gyngell and Michael Wesley, "Regional Diplomacy Has New Impetus", *The Australian Financial Review*, 3 April 2008, p. 79.

17. Ibid.

18. John McDonnell, "Special Relationships Are Fraught", *The Australian*, 14 April 2008.

19. Ibid.

20. Ibid.

21. http://blogs.theaustralain.news.com.au/paulkelly/index.php/theaustralian

22. Ibid.

23. Ibid.

24. Hugh White, "Conflict in Asia: Why War In Asia Remains Thinkable", speech given at the IISS-JIIA Conference in Tokyo, Japan, 3–4 June 2008.

25. Ibid.

26. Christian Caryl and Akiko Kashiwagi, "This Nation Is An Island", *Newsweek* (International Edition), 12 May 2008.

27. Ibid.

28. Ibid.

29. Editorial, "East Asia Community: Japan Should Work To Give Shape To Such A Bloc", The Asahi Shimbun, 21 Novermber 2007, p. 25.

30. Seiichiro Takagi, "Japan-China Relations: How To Build A "Strategic Relationship of Mutual Benefit", The Association of Japanese Institutes of Strategic Studies, 13 February 2008.

31. Ibid.

32. Ibid.

33. Ibid.

34. Tomohide Murai, "SDF Peace Missions For Stable Japan-China Relations", The Association of Japanese Institutes of Strategic Studies, 20 February 2008.

35. Ibid.

36. Hiroyasu Akutsu, "A New Era For Japan-ROK Relations", The Association of Japanese Institutes of Strategic Studies, 14 March 2008.

37. Hahm Chaibong, "The Two South Koreas: A House Divided", *The Washington Quarterly*, Summer 2005.

38. Ibid.

39. Ibid.

40. Editors, "Special Report: The Cold War in Asia—In Dangerous Waters", *The Economist*, 7 October 2006.

41. Ibid.

42. Ibid.

Chapter Two

EASTO: East-Asia Security and Trade Organization

This organization does not exist—for now. It is a hypothetical regional institution that I created in an effort toward making a larger argument within this chapter. That is, in truth, Asia-Pacific is indeed ascending to a new level of organization and purpose at the beginning of the 21st century. Though the U.S. remains deeply engaged at all levels within region and is still viewed as the most powerful nation within Asia-Pacific, nevertheless, America is irrefutably witnessing a fundamental shift in the region's power dynamics. Henry Kissinger, former U.S. Secretary of State during the Nixon and Ford Administrations (1973–1977), stated in an article published in *The Washington Post*, in April 2008, that the global balance of power has shifted from the Atlantic to the Pacific. And, America, particularly, must deal with this fact.[1]

Yet, the U.S. foreign policy establishment has shown some reticence in accepting this inescapable truth. For those who have truly moved beyond the Cold War, they are faced with a new set of challenges and dangers associated with this geopolitical shift. Thus, the inevitable question is asked, 'What does this geopolitical and historic epoch mean for American interests in the Pacific region?' Since the Spanish-American War, in 1898, the U.S. has viewed the region as being an invaluable part of its global empire.

Therefore, the primary focus of this chapter will be two-fold. First, I will examine to what extent—if any—American influence has actually declined within the region. Secondly, I will focus upon the potential ramifications of a new and significant security and trade organization being developed as a counter-weight to the powerful U.S. presence in Asia-Pacific. And, if such an organization were to be created, would this in and of itself represent the decline of U.S. influence throughout the region?

THE AMERICAN EAGLE: A NEW REALITY IN ASIA-PACIFIC

Joshua Kurlantzick, a Fellow at the Pacific Council on International Policy, believes the transformation of Asia-Pacific is already underway. And, America must recognize this process and make some fundamental changes to remain a major player within the region. Kurlantzick, writes,

"Across East Asia, governments and leaders are developing their own institutions and intraregional trade patterns. They even have begun holding their first truly regional meeting, the annual East Asia Summit (EAS), which first convened in December 2005. Outside government, average people have developed a growing pan-Asian consciousness, the result of closer commercial links, the rise of an East Asian middle class, and the penetration of Asian pop culture products in households. In subtle ways, people across East Asia, like Europeans after WWII, are beginning think of themselves as citizens of a region."[2]

This perception and structural evolutionary process within the Asia-Pacific region are seen by various U.S. observers as part of a natural post-Cold War development that reflects the interests and thinking of those living in this region. Most do not see this development as an overt threat to the American presence, but instead represents a realistic re-evaluation of the current realities confronting the leaders and the people in Asia-Pacific. Dick Nanto, an analyst on East Asia for the Congressional Research Service, an invaluable source of information for the United States Congress, writes,

"(After WWII,) the political and security arrangements that were formed among East Asian nations . . . tended to be anti-China or anticommunist in nature. ASEAN (Association of South East Asian Nations) or SEATO (South East Asia Treaty Organization) are two cases in point. Currently, however, the economic and political arrangements are crossing philosophical lines, and China is emerging as a regional hegemon in Asia. These changes are manifest in intra-Asian organizations such as the East Asia Summit, ASEAN Economic Community, ASEAN+3 (ASEAN plus China, Japan, and South Korea), the ASEAN Regional Forum, and the six-party talks, as well as track-two for a, such as the Shangri-La Dialogue or the Northeast Asia Cooperation Dialogue."[3]

What Kurlantzick and Nanto are trying to convey to fellow scholars who study Asian affairs, or to the members of the U.S. Congress, is that the leaders, people and nations within the Asian-Pacific region are indeed energizing and mobilizing the region to meet their present and future interests. The U.S. still represents a major factor within their calculations on matters concerning Asia-Pacific. However, their interests—regional interests—are no longer viewed as secondary or peripheral. In short, this collective entity, though still divided by geography, history and power on many issues, has found enough common ground to make these regional institutions and organizations take on a new importance. An importance that the U.S. dare not underestimate; the Cold War era is over for the nations of Asia-Pacific. Do the U.S. government and its foreign policy establishment truly understand this fundamental and geographic reality?

Fortunately, it appears that there are a few regional observers within the U.S. foreign policy establishment who understand. Jason T. Shaplen and James Laney wrote an article in *Foreign Affairs*, in November/December 2007, which proclaimed America's influence in the Asia, particularly in Northeast Asia, was in a state of transition. Shaplen, a former policy adviser at the Korean Peninsula Energy Development Organization, and Laney, a former U.S. Ambassador to South Korea from 1993 to 1997, write,

"After 60 years of U.S. domination, the balance of power in the region is shifting . . . For the past half century, the United States has relied almost exclusively on bilateral alliances to promote its interests in the area . . . To maximize its influence going forward, Washington must acknowledge that the transition is inevitable, identify the trends shaping it, and embrace new tools and regimes that broaden the base the United States relies on to project power."[4]

In September 2005, American economist C. Fred Bergsten, Director of the Institute for International Economics gave an insightful speech at the National Press Club in Tokyo, Japan. Dr. Bergsten observed that economic integration throughout the East Asian region has been steadily progressing without much fanfare—even in Asia. Yet, he said, "It seems that the countries of East Asia are heading steadily if slowly toward the creation of a regional community, or at least an East Asia Free Trade Area (EAFTA). It will take considerable time to reach that ultimate goal . . . But the rest of the world, and many Asians themselves, may not realize the progress that East Asia is making toward construction of a functional regional economic zone. *Virtually every possible combination of the core Asian group—consisting of the original members of the Association of Southeast Asian Nations (ASEAN) along with China, Japan and Korea—is already engaged in active integration efforts* (the author italicized this sentence within his speech).[5]

In terms of strategic security, and the future role of the U.S. in the Asia-Pacific region, well respected research analyst Bruce Vaughn authored a report, in January 2007, which spoke directly to this critical issue and what it means for the American government. Vaughn, an analyst on Southeast and South Asian Affairs within the Congressional Research Services which is affiliated with the Department of Foreign Affairs, Defense, and Trade Division, is clearly concerned that U.S. officials and strategists are not paying enough attention to the regional events and are oblivious to the pace of change which is occurring almost on a daily basis. Thus, his report goes right to the heart of the matter with little jargon or subtlety to hide his intent to shake the U.S. government out of its 9/11 induced trance.

Vaughn states in the summary of his report, "Many Asia-Pacific analysts and observers, both in the region and in the United States, feel that the United States is preoccupied in the Middle East and as a result is not sufficiently focused on the Asia-Pacific at a critical point in the evolution of what may prove to be a new era in Asia."[6] He points out that the post-WWII security alliances established to prevent the spread of communism had also assisted the U.S. in maintaining its Asia-Pacific presence. However, at the end of the first decade of the 21st century, Vaughn feels they are either passé or in need of a serious policy re-evaluation. He writes, "The circumstances under which these alliances were forged have changed dramatically. The fall of the Soviet Union, the post-Cold War world, the Asian financial crisis, the rise of China, and the emergence of violent Islamist extremists have all done much too significantly alter the geopolitical landscape of Asia."[7]

In the end, what these analysts and scholars are trying to convey is that the Asia-Pacific region is changing dramatically, but the U.S. government has not presently formulated, nor seriously deliberated about, their next move within the region. Yes, the 'War on Terror' and its manifestation within Iraq and Afghanistan are recognized quite correctly as disasters and geopolitical missteps. Yet, this does not excuse the American government's shocking degree of ignorance in understanding of what is commonly viewed as the new fulcrum of global affairs—the Asia-Pacific region.

Upon closer inspection, the dramatic economic development and societal transformation occurring within the Asia-Pacific community are actually a reflection, to a significant degree, of Western principles and values. In short, what the world at-large is currently witnessing is the manifestation and absorption of economic and political values within an Asia-Pacific framework. With more than a bit of historic irony beckoning, the region in the 21st century is basically a mirror image of what the West has sought to achieve and promote for itself during the past two hundred years. That is to exercise its dominant position culturally, economically and militarily throughout the world. To bring this argument full-circle, Asia-Pacific's rise to greater international stature is fundamentally due to the internal changes and modernization occurring within the individual countries in this region. And, it is this 'modernization' process that has transformed these societies by giving them the capacity, and their respective citizens the critical economic skills and tools to achieve unprecedented domestic prosperity and to collectively re-establish themselves in international affairs.

However, Fareed Zakaria, author of *The Post-American World*, believes that the liberation of women, within individual societies, has also greatly contributed toward their dramatic transformation. In short, the West has supported such values within Asia-Pacific and this has contributed toward women having a larger and more significant role within their respective societies. Zakaria, a rising star within the ranks of U.S. foreign policy analysts, notes, "When Asian leaders today speak of the need to preserve their distinctive Asian values, they sound just like Western conservatives who have sought to preserve similar moral values for centuries . . . After all, the appeal of tradition and family values remains strong in some very modern countries—the United States, Japan, South Korea. But, in general, and over time, growing wealth and individual opportunity does not produce a social transformation. Modernization brings about some form of women's liberation. It overturns the hierarch of age, religion, tradition, and feudal order. And all of this makes societies look more and more like those in Europe and North America."[8]

ASIA-PACIFIC: THE FUTURE IS NOW

After centuries of humiliation, repression and servitude to Western interests and power, the Asia-Pacific region is beginning to re-emerge as a significant player in global affairs. An argument can be made that the region experienced a 500-year aberration due to tragic domestic political decision-making and cold-blooded foreign exploitation. Altogether, the Asia-Pacific region fell into a half-millennium black hole which it is only now emerging. Ellen Frost, a Visiting Fellow at the Peterson Institute for International Economics, wrote in her new book, *Asia's New Regionalism*, that what we are witnessing is "the resurgence of a pre-colonial "Maritime Asia"—the sweep of coastal communities, port cities and towns, and waterways connecting Northeast and Southeast Asia, India and now Australia. Maritime Asia is the locus of Asian wealth and power. It is where 60 to 70 percent of Asians live, the biggest cities are and globalization-driven investment is concentrated. The world's six largest ports are all Asian."[9]

Asia-Pacific's rise is not a mystery, nor an historic aberration. Instead it represents a pragmatic and subtle shift in attitudes and strategy. The end result, many speculate, will be a new and determined region that is dedicated toward changing its destiny in the 21st century, and the West is going to help them achieve this objective. Greater regional autonomy and self-determination will become increasingly evident to the West as the new century unfolds. In short, many Asia-Pacific observers believe the West is in for a major geopolitical wake-up call.

Parag Khanna, who directs the Global Governance Initiative in the American Strategy Program of the New America Foundation, believes the West has inadvertently played a key role in its own geopolitical dilemma which is, quite simply, that they have created and inspired the re-emergence of a powerful Asia-Pacific. Khanna asks, "How did East Asia become the cockpit of global change, a world region on a par with North America and Europe?"[10] He answers this question by writing, "China and Asia are merely absorbing Western knowledge to accelerate the construction of an Eastern order. American skeptics argue that a "Concert of Asia" is impossible due to simmering rivalries, but Asian confidence has already evolved to the point where America may speak only when invited—when the East Asian Summit first convened in Kuala Lumpur in 2005, the United States was not invited at all."[11]

Khanna was born in India but was raised in the United Arab Emirates, the United States and Germany, thus, it is no surprise that he values geography and its role in shaping history and the future. He mentions the French sociologist Auguste Comte, who saw a direct association and correlation between demography and human destiny. Comte observed that Asia has the oldest cultures, the most people, and by certain measures, the most money of any region in the world. Khanna, in agreement with Comte, writes, "Asia is shaping the world's destiny—and exposing the flaws of the grand narrative of Western civilization in the process. Because of the East, the West is no longer master of it own fate."[12] If true, this means that the 500-year period of Western dominance is coming to an end in the relative near future. Is the West ready for this historic transition?

The Lowy Institute in Sydney, Australia, published a policy brief, in July 2007, which dealt with Asia-Pacific's future regional architecture and what it means for the nations involved. The policy brief also identified the (3) primary reasons for the shift in the thinking concerning Asia-Pacific regionalism:

1. Globalization
2. Rise of China
3. 1997/1998 Asian Financial Crisis[13]

Neil Francis, the former Australian Ambassador to Croatia and Fellow at the Whitehead Center for International Affairs at Harvard University, believes that some form of an East Asian community would be a very positive development for regional stability. Francis writes,

"An East Asian community composed of the 16 EAS (East Asian Summit) participants would represent more than 60 percent of the world's population and possess a combined GDP greater than the European Union. It could provide significantly increased trade benefits to its members, help dampen Sino-Japanese rivalry, ease the present tensions in the region over Japan's Pacific War, encourage more cooperative attitudes toward the issue of natural resource exploitation in East Asia, promote engagement over containment, and prevent domination of the region by any power."[14]

Perhaps, it would be appropriate, at this time, to examine the primary reasons for the shift in attitudes and thinking with concern to Asia-Pacific's future. On the issue of globalization, obviously this is the new religion in the world of finance. To criticize or question its fundamental presence or purpose in the world's business and political communities is to invite derision and condescension of the first order.

From a historical standpoint, national economics and domestic politics remain, and always will be joined at the hip. Therefore, those observers stating that nation-states are no longer major forces in global affairs, that their overall influence has diminished, and that globalization has become a force unto itself are simply delusional.

Point in fact as I write this chapter, in January 2009, the U.S. government has just bailed out numerous failing financial institutions and banks to the tune of over $800 billion dollars. And, U.S. carmakers have also received a government loan (it's a bailout). If most economists are correct in their determinations, this will not be the end of it. Global markets have plummeted and the entire world's financial architecture has been called into question. As expected, this financial meltdown will have serious political ramifications in all regions of the world, and democratic and non-democratic nations will be affected regardless of their political apparatus. However, it appears that the nation-state is making a comeback, of sorts, because millions of citizens are demanding their respective governments to do something, now, to relieve their economic (unemployment) and personal pain (foreclosure of their home) due to the global financial collapse.

David Skilling, the Chief Executive of the New Zealand Institute, states in his article, "*An Asia-Pacific Century?,*" that politics still matters and globalization does not operate within a vacuum. Skilling writes, "Often the trend of globalization is painted as an inexorable and irreversible force, proceeding in a smooth manner as people pursue shared commercial interests. But economics does not proceed in a vacuum. Economics and politics cannot easily be separated as the events of 1914 should indicate. Determinism of any sort, be it economic or technological, is generally a caricature of reality. Politics continues to matter, and the actions of government—or the absence of action —remain vitally important."[15] Obviously, despite the overall prosperity enjoyed in the Asia-Pacific region during the past quarter-century, the future of globalization, though presently important, remains uncertain.

The rise of China has certainly attracted the undivided attention of the U.S. government. Clearly, American analysts are deeply concerned about the future U.S. position in Asia-Pacific. Bruce Vaughn wrote a CRS Report for Congress titled, *"East Asian Summit: Issues for Congress"*, in early December 2005. This report was published a couple of weeks before the first-ever East Asia Summit gathering at Kuala Lumpur, Indonesia, that took place in late-December 2005.

In his summary, Vaughn cautiously warns that there are undeniable shifts and trends occurring within the region and the U.S. must recognize this reality and act upon them. Vaughn writes,

"Fundamental shifts underway in Asia could constrain the U.S. role in the multilateral affairs of Asia. The centrality of the United States is now being challenged by renewed regionalism in Asia and by China's rising influence . . . Although there are a number of obstacles to the realization of an East Asian bloc that would limit American influence in the region, some observers are of the opinion that the United States should take further steps to reinforce its own regional role and revitalize ties to with allies, friendly countries, and others to deter that possibility."[16]

In 2007, the 10th anniversary of the Asian financial meltdown was duly noted throughout the region. However, most saw little to celebrate because it represented another embarrassing moment in the Asia-Pacific region's history. Countries, such as Indonesia, South Korea and Thailand, suffered enormously as they watched their respective currencies plummet in value before their eyes. Economic activity slowed to a crawl.

I remember visiting Bangkok, Thailand and Seoul, South Korea during 1998. In both cases, the dramatic slowdown in economic activity was quite dramatic. In Bangkok, Thailand, I saw numerous sky-cranes and unfinished building projects throughout the city. I remember talking to taxi cab drivers who used to be white-collar workers until the economic meltdown cost them their jobs. I remember traveling through Kimpo International Airport in Seoul, South Korea during the Christmas season. I had expected huge crowds consisting of international travelers, family members being dropping off or picked up, security personnel, individuals representing airlines, car rentals, and various food and travel businesses. Not on that day. I was literally taken aback, asking myself, "Where are all the people?"

Not many people were smiling in either one of these Asian mega-cities. There was a kind of hush looming over them. You felt the embarrassment, humiliation and suffering of these proud people due to their precarious financial situations. Once again, Asia was dependent upon the West to save them from a calamity from which they could not save themselves. It was a difficult moment that has not been forgotten by the people of Asia-Pacific.

Walden Bello, professor of sociology at the University of the Philippines at Diliman, writes, "Ten years after the Asian financial cataclysm of 1997, the economies of the Western Pacific Rim are growing, though not at the rates they enjoyed before the crisis. There is no doubt that the region has been indelibly scarred by the crisis, the key indices being greater poverty, inequality, and social destabilization than existed before the crisis."[17] Professor Bello noted in another article that "Globalization has failed to provide capital an escape route from its accumulating crises. With its failure, we are now seeing capitalist elites giving up on it and resorting to nationalist strategies of protection and state-backed competition for global markets and global resources, with the U.S. capitalist class leading the way."[18]

Globalization, the rise of China and the painful memories of the 1997–1998 economic meltdown, are all contributing factors that eventually led to the first Asian Summit Conference held at Kuala Lumpur, Malaysia, in December 2005. However, does this regionally-based conference represent the new trends concerning the economic future and geopolitical perceptions within the Asia-Pacific region? I believe the answer to this critical question is yes and no. In short, the jury is still out on whether future Asian Summits will have a significant impact on the region. One of the common complaints throughout the region right now is that there are too many "alphabet" conferences and meetings already. Leaders throughout the region have simply too many other commitments and responsibilities to be able to attend all of them. Thus, future Asian Summits will have to prove that concrete results can be obtained by the attendance of these leaders to justify its existence and importance to this complex and vast region.

The Asian Summit meeting that occurred, in December 2005, was the brainchild of former Malaysian Prime Minister Mahathir bin Mohamad. He had advocated for years that such an Asian-only summit should be created to discuss the critical issues facing the region. Mahathir also saw the Asian Summit as a substantive symbol indicating to the West that a new Asia has emerged since the end of the 20th century. And, that Asians—alone—should have a serious venue in which to discuss the future challenges confronting Asia in the 21st century.

Prime Minister Mahathir wrote, in 2002, that the theory of globalization was not a "God-given, iron-clad law of nature or humanity. It is a set of concepts and policies made by human beings and, therefore, can also be re-conceptualized, reshaped and changed."[19] Prime Minister Mahathir went on to describe what he believed was the real origins of this global phenomena that was taking the world of finance to a new level of integration by stating in an article, "In reality, this concept was designed by the developed countries on behalf of their companies and financial institutions to overcome the regulations set up by developing countries to promote their domestic economy and local firms, which had been marginalized during colonialism."[20]

Simply put, Mahathir believes that globalization was a "risk" because it could produce, with equal rapidity, new wealth or financial disaster for those who fully accepted and participated in this economic concept without caution or study. Hence, the financial meltdown in East Asia, in 1997-1998, which Mahathir points to as a clear example of such a "risk" that went very badly for the region.[21] Thus, an Asian Summit became increasingly necessary for comprehensive discussions and consensus-based strategizing by Asian leaders on where the region should go in the 21st century and beyond. An agenda was published by the Institute of Defence and Strategic Studies in Singapore, in November 2005, just a month before the first Asian Summit commenced , that offered (30) recommendations for the visiting summiteers.

The contributors to this detailed report had written in their Executive Summary that their recommendations were designed toward "East Asia Summit's evolution from an nascent regional institution for addressing broad concerns of an intramural nature to, it is hoped, a regional mechanism not only for generalized confidence building, but one armed with a thematic and problem-solving agenda and empowered by its trustees to engage with and functionally manage the serious challenges confronting the region."[22]

Early skeptics such as Ryu Jin, a *Korea Times* correspondent, reported that the inaugural meeting "revealed the rocky path ahead as some have already begun struggling for leadership."[23] Ryu's reporting also exposed one of the future obstacles for the East Asia Summit is the issue of membership, he writes "The dispute, international relations say, reflects the behind-the-scenes mechanisms of world politics, which have become increasingly acute in East Asia due to, along with other minor causes, the invisible competition between China and the United States."[24] Patrick Walters, a correspondent for *The Australian*, wrote that the inaugural East Asian Summit was not a threat to the longer established ASEAN forum which was established in 1967. However, Walters indicates that the first East Asian Summit does represent a changing-of-the-guard in the region's power structure, his report states "the summit has clearly delineated China's rapid ascent to become the dominant strategic influence in the region, eclipsing Japan which has long been ASEAN's biggest investor, trading partner and aid donor."[25]

However, in 2008, it appears that the annual Asia Summit may have already achieved a greater stature than its critics had anticipated within Asia-Pacific. During *"The Shangri-La Dialogue"* which represented the 7th International Institute for Strategic Studies (IISS) Asia Security Summit, held at Singapore in May–June 2008, the final report for this summit indicated that the Asia Summit was now considered to be in the same league as the ASEAN

Defence Ministers and the Shanghai Cooperation Organization.[26] Not bad for a regional gathering that had its initial meeting only three years earlier.

EAST ASIA SECURITY AND TRADE ORGANIZATION (EASTO): ASIA-PACIFIC'S NEW PARADIGM IN THE 21ST CENTURY

Perhaps, my idea of creating the East Asia Security and Trade Organization (EASTO) is not too far-fetched of an idea after all. The regional dynamics are changing at lightening speed. Also, the new global imperatives and regional challenges directly affecting Asia-Pacific appear to favor such an organization that could comprehensively deal with the most pressing problems confronting this culturally and politically complex and diverse region within one policy structure. Why? In my opinion, ALL the existing global and regional dilemmas and difficulties are intertwined, to one degree or another. Having so many different forums and summits is a wasteful division of labor and time. And, at this moment, time is the enemy of mankind because many of the global problems such as the environment, food and water shortages and a fast-approaching energy crunch, just to name a few of the breath-taking challenges before us, makes the waste of human labor and time almost criminal. The leaders of Asia-Pacific, in the 21st century, will also, I believe, need to direct their finite energies increasingly toward growing domestic demands and needs. In short, maintaining social harmony and stability will be increasingly a challenge for ALL governments in the region.

Therefore, if EASTO could achieve anything, it would be an organization where Asia-Pacific's leaders and their ministers could come together under one roof—literally and regionally—to address the emerging economic, environmental and security issues that will affect them all. And, EASTO will also represent a real opportunity for the U.S. to be a direct participant within an organization that truly recognizes the new role and stature of the Asia-Pacific region in the 21st century. Hence, EASTO could very well, in the eyes of the world, be the geographic, hegemonic and political foundation of what many are calling—'The Asia-Pacific Century'.

NOTES

1. Henry Kissinger, "The Three Revolutions", *The Washington Post*, 7 April 2008, p. A17.

2. Joshua Kurlantzick, "Pax Asia-Pacifica? East Asian Integration and Its Implications for the United States," *The Washington Quarterly*, Summer 2007, pp. 67–68.

3. Dick Nanto, "East Asian Regional Architecture: New Economic and Security Arrangements and U.S. Policy", CRS Report for Congress, Congressional Research Service, 4 January 2008.

4. Jason T. Shaplen and James Laney, "Washington's Eastern Sunset: The Decline of U.S. Power in Northeast Asia", *Foreign Affairs*, November/December 2007.

5. C. Fred Bergsten speech, *"Embedding Pacific Asia in the Asia pacific: The Global Impact of an East Asian Community"*, Japan National Press Club, 2 September 2005.

6. Bruce Vaughn, *"U.S. Strategic and Defense Relationships in the Asia-Pacific Region"*, CRS Report for Congress, Congressional Research Service, 22 January 2007.

7. Ibod.

8. Fareed Zakaria, *The Post-American World* (New York: W.W. Norton & Company, 2008), pp. 80-81.

9. Ellen Frost, "Designing Asia: Chinese-led Integration of East Asia Spurs An Economic Boom and Diminishes U.S. Role in the Region", *YaleGlobal*, 12 May 2008.

10. Parag Khanna, *The Second World: Empires and Influence In The New Global Order* (New York: Random House, 2008), p. 262.

11. Ibid.

12. Ibid.

13. Neil Francis, "For An East Asian Union: Rethinking Asia's Cold War Alliances", *Global Catastrophe*, Volume 28 (3)—Fall 2006, Harvard International Review website.

14. Ibid.

15. David Skilling, "An Asia-Pacific Century?", The New Zealand Institute, 21 April 2006.

16. Bruce Vaughn, "East Asian Summit: Issues for Congress", CRS Report for Congress, Congressional Research Service, 9 December 2005.

17. Walden Bello, "All Fall Down: Ten Years After The Asian Financial Crisis", www.zmag.org, 13 August 2007.

18. Walden Bello, "The Post-Washington Dissensus", *Foreign Policy in Focus*, 24 September 2007.

19. Mahathir bin Mohamad, "Globalization: Challenges and Impact on Asia", a chapter within the book, *Recreating Asia: Visions for a New Century*(Singapore: John Wiley & Sons (Asia), 2002), pp. 5–11.

20. Ibid.

21. Ibid.

22. See Seng Tan and Ralf Emmers, editors, "An Agenda for the East Asia Summit", *Institute of Defence and Strategic Studies* (Singapore, November 2005), Executive Summary.

23. Ryu Jin, "Asia Summit Augurs Power Struggle", *The Korea Times*, 14 December 2005.

24. Ibid.

25. Patrick Walters, "East Asia Summit 'No Threat'", *The Australian*, 14 December 2005.

26. International Institute for Strategic Studies, "The Shangri-La Dialogue", Asia Security Summit, May–June 2008, Singapore.

Part II

SIGNIFICANT POWERS
IN ASIA-PACIFIC

Chapter Three

Australia: The Age of Rudd

Australia, at first glance, can be very deceiving to an outside observer. This large continent-nation has been blessed with a multitude of resources and a wildlife and vegetation that is unique only to itself. Yet, upon a closer look, one can see a harsher country due to a challenging environment which limits its capability of maintaining a functioning population. Jared Diamond, the globally renowned geographer who teaches at the University of California at Los Angeles, wrote in his international bestseller, *Guns, Germs, and Steel*, "Agriculture was another nonstarter in Australia, which is not only the driest continent but also the one with the most infertile soils. In addition, Australia is unique in that the overwhelming influence on climate over most of the continent is an irregular non-annual cycle, the ENSO (acronym for El Nino Southern Oscillation), rather than the regular annual cycle of the seasons so familiar in most other parts of the world."[1]

It is a nation that was originally isolated geographically, developmentally and indigenously from the mainstream of global affairs. Yet, in 2009, it finds itself ranked within the top twenty economies worldwide. Its stature is on the ascendance in the Asia-Pacific community. Australia, after maintaining the infamous 'whites only policy' with concern to its immigration policies since 1901—especially toward Asians—is now being steadily absorbed into the East Asian Hemisphere. As a result, the Australian political leadership in ALL the major political parties now views Asia-Pacific as their long-term savior, economically and militarily. The road for Australia since Federation, consummated in 1901, has certainly been a long and torturous one in respect to its embracement of its immediate Asian neighbors. The Australians were the 'white neighbors' in an Asian neighborhood who held them at arm's length due to its historical origins. Race, according to Paul Kelly, Australia's pre-eminent political commentator for *The Australian*, was the overwhelming issue for the new nation. Kelly wrote,

"In Australia love of country and pride of race became a united faith. At Federation the most powerful single element in Australian nationalism was racial unity. White Australia was the first policy of the new commonwealth; it was the first plank in the platform of the new Labor Party; it was the core requirement in the workplace of the new nation. To conceive of White Australia as just a policy is to misinterpret the situation. It was a policy but even more than a policy: it was the essence of national identity."[2]

I mention this historical fact concerning 'White Australia' and its racist overtones because Australia has dramatically come full circle as a nation— especially in its relations with its Asian neighbors. Not only has it shed its racist immigration policy, beginning in the 1960s, but it elected, in November 2007, a prime minister, Kevin Rudd, whose academic and professional backgrounds are deeply embedded in Asian affairs; China to be more exact. Indeed, Australians elected the first leader in its history who speaks Mandarin fluently. In fact, Kevin Rudd is the only Western leader to speak Mandarin. The timing could not have been better. In 2007, China became Australia's top trading partner, not just within Asia, but in the world.[3] French may be the language of diplomats, but Mandarin is increasingly the language of business in the Asia-Pacific community.

Australia is considered a 'middle-power' in the global hierarchical jungle of power politics. Again, the Land Downunder is somewhat incongruous to outsiders because, though its territorial size is considerable, its population is a meager 21 million. In short, lots of land but few people to defend it. I first traveled to Australia in January 1977. I had been assigned to serve at the Harold E. Holt Naval Communications Station in Western Australia. It was a facility shared by U.S. and Australian military personnel that was located upon the northwest cape of this immense state.

Though, quite clearly from the very beginning, I realized that the Australians were the junior partner at this 'joint-facility'. I was stationed at this facility for two years. During my tenure at this base, I traveled widely throughout Western Australia; from Port Hedland in the north, to Newman a mining town in the central region of the state, to the stunningly beautiful and sun-drenched city of Perth in the south; what I found was a beautiful and gritty nation and a people as wonderful and tenacious as the land they occupied.

In 2009, Australia is trying to define its economic and military positions in Asia-Pacific. The rise of China, during the past thirty years, is fundamentally changing the political landscape and the post-World War II relations between nations throughout the region. In essence, where is Australia's place in this newly forming constellation of nations in the most dynamic and diverse region in the world. It is a question that is being debate within all quarters of the Australian government and society.

A NEW VISION FOR AUSTRALIA AND THE ASIA-PACIFIC COMMUNITY

Prime Minister Rudd, in June 2008, gave a speech at The Asia Society Australasia Centre, in Sydney, titled, "It's Time to Build an Asia Pacific Community", that clearly spells out Rudd's new vision for Australia as the 21st century unfolds. The newly elected Australian prime minister spoke directly to what he perceives as the fundamental challenges and opportunities awaiting Australia,

"The Government's mission is to build a strong and fair Australia capable of meeting the new challenges of the 21st century...But Australia faces additional regional and global challenges also crucial to our nation's future—climate change, questions of energy and food security, the rise of China and the rise of India...When Australia looks to the Asia-Pacific region, we can see significant future challenges...A core challenge for Australia is—how do we best prepare ourselves for the Asia Pacific Century—to maximize the opportunities, to minimize the threats and to make our own active contribution to making this Asia-Pacific Century peaceful, prosperous and sustainable for us all."[4]

Prime Minister Rudd's vision for the region is not based upon vague or fuzzy perspectives, he sees Asia as the fastest growing region—economically and militarily. He also stated in his speech "by 2020, according to a study in 2007, that Asia will account for around 45 per cent of global trade . . . it will account for around one-third of global trade...Asia's share of global military spending will have grown to nearly one quarter. Put simply, global economic and strategic weight is shifting to Asia."[5]

Finally, Rudd identifies the three pillars on which Australian foreign policy is founded upon:

1) The ANZUS Treaty (Australia—U.S. Security Alliance)
2) The United Nations (Rules Based International System)
3) Comprehensive Engagement in the Asia-Pacific Region[6]

The Australia—U.S. security alliance remains the primary foundational pillar upon which Australia's existence and influential stands on. It is true that China has become Australia's top trading partner, but it is America who provides the protective shield from which Australians operate within the

Asia-Pacific region with certainty and confidence. The Australian government also understands it has an obligation to maintain to the best of its ability
a credible military force to assist the United States in a region that has a pro-
pensity for the unpredictable. And, this reality requires that Australia spend,
according to its ability, the proper amount of its GDP in the promotion and
development of its own security. The Australian defense budget for 2007-
2008 was a reflection of the seriousness that the government takes its responsibility toward this objective. The overall defense budget will be increased by
10.6% - the largest in thirty years. Patrick Walters, the national security editor
at *The Australian*, writes, "For the first time in more than a decade defense
spending has hit 2 per cent of GDP as the government continues the most
sustained defense buildup Australia has seen since WW2."[7]

Why does the Australian defense budget need to grow at an almost unprecedented (post-WWII) rate? What are the primary potential threats that
Australia confronts at the beginning of the 21st century? Of course, there
is the ever-present scourge of terrorism. A point of fact, since 9/11, almost
100 Australians has been killed by terrorist bombs directed toward them and
other westerners at resorts, such as Bali, in Southeast Asia. Yet, I believe the
primary motivator for the large increases in the Australian defense budget is
due to the budgetary double-digit modernization of the Chinese military. I do
not believe it has anything to do with the reemergence of historic fears relating to 'yellow peril', which has existed, to one degree or another, throughout
Australian history—certainly since its Federation in 1901.

Instead, I believe the Australian budgetary and geopolitical approach is
based upon a more pragmatic and proper analysis that views of an emerging hegemonic power, such as China, with a proper degree of respect and
skepticism. And, as expected, it is the 'China Factor' that is now dominating
conversations within the Australian government, particularly its foreign ministry and defense establishment. Alexander Downer, the former and longest
serving (1996-2007) Australian foreign minister in the nation's history, commented during an interview, in 2006, "the Chinese can be quite aggressive;
they want to see how tough you are at diplomacy. They tried to soften our
U.S. stance, but they came to respect our commitment to the U.S."[8]

As far as China's future involvement in Asia-Pacific affairs, Downer, who
currently represents the United Nations as a Special Envoy to Cyprus, does
not mince words on this important topic, "China has substantially strengthened its position in Asia-Pacific. Its stature has grown tremendously. China
has more prestige than Japan within the region. The 'China factor' is very
significant, and its growing power needs to be balanced within the (Asia-
Pacific) region, perhaps through institutions such as the East Asia Summit."[9]
Finally, Downer, who remains highly regarded throughout the Asia-Pacific

region, sees Asia-Pacific experiencing dramatic change in the near future. He noted at the end of our interview, in Canberra—the nation's capital, "I believe, over time, that a growing political momentum for an Asian Free Trade Area (AFTA) will emerge. And, I suspect the free trade area will extend from North China to New Zealand. However, a similar type of agreement concerning regional security will be harder to achieve."[10]

On matters concerning the Australian military and its future capabilities and objectives, I spoke with the former General of the Australian Army Peter Abigail. General Abigail views China's recent build-up and modernization as a process of "catch-up."[11] He agrees that China is indeed re-building its military to meet its security needs—domestically and internationally. However, he does not foresee any Chinese attack on any of its (14) neighbors. The primary reasons for his analysis are that he believes, "the way power is used in Asia is changing due to China and other important factors: Japan's 'normalization' dilemma; potential Korean unification; growing Russian power in Siberia."[12] General Abigail also believes the following geopolitical and regional events will occur in the relatively near future:

1) Taiwan receiving some type of Hong Kong-type of deal (Special Administrative Region) from mainland China.
2) The Koreans will, in the end, make their own decisions concerning the fate of the Korean Peninsula. Though, he notes that China would like to see U.S. troops off the Korean Peninsula as well.
3) Fewer U.S. military bases in Japan
4) U.S. strengthening its military and security capabilities in Singapore, Malaysia, Thailand and the Philippines
5) The Shanghai Cooperation Organization (SCO) is designed to get the U.S. out of the 'stan' countries in Central Asia which are located on China's western border[13]

Finally, General Abigail discusses the matter of Australia's current military capabilities and its future plan for being effective within the Asia-Pacific region. The former General of the Australian Army had some observations concerning the present-day use of the military, and what should be done about it. Abigail mentioned immediately that the Australian Army, and the other military branches, needs to be bigger because "Australia is in too many places, especially in the South Pacific. Australia has troops upon, or has sent troops to, such places as East Timor, Papua New Guinea, Solomon Islands and West Papua. All of these islands are 'fragile states'. Plus, we have troops in Iraq and Afghanistan as well. We are simply 'overstretched'. And, to provide proper intelligence coverage is very difficult. Remember, the Australian

Army is approximately 25,000 and the overall military has about 51,000 troops. New York City has a larger police force than the entire Australian military, but the New York City police force does not have to send its forces to different locations throughout the state of New York."[14]

To meet some of the growing demands upon the Australian military, as identified by General Abigail during our interview in May 2006, the (John) Howard government announced, in May 2007, that the nation's defense budget would be increased 10.6 per cent. Patrick Walters, the national security editor at *The Australian*, wrote that the double-digit spending surge represented the largest military spending increase in thirty years and that "an extra $14 billion has been committed over the next decade on equipment, personnel, logistics and continuing military operations offshore led by Afghanistan and Iraq."[15]

Australia's defense budget soared to $22 billion during the fiscal year 2007–2008. I know this size of a budget sounds like a joke to American readers who are used to reading about this level of expenditure in less than a *single* month for the U.S. military, but Australia, despite being a country relatively close to the size of the U.S., has a very small overall population—21 million.

General Abigail's observations concerning the (lack of) size of the Australian military, especially its army, with concern to its use in multiple military campaigns was addressed directly by this new budget. Walters writes, "The aim is to grow the overall size of the defense force by 6,000 to 57,000, by 2016, including a 30,000 strong army and rebuild the navy's strength which currently is 1000 below the targeted ceiling."[16] In an article written a year later, in April 2008, Walters notes that Australia has seriously invested in its 'hard power' capabilities, such as its armed forces and its key security agencies, and cut back on its 'soft power' entities such as the Department of Foreign Affairs and Trade (DFAT) in recent years. He points out that the Australian military budget has increased 55% since 2001 and the nation's key security agencies have seen their respective budgets more double in the same timeframe. Walters quotes Prime Minister Rudd saying, "The truth is that Australia has been too quiet for too long across the various councils of the world. That is why during the course of the next three years the world will see an increasingly activist Australian international policy."[17]

It is an interesting bit of irony, in my opinion, that Kevin Rudd who trounced the incumbent Prime Minister John Howard, in the November 2007 elections, due to what many Australians perceived as a misguided activist internationalist foreign policy. Now see the new Prime Minister Kevin Rudd maintaining the same activist and aggressive foreign policy of his predecessor. It reminded me of a prescient comment made by then Australian Foreign Minister Alexander Downer after I had finished interviewing him in May 2006. We were walking out his office and down a short hallway and he said to me if the Labor Party came to power in 2007 that Australia's national security would not be endangered at all. There might be a reduction in the scope of Australian foreign policy but the basic concept and strategy would remain the same.[18] It appears that his analysis concerning Australia's future foreign policy activities and initiatives was quite correct.

THE RISE OF CHINA AND THE ASIA-PACIFIC REGION

Prime Minister Rudd's new vision for the Asia-Pacific community and the enhancement of the Australian military to meet the potential demands and needs within the region are all part of a process in dealing with an emerging reality that will only become more intense and relevant to Australia and its citizenry in the immediate future. How does the Rudd Government handle the hegemonic rise of China within the Asia-Pacific region? How will this geopolitical fact alter its key alliances and relations with America and Japan? Can Australia, diplomatically and militarily, find the necessary and proper balance and positioning between these major powers—America, China and Japan?

First, let's look at the 'China Factor' in terms of what Australia is dealing with in geopolitical terms. Prime Minister Rudd, and many others within the Australian foreign policy establishment, believes that this may be the best opportunity and time for Australia to solidify its relations with China—the most dynamic economy in the Asia-Pacific region. The Prime Minister gave a speech at The Asia Society Australasia Centre, in Sydney, on 4 June 2008. Rudd spoke directly to the issue of Australia's role in the Asia-Pacific region and the 21st century. He stated, "The (Rudd) Government's mission is to build a strong and fair Australia capable of meeting the new challenges of the 21st century . . . But Australia faces additional regional and global challenges also crucial to our nation's future—climate change, questions of energy and food security, the rise of China and the rise of India . . . When Australia looks intrinsically to the Asia-Pacific region, we can see significant future challenges."[19]

Prime Minister Rudd also addressed the primary issue confronting Australia at the beginning of the new century, he stated, "A core challenge for Australia is—how do we best prepare ourselves for the Asia-Pacific Century—to maximize the opportunities, to minimize the threats and to make our own active contribution to making the Asia-Pacific Century peaceful, prosperous and sustainable for us all."[20] Though mentioned earlier in this chapter, I believe these primary points deserve to be presented again; Rudd identifies (3) factors associated with Asia's global standing by 2020:

1) Asia will account for around 45% of global GDP
2) Asia will account for around one-third of global trade
3) Asia's share of global military spending will be nearly 25%[21]

Prime Minister Rudd finished his speech by stating, "We in this nation have a unique requirement to fully comprehend and engage with the great new global dynamics of the Asia-Pacific Century. Australia must play its part in shaping the region's future. And that is what the new (Rudd) Australian Government intends to do."[22]

The Prime Minister's plan to have Australia participating in the construction and shaping of the Asia-Pacific Century is generally viewed as a positive step by the Australian people and within various government ministries. However, the biggest question is how does the Rudd Government steer a constructive and pragmatic course for Australia as the Asia-Pacific region becomes the fulcrum of global affairs in the 21st century? And, how should Australia handle the 'China Factor' which, in the minds of most regional observers, will be the main issue to confront the nation and the region throughout the present century? The views concerning these questions and others are presented within this section of the chapter. Thus, it is understood, that there is a great deal at stake for Australia—especially in terms of its future economic sustainability and national security.

Hugh White, a Visiting Fellow at the Lowy Institute for International Policy, is rather dubious about Prime Minister Rudd's vision of an 'Asia-Pacific Community'. He does not mince words about his thoughts concerning Rudd's visionary aspirations and intentions. White, who is also a Professor of Strategic Studies at the Australian National University, writes "First, I do not believe he is serious about the whole thing. Everything that Rudd has said and the way he has said it about the Asia-Pacific Community suggests that this was an idea dreamed up on the run to provide a story lead for his Asia Society speech and a news peg for his trip to Japan and Indonesia . . . Second, I don't much like the Asia-Pacific Community idea, even if Rudd is serious about it, because I do not think it is an effective way to address the real risks and challenges we fact in Asia...The forums themselves have at most a marginal effect. Does anyone really believe that strategic competition is growing between the U.S. and China because they have not found the right shaped table to sit down at yet?"[23]

Perhaps, the skeptical comments made by veteran Australian diplomat and former ambassador, Richard Woolcott, and Paul Kelly, Australia's pre-eminent political commentator, should be noted at this time. Ambassador Woolcott, in July 2008, talked with U.S. Deputy Secretary of State John Negroponte about Rudd's idea of creating a new Asia-Pacific Community forum. Woolcott conveyed to Kelly what Negroponte must have alluded to during their meeting in Washington, DC on this topic. Woolcott, the longtime Australian diplomat stated, "I think this is a real issue. It applies particularly to the U.S. The President has got to work out what meetings he goes to and which ones he doesn't. China, Japan and I suppose India and Indonesia already have a lot of commitments. This issue needs to be worked out."[24] This is diplomatic-speak for saying that the idea has merit but it requires a great deal more thought and development.

Paul Kelly, one of Australia's most astute observers of its politics—domestic and foreign, also questions the whole concept and he is simply unsure how receptive the region will be toward creating another forum for regional issues. Kelly writes,

"The Prime Minister is right to argue the Asia-Pacific, ideally, needs a new inclusive body that embraces the economic, political and security agendas. But this involves a triple test: whether the time is ripe in political terms, whether Rudd has the standing to persuade other leaders and whether the regional architecture option is the wisest foreign policy initiative for Australia at this point. Rudd wants to think big, but there is no obvious sign that the region will warm to this."[25] What Woolcott and Kelly are simply saying is that the Asia-Pacific Community idea is worth pursuing but it needs a great deal more planning and work.

The 'China Factor' is another issue that is hotly debated within various governmental and think-tank circles. The following questions keep Australian foreign policy practitioners busy into the late-hours of the night: To what degree, should Australia engage China? What are the geopolitical risks for going too far in reaching out to China? And, the China economic juggernaut and its increasing need for Australia's natural resources are one of the fundamental reasons for Australian economic prosperity since the early 1990s. Thus, a fundamental and inescapable question arises, is Australia ready to risk its future *economic* viability to preserve its future *security* alliance with the U.S.?

These questions are no longer discussed philosophically or theoretically. They are literally forcing themselves into the daily conversations amongst Australians and its representative government. However, the answers to these critical questions are becoming increasingly difficult to ascertain. In short, there is a growing perception that real consequences will be endured if the present stability within Asia-Pacific is rocked or shaken by some unexpected event or occurrence. And, Australia, if innovative and proper planning and thinking have not been done with concern to the questions mentioned above, could find itself in a great deal of trouble—economically and geopolitically.

On the matter of China, there are arguments supporting varying degrees of Australian engagement with the 'Middle Kingdom'. Rowan Callick, longtime foreign correspondent for *The Australian*, identifies Australia-China relations as the premier international relationship that must work. Callick writes, "There is no more important area of international affairs for Australia than its relationship with China and the ownership, production and trade of iron ore. It weighs heavily on Australia's earnings, its security and its influence. Getting it right will take wisdom, perseverance and nerve."[26]

Greg Sheridan, foreign editor at *The Australian*, wrote about Prime Minister Rudd's visit to China in April 2008. Sheridan, a conservative columnist who believes that Australia must remain actively engaged in Asia, saw Rudd's actions and statements in China as a possible harbinger for future relations with this powerful hegemonic power. Sheridan writes, "Kevin Rudd this week has produced his own cultural revolution. He may have transformed the way the world deals with China. He may have produced a great leap forward in the broad international project of making China a normal nation."[27]

Sheridan, one of the leading voices concerning Australian foreign policy, views Rudd as being a unique Western leader who can criticize China without being seen as an enemy of China due to his academic and personal connection to the country. The Australian prime minister has shown, so far, not to be afraid of a Chinese backlash for his public utterances concerning Chinese human rights abuses against its own people in Tibet. Sheridan, in admiration, writes, "No Western leader, with the partial exception of U.S. presidents, does what Rudd did this week: criticize the Chinese over human rights abuses in Tibet before he arrives, in fact in a joint press conference with U.S. President George W. Bush. Repeat the criticism in London. Absorb furious official Chinese protests in Beijing and Canberra, then go to China and repeat the offense in public, in front of a Chinese audience."[28]

However, John McDonnell, a trade adviser to the Chinese government between 1986 and 1989 during the reign of the Hawke Government, reminds readers that Prime Minister Rudd walks upon a very thin line between being too close to the Chinese leadership and maintaining a tough negotiating position on matters of great important to Australia. McDonnell, who wrote in a column for *The Australian*, "The Prime Minister, as someone who knows and understands China, must realize that he has to clarify, for Australians as well as the Chinese public, the basis on which he deals with the leadership in Beijing . . . The PM is in an invidious position; he must demonstrate that he has an arm's-length relationship with the Chinese Government while at the same time building on his reputation as the Western leader who is closest to China."[29] Yet, McDonnell, at the end of his column, reminds his fellow Australians, but especially Prime Minister Rudd, on what the former U.S. Secretary of State Henry Kissinger once said many years ago, that you must be willing to walk away from the negotiating table if you feel the Chinese are not meeting, or recognizing, your fundamental national interests.[30]

Nevertheless, Allan Gyngell and Michael Wesley, both longtime and highly respected foreign policy scholars, believe that Prime Minister Rudd represents a completely new image for Australia in its foreign relations with China. Gyngell and Wesley, both members of the Lowy Institute, wrote in *The Australian Financial Review*, "Kevin Rudd will arrive in Beijing with something like celebrity status—no previous Australian prime minister has had anything like the public profile in China of Lu Kewen (Rudd's Chinese name)...China is central to his foreign policy experience. He studied Chinese history and language, was posted to the Australian embassy in Beijing and has worked in China as a business consultant...This is good news for us. The Prime Minister can communicate an image of modern Australia directly to the Chinese public . . . The question for Australia (and the immediate foreign policy challenge for Rudd) is how this personal narrative can be harnessed for a broader and more difficult purpose: reshaping and giving new depth to the Australia-China relationship."[31]

In regional geopolitical terms, Prime Minister Rudd showed strong enthusiasm for the American idea of creating a permanent security body consisting of the nations (the U.S., China, Japan, Russia and North and South Korea) who participated in the six-party talks that were related to the evolving nuclear situation inside North Korea. In April 2008, Rudd discussed this new American security initiative for North Asia during a visit to Washington, DC, with U.S. President George W. Bush and U.S. Secretary of State Condoleezza Rice. The Prime Minister afterwards commented, "We should welcome any efforts by the U.S., China, Japan and others to extend the six-party talks mechanism into a broader security mechanism, one that would later be broadened to include other countries."[32] Rudd also stated, "Given Australia's strong economic and strategic interests in north Asia, we would see ourselves as a participant in any such mechanism at the earliest opportunity."[33]

Actually, this idea of creating a regional security entity is not really a new concept at all. In June 2007, a similar concept had been proposed by then Australian Foreign Minister Alexander Downer during a visit to Tokyo, Japan. Downer stressed the need for Northeast Asia to have a permanent security forum to deal with potential flash points like the Korean Peninsula and the Taiwan Strait. The then Foreign Minister stated, "Australia is interested in the question of the possible evolution of a Northeast Asian security mechanism . . . For Australia, no region is more important to our future than North Asia."[34]

Perhaps, foreign policy scholar Hugh White has put his finger on the main concerns for Australia and its citizenry. Professor White wrote in a white paper for the Lowy Institute, in 2006, titled, "Beyond the Defense of Australia", that "we live in an era of profound change in the global distribution of power among states, especially in Asia, with uncertain strategic consequences. It is quite unclear how the international system will accommodate the growing power of China, India and perhaps others. There is a real risk that the stable Asian international order of recent decades, on which Australia's security and prosperity depends, will be undermined. This raises questions about how to protect Australia's security in a more unsettled Asia of powerful and potentially hostile states."[35] Perhaps, indeed, the time to create a more formalized and substantial organization that deals directly with security matters in North Asia has finally arrived.

Former Australian Defense Chief General Peter Cosgrove participated in Prime Minister Rudd's 'Australia 2020 Summit' gathering in April 2008. According to the initial summit report (introduction), "The Australia 2020 Summit was designed to harness the best ideas from across the nation and apply them to challenges before us, to create a better future for Australia."[36] In essence, the summit was taking a 'Big Picture' approach to the major problems confronting Australia today and in the future. General Cosgrove participated in a group of about 90 individuals discussing Australia geopolitical challenges. He commented, in *The Australian*, on the geopolitical consensus that had formed within the group, "we have to build an independent international relations policy. This is not a code for no more alliances. We have to have an Australian view which is specific to our own future. To have our voice heard, we have got to earn the leadership. We believe that we should aim for a cultural step where we are the most open and the more diverse culture in the world. It is very much the engagement on every plane of nation states, one with the other."[37]

THE AUSTRALIAN MINERAL INDUSTRY: MONEY IN THE BANK

In order for Australia to have a bigger voice in Asia-Pacific affairs it will have to maintain it's expanding and highly productive economic base. Point in fact, financial prowess is a basic and fundamental requisite toward possessing a larger presence in global affairs. In the case of Australia, both major political parties (Labor and Liberal) wish for their country to play a substantial role in regional affairs concerning Asia-Pacific. Perhaps, in some cases, to even influence and participate in the eventual outcome of critical global issues as well. Australia also desires to be seen as an independent broker amongst the more powerful and influential players in the Asia-Pacific region. However, I believe there are two major obstacles that stand in the way of fulfilling this geopolitical objective.

First, it remains a Commonwealth nation that technically has the British monarch, Queen Elizabeth, as its head of state. Despite vigorous protestations that Australia is a thriving democracy, with a directly elected representative government which is completely capable of deciding the issues confronting the nation, once again, recent history contradicts and haunts this nationalistic defense. On 11 November 1975, then Labor Prime Minister Gough Whitlam and his elected government were essentially fired by Queen Elizabeth's then representative in Australia, Governor-General John Kerr. It is an event that still disturbs and haunts Australian society.

I know this for a fact, because I gave a paper on the dismissal of the Whitlam Government at the annual Australian-New Zealand Studies conference, in 2006, which was held at Georgetown University. I clearly demonstrated that indeed there was irrefutable evidence which indicated external interference emanating from both the U.S. and British governments. This was very unsettling for some of the Australians in the audience, though there were several who nodded in agreement with my historical analysis.

Yet, later on that day, a troubling occurrence took place at the conference concerning this very same topic; an older woman who attends the annual conference every year and is also a major contributor to its success—motioned with a slashing movement with her hand across her throat while looking at the chairperson who was overseeing the panel discussion. In short, she told him to end the conversation now!

And, indeed, the discussion came to an abrupt halt. The audience was taken aback and shocked by this heavy-handed disciplinary action. Three years later, I have certainly not forgotten the incident. In retrospect, I realize that these individuals who believe they can simply expunge or hide from history and memory, are always angered and surprised when these related human elements constantly interject themselves into present-day affairs, whether we want them to or not.

The second major obstacle confronting Australia's desire to be a more independent and influential voice in geopolitical affairs is its growing dependence upon China and other Asian nations to purchase its almost infinitely available mineral resources. Australia is the driest continent—except for Antarctica—in the world and it has not been blessed with exceedingly fertile soils with the capability to naturally grow an abundance of food. However, this beautiful island-continent does possess an enormous amount of various minerals that are greatly in demand, especially by the dynamic and growing economies within Asia. Yet, a real danger exists for Australia and its future status in Asia-Pacific.

History has shown that the foundational base for any nation's ability to project influence and power is its economy. Australia's industrial base is relatively small, due in part, to having a small domestic market. The country has only 21 million citizens. Overall, the Australian economy ranks 16th in the world in terms of total GNP. Like much of the developed world, Australia has lost manufacturing jobs to their Asian neighbors who possess an almost limitless source of cheap physical labor. In short, Australia's economy is becoming increasingly one-dimensional. Though, I do recognize that Australia exports wool, commercial goods and various food products, yet, the real money that drives the nation's economy forward is its prodigious mineral-exporting industries. In fact, one can make a strong argument that the growth of the Australian economy over the past seventeen years would never have occurred without the huge and growing mineral demands from developing countries such as China and India.

Put simply, in 2009, it is the selling of Australia's natural resources, primarily located in the state of Western Australia, that have become the backbone of the modern Australian economy. China, in particular, has invested billions into the Australian outback hoping to have first access to any future oil and gas discoveries, and they have signed long-term multi-billion dollar contracts for the continued importation of Australia's valuable minerals that Chinese manufacturing so desperately needs to maintain the nation's high economic growth rates. In May 2007, Sid Marris, an economic correspondent for *The Australian*, writes, "Booming economies in China and India will keep demand for Australian resources growing at a healthy pace despite increasing competition from other mining nations, according to then Australian Treasurer Peter Costello."[38] Marris also writes, "China, with its fourth straight year of double-digit economic growth—rising 10 per cent last year—remains the most important resources market for Australia after this month overtaking Japan to become our biggest trading partner."[39]

According to Ross Garnaut, who some consider Australia's most influential economist, Australia is going to greatly benefit from the continued growth of China.[40] Rowan Callick, a correspondent for *The Australian* stationed in China, writes, "Australia's most influential economist, Ross Garnaut, forecasts in a report that China is at an historic economic and social turning point that will lead to an even bigger appetite for resources at higher prices."[41] Garnaut, who was chief economic adviser to former Australian Prime Minister Bob Hawke and later appointed as the nation's ambassador to China, drafted a report, along with colleague Associate Professor Song Ligang at Australian National University, which was based upon economic studies concerning Australia's regional neighbors such as Japan, South Korea, Singapore and Taiwan at similar stages of their own development. Garnaut and Song concluded the China is approaching a "period of resource-intensive demand unique in world history."[42] The two scholars also believe that China has the potential to increase its economic output by a multiple of eight over the next two decades. This economic speculation is based upon China's growth patterns over the past twenty years—its economy has enlarged by a multiple of six.[43]

LIVING AMONG GIANTS IN THE 21ST CENTURY

Despite the continuation of Australia's economic prosperity and, in November 2007, electing a new prime minister who is attempting to create a greater and more meaningful role for Australia in the Asia-Pacific region, I sense a nation that is approaching the 21st century with cautious optimism. I have lived, or have visited many times, Australia since 1977. The Australian people have always been portrayed as a group of independent minded roustabouts who take life as it comes. This image is true. Yet, they are also a quiet people who have a strong sense of themselves. They are a people who have no illusions about their place, or their country's place, in the universe of mankind. In short, Australians have learned to be realists in a world that represents uncertainty, perhaps, even danger. They didn't create the world, but they have learned to survive in it.

A poll published in September 2008, taken by the Australian-based Lowy Institute, showed that a growing number of Australians now have a favorable view of the U.S. and a growing wariness of China. This poll does not represent an anti-China sentiment, but it does indicate that China's continued growth as a major power in Asia-Pacific has created some concern. It also appears that Australians are now slowly moving back toward their two most important allies in the region: America and Japan. Allan Gyngell, Lowy Institute Executive Director, stated, "Trust in the United States also appears to have improved slightly. This year the United States tied with Japan when it comes to overall trust to act responsibly in the world. That's ahead of India, Russia and China."[44]

During my many visits to this wonderful land, and from my many conversations and interviews with Australian citizens, I always came away with the sense that Australians maintain a keen awareness of their precarious situation in Asia. They are a former British colony that has not become a totally independent republic in the 21st century. Yet, their stature has grown within the Asia-Pacific community due to the nation's successful domestic economy and democratic politics, and for their expansive and visionary foreign policies - which reflects Australia's coming of age. As a result, the Australian government is increasingly introducing regional initiatives, participating in regional forums and meetings, and reaching out to their neighbors in constructive ways that produce and promote friendship.

It is my firm belief that Australians realizes that their *long-term* survival will be dependent upon their direct involvement and participation at all economic and political levels with their Asian brethren. Thus, the convergence of hegemonic aspirations, regional geography and domestic and international politics can quite possibly produce a new Australia. Perhaps, *The Age of Rudd* will represent an historic epoch. In short, a period when the fundamental re-transformation of Australian society occurred, and its destiny within the Asia-Pacific region was redirected in the 21st century.

NOTES

1. Jared Diamond, *Guns, Germs, and Steel: The Fates of Human Societies* (New York: W. W. Norton & Company, 2005), p. 308.

2. Paul Kelly, *100 Years: The Australian Story* (New South Wales: Allen & Unwin, 2001), p. 52.

3. C. Fred Bergsten, Charles Freeman, Nicholas R. Lardy and Derek J. Mitchell, *China's Rise: Challenges and Opportunities* (Washington, DC: Peterson Institute For International Economics, 2008), p. 221.

4. Speech by Australian Prime Minister Kevin Rudd, The Asia Society Australasia Centre, Sydney, 4 June 2008, titled, "It's Time to Build an Asia Pacific Community."

5. Ibid.

6. Ibid.

7. Patrick Walters, "Defense Spending Jumps 10.6pc to $22 billion", *The Australian*, 8 May 2007.

8. Interview with Alexander Downer, Australian Foreign Minister, Canberra, ACT, 22 May 2006.

9. Ibid.

10. Ibid.

11. Interview with Peter Abigail, former Australian Army General, Canberra, ACT, 22 May 2006.

12. Ibid.

13. Ibid.

14. Ibid.

15. Patrick Walters, "Defense Spending Jumps 10.6pc to $22 Billion", *The Australian*, 8 May 2007.

16. Ibid.

17. Patrick Walters, "Cuts Will Weaken Our 'Soft Power'", *The Australian*, 11 April 2008.

18. Interview with Australian Foreign Minister, Alexander Downer, 22 May 2006.

19. Speech by Australian Prime Minister Kevin Rudd, "It's Time To Build An Asia-Pacific Community", The Asia Society Australasia Centre, Sydney, Australia, 4 June 2008.

20. Ibid.

21. Ibid.

22. Ibid.

23. Hugh White, "Rudd's Asia Plan Lacks Conviction", The Lowy Institute Blog, 16 June 2008.

24. Paul Kelly, "Time May Not Be Ripe", *The Australian* Blog, 9 July 2008.

25. Ibid.

26. Rowan Callick, "Strong Ties With China Are Critical', *The Australian*, 17 March 2008.

27. Greg Sheridan, "PM Makes Great Leap On China", *The Australian*, 12 April 2008.

28. Ibid.

29. John McDonnell, "Special Relationships Are Fraught", *The Australian*, 14 April 2008.

30. Ibid.

31. Allan Gyngell and Michael Wesley, "Regional Diplomacy Has New Impetus", *The Australian Financial Review*, 3 April 2008, p. 79.

32. Dennis Shanahan, "Move to Join Security Group", *The Australian*, 2 April 2008.

33. Ibid.

34. The Associated Press, "Australia Calls For Security Forum: Regional Link Sought for Northeast Asia", *International Herald Tribune*, 7 June 2007, p. 3.

35. Hugh White, "Beyond the Defense of Australia: Finding a New Balance in Australian Strategic Policy", Lowy Institute for International Policy, Lowy Institute Paper 16, 2006.

36. Australia 2020 Summit, Initial Summit Report, April 2008.

37. Editorial, "Security 'Key to Australia's Future", *The Australian*, 19 April 2008.

38. Sid Marris, "China to Continue Feeding the Boom", *The Australian*, 8 May 2008.

39. Ibid.

40. Rowan Callick, "China Close to Turning Point", *The Australian*, 2 August 2007.

41. Ibid.

42. Ibid.

43. Ibid.

44. Lowy Institute For International Policy, "Australians Turn to the United States But Are Increasingly Wary of China: Lowy Poll 2008", 28 September 2008.

Chapter Four

Japan: The Uncertain Rising Sun

It is not a cliché to say that Japan is truly an enigma to much of the world. It is presently the second most powerful economy in the world, and its military, though limited by its post-World War II (U.S.-designed) constitution, is one of the most technologically advanced in the world. Yet, Japanese domestic politics rivals Italy's in terms of instability and incoherence. Japan is a country that is experiencing a tumultuous period in its history for several reasons:

1) The rise of China
2) A nuclear armed North Korea
3) An America overstretched - financially and militarily

As a consequence, it may be time for the Japanese to develop and implement a new and revised stratagem for itself within the Asia-Pacific paradigm. Simply put, Japan finds itself caught within the unmerciful riptides of history. Yet, its government is suffering from an acute case of paralysis from analysis, and it is this institutional gridlock which is undermining future Japanese domestic and foreign policies. Questions such as: Which geopolitical direction does Japan embark upon in the 21st century? Is Japan capable of breaking out of its post-WWII constitutional and geopolitical confinement? Can U.S.-Japan relations survive such a fundamental reconfiguration of Japan's role in Asia-Pacific? Will the answers to these questions lead to conflict with China in the near future?

In terms of its defense and foreign policies, Japan has been seriously restricted for approximately the past 60 years since the signing of the San Francisco Peace Treaty in 1951. This treaty officially ended WWII between the United States and Japan. Since the treaty's implementation, in 1952, the

Japanese, like most of their Asia-Pacific neighbors, have functioned quite well within the American constructed 'hub-in-spokes' Asia-Pacific security framework. Also, the signing of the San Francisco Peace Treaty tied together the destinies of these two powerful nations within the Asia-Pacific region for over a half-century.

Upon reflection, it appears that both nations have greatly benefited from this arrangement during the past 60 years. America built numerous military bases in Japan with the purpose of maintaining its position in East Asia, as well as preventing a possible resurgence of Japanese militarism. And, in return, Japan was able to rebuild its economy (with U.S. aid) without committing large expenditures for its own defense due to the U.S. accepting this responsibility willingly. It should also be noted that U.S. policies, in this regard, during this period, were met with quiet approval by almost all East Asian nations—including Communist China. Thus, the containment of post-WWII Japan was fully supported.

However, in 2009, the dynamics and geopolitical environment within the Asia-Pacific region has changed significantly. The U.S.-Japan security alliance is now being seriously re-evaluated by a growing number of Japanese politicians and scholars. The *relationship* is still very important to both nations, but recent global developments and events have made many Japanese feel that America's influence is on the wane. In addition, the geopolitical situation in East Asia is increasingly daunting and unsettling to Japan's political establishment. Recently, the U.S. has requested that Japan expand its military capabilities within East Asia—especially its coast guard fleet. This new maritime development, so far, has not unnerved nor has it triggered an arms race amongst the major powers in the region: China, North/South Korea, Russia or Vietnam.

However, if Japan keeps expanding its military footprint within the region, questions will be asked about its ultimate objective(s) with concern to Asia-Pacific. And, what future role will the U.S. play in terms of keeping the Japanese within acceptable boundaries—militarily speaking. Finally, you can count on the Chinese, Koreans, Russians and the Vietnamese to enhance their military capabilities. Unlike Americans, WWII is still very much on the minds of Japan's victims from this bloody and destructive period of Asian history.

Richard Samuels, author of *Securing Japan*, writes in the conclusion of his well-received book that the U.S. and Japan are in the process of re-evaluating their almost 60-year alliance due to the changing circumstances within Asia. Samuels, the Ford International Professor of Political Science and Director of the Center for International Studies at the Massachusetts Institute of Technology, does not perceive any anti-American sentiments within the Japanese establishment, but instead Japan is simply being pragmatic about the real strategic value of its alliance with America.

Professor Samuels writes,

"Washington understands that Tokyo will work hard to reconcile its Asian diplomacy and economic interests with its global diplomacy and military interests. It knows that its friends in Japan's military establishment are doing rhetorical battle with those in the economic establishment who are less convinced of the value of the "globalized" alliance. Thus, recent agreements concerning "alliance transformation" notwithstanding, it is by no means a foregone conclusion that either Japan or the United States will continue to see an enhanced militarized alliance as its best choice. Having examined Japanese strategic options, then, it is useful to glance at those of the United States as well."[1]

The U.S. situation in the Asia-Pacific region is indeed increasingly complex and delicate. Historically, the American presence in this region has been vitally important to its economic and geopolitical interests since the 19th century. America has dedicated enormous resources in maintaining its presence in the region. In fact, the U.S. has shed a considerable amount of blood to ensure its position in Asia-Pacific. Yet, in 2009, this geographic, historic and strategic situation is now being re-assessed by the U.S. itself because the region's 'power equation' has been altered with the arrival of a new hegemonic power—China.

As a result, according to Professor Samuels, the 21st century in Asia-Pacific will very much depend on how the U.S. reacts to this 'game changing' development within the region. The entire American security network will be affected—perhaps dramatically—if the U.S. responds too aggressively or inappropriately to suit the vital interests of the nations directly involved, especially the U.S.-Japan alliance. Samuels writes,

"Ever since Alfred Thayer Mahan elaborated his maritime strategy for the United States, U.S. strategists have sought to establish Pacific outposts to secure American commerce and to balance against a rising hegemon in the region. In so doing, the United States found itself in successive Pacific wars—the first with Japan in the 1940s, then with China on the Korean Peninsula in the 1950s, and finally with Vietnam in the 1960s and 1970s. Since then, though, only after construction of a series of 'hub and spoke' alliances through which the United States could ensure its relationship with each of the region's powers was more robust than any of the relationships among them, the regional balance has been stable . . . Now, however, China is poised to become a peer, and its rise would ensure a relative decline of U.S. power that could destabilize the region . . . (And,) it is of vital importance to the

United States that China become a great power without alarming Japan and
its neighbors."[2]

JAPANESE POLITICS: ORGANIZED CHAOS

When I started this book, in 2007, the Japanese prime minister was Shinzo
Abe. By late-2008, Japan would already have two successors to Abe. Indeed,
within twenty-four months, the Japanese would witness the fall of Abe and
his successor Yasuo Fukuda; and the rise of Taro Aso. How long will Prime
Minister Aso's tenure be is anybody's guess. If recent history is any kind of
barometer to judge Aso's longevity, the Japanese would be wise to not invest
too much political capital upon any of his long-term commitments—even his
short-term commitments are suspect in the present political environment.

Not to be too irreverent on such an important subject, but, in the last two
decades, Japan has experienced a succession of prime ministers. In recent
times, Japanese politics appears to be almost irrelevant. How can a foreign
government negotiate with Japan on a serious matter when they know the
current leader could very well be gone within a year!?! And, the even more
troubling aspect about this mind-boggling situation is that ALL the prime
ministers come from the *same* political party in Japan—the Liberal Democratic Party (LDP). This party has been in power for almost the entire period
of Japanese history since 1955.[3]

In my opinion, this represents the heart of Japan's political nightmare. In
the late-1990s, I lived in Japan (including Okinawa) for over three years while
teaching history and government for the University of Maryland. In 2007, I
made two separate visits to Tokyo (International Christian University) and
Nagoya (Aichi University), respectively, to make presentations at two highly
respected academic institutions—while representing Central Michigan University. I always ask my hosts why Japan doesn't have more political competition
and stability. Their response was usually a simple shrug of the shoulders. Japan
has essentially evolved into a fragmented one-party democracy.

(Note: I returned to Aichi University, in May 2009, to do research and
study China at the International Center for Chinese Studies - which is affiliated with Aichi University)

Yes, there are other viable political parties, and they indeed have represen-
tation within the Japanese Diet, but none of them have ever been able to win
the prime minister-ship as an individual party, and only briefly as a coalition,
in the 1990s, since the mid-1950s.[4] Therefore, a suffocating political gridlock
has enveloped and stymied Japanese politics preventing much needed new
ideas or reforms to reach Japanese society.

In 2006, Shinzo Abe was elected prime minister in Japan. He promised to revise the Japanese Constitution—especially Article 9—once he took office. Abe stated, at a regional party convention in Hiroshima, "As the next LDP president, I'd like to take the lead to put revision of the Constitution on the political agenda."[5] He told the attendees that revising the Japanese Constitution was a deeply personal matter, by stating "I'd like to draft a new Constitution with my own hands."[6] It was Article 9 that prohibited Japan from initiating or participating in a war. It had served Japan well for close to sixty years before Abe's election to the prime minister-ship. Even today, it can be stated that this specific constitutional article, and the U.S. providing the necessary military security for Japan after they signed the San Francisco Peace Treaty in 1951, has brought a significant degree of comfort and stability to the people of the Asia-Pacific community.

Upon hindsight, the possibility of a resurgent Japan after WWII created a considerable amount of consternation throughout the region. In fact, one of the driving forces that eventually produced the ANZUS Treaty (1951)—involving America, Australia and New Zealand—was the issue of a resurgent Japan in the post-war period.

Yet, in 2006, Abe's proposal to revise this section of the Japanese constitution was generally acceptable to most Japanese because he also stated that he would maintain the tough foreign policies of his predecessor Koizumi toward China and Korea. Abe stated publicly that his dual foreign policy aims were "Japan should seek a larger role in the world and further strengthen its alliance with the United States."[7] Thus, Abe sought to revise the Japanese constitution and also promote reassurance throughout Asia, simultaneously, with concern to Japan's future foreign policy capabilities.

Shinzo Abe had replaced the somewhat flamboyant and eccentric Junichiro Koizumi, known for his Lion-King mane of hair and his love for Elvis Presley's music. But, he was also a controversial figure on two sensitive issues. First, he was the first Japanese prime minister to send a Japanese military contingent force into a foreign theater since WWII. Koizumi sent this contingent that represented Japan in support of the U.S. efforts in Iraq. And, secondly, the former prime minister occasionally created a firestorm of protest from China and Korea when he visited the Yasukuni Shrine which has a number of convicted war criminals interned there. Despite these controversial decisions, Koizumi, by most Japanese, was clearly perceived as being a successful prime minister who served 5 and half years in office. Considering the chaotic nature of Japanese politics since the fall of the Berlin Wall in November 1989, his tenure in office was viewed as providing much needed stability to a body politic that was fragmented and stifled by indecision concerning the nation's future direction.

At 51, Abe portrayed himself as an aggressive nationalist. He was the youngest Japanese prime minister elected in the post-WWII era.[8] The new prime minister was born in 1955, thus, he represented a new generation in Japan that had no direct ties to WWII (1941-1945) or to the post-war U.S. occupation of Japan (1945-1952). It was a generation that had come of age during the stunning economic resurgence of Japan in the 1970s and 1980s. The Japanese economic juggernaut had created a great deal of pride throughout the nation, but it also produced new voices within its business and political establishments questioning whether it was time for Japan to become a *'normal'* nation.

The most famous publication that expressed this sentiment amongst likeminded Japanese, in 1989, was an essay titled, "The Japan That Can Say No". It was written by Akio Morita, the co-founder of Sony, and Shintaro Ishihara, who is currently the governor of Tokyo. This controversial essay received a huge response throughout Japan. The essay essentially stated that the term *'normal'* meant that Japan must regain its autonomy and independence as a nation in its domestic and international affairs.[9] Of course, this emerging dialogue and grassroots nationalism, occurring within Japanese society, took place under the watchful gaze of the U.S. military which had numerous bases situated throughout the country.

Thus, a generation later, Prime Minister Abe, in 2006, proposed a new initiative to revise the Japanese Constitution. He had absolute majorities in both houses of the Diet (Japan's parliament). An idea that had percolated to the surface of Japanese society, in the late-1980s, was now being directly acted upon at the beginning of the 21st century. In short, it was not a new idea but it was certainly an idea that had remained in the consciousness of many Japanese businessmen and politicians. After eight months in office, in May 2007, Prime Minister Abe made his move to begin the process that would eventually lead to the revising of the U.S.-constructed Japanese Constitution. The Japanese Diet approved a three-year process to rationally debate the new reforms concerning the Constitution—especially its provisions restricting the development of Japan's military. Jin Xide, a researcher at the Institute of Japanese Studies affiliated to the Chinese Academy of Social Sciences, stated, "For Abe's ambition to revise the constitution, it is the first concrete step; it is a breakthrough, but it cannot guarantee revision."[10]

Three months later, Prime Minister Abe's dreams of redefining Japan in terms of patriotism and nationhood fell apart badly due to the national elections held on 29 July 2007; half of the upper house seats in The Diet were up for grabs. Though, most voters are generally supportive of Abe's reforms concerning the implementation of patriotic education, rewriting Article 9 of the national constitution, and even expanding the role and scope of the Japanese armed forces, it did not prevent the LDP from suffering one of its worst electoral setbacks in the party's history. It appears economic issues such as quality jobs for youth, rising health-care costs nationwide and uncertain pensions for the aged had clearly trumped Abe's visionary constitutional and patriotic reform agenda. Politically, Abe was badly wounded by this political debacle that called into question his ability to lead the LDP party and the nation. The LDP was especially devastated in the rural areas of Japan—they lost 17 seats amongst the 23 party incumbents.[11]

Upon retrospect, the telltale signs indicating a political disaster was metastasizing throughout Japan were clearly evident but Prime Minister Abe chose to ignore them. Despite Abe's confident statements that Japan's economy would eventually fix itself, the public did not have, or hold, the same confidence or perspective as the prime minister. Thus, the declining national economy became extremely problematic for the LDP as the July 2007 upper house elections drew closer. Yet, Abe remained focused primarily on his narrow political agenda, despite an increasing number of voters telling pollsters that their economic lives were worse or not improving since Abe's election in September 2006.

Richard Katz and Peter Ennis, co-editors of *The Oriental Economist Report*, a monthly newsletter in Japan, wrote that Prime Minister Abe's approval rating had dropped dramatically since his election, in September 2006, from 70% to 27% on the eve of the July 2007 elections. Those unhappy about their economic fortunes were growing in numbers. Pollsters showed that 42% of respondents felt they were worse off than before Abe became prime minister, and 54% indicated that they were no better off.[12] Thus, the LDP faced falling approval ratings for its prime minister, rising disgruntlement amongst voters and a faltering economy. A perfect storm was brewing amongst Japanese voters and the LDP stood in its path. Afterwards, though the LDP maintained its political leadership of the nation, its voice was undeniably weakened by the election results. Abe defiantly stated that he would not step down as leader, but, in September 2007, he was gone. Katz and Ennis wrote, "Ever since the fall of the Berlin Wall and the popping of Japan's late-1980s (real estate) bubble, Japan has suffered from political instability."[13] It appeared that it was time, once again, to find a new prime minister.

The LDP determined that youthful vigor and vision was not the answer for Japan and its current challenges and problems. This time the party looked to its past to save its future standing with the Japanese people. Yasuo Fukuda, a 72-year old former Chief Cabinet Secretary and then president of the LDP, received 62.6 % (330 votes out of 528 votes cast) of the vote in The Diet to become the 91st prime minister of Japan. The Fukuda family is well-known within the history of modern Japanese politics. His father, Takeo Fukuda, was the 67th Japanese prime minister from December 1976 to December 1978.[14] Now, the LDP turned to his son, Yasuo, to stabilize the party and restored its reputation with Japanese voters.

Unlike his predecessor, Prime Minister Fukuda reached out to the Chinese and Koreans and attempted to improve relations, despite the fact that relations with these two neighbors in northeast Asia have often been strained, if not hostile, in recent years. For a time, though, things looked promising for Fukuda. In May 2008, Chinese President Hu Jintao arrived in Japan for a 5-day state visit. President Hu was the first Chinese head of state to visit Japan in a decade. Many observers in China and Japan called the visit between Fukuda and Hu the "warm spring".[15] Most analysts considered the 5-day state visit a diplomatic success. Zheng Donghui, an expert on Japan studies at the China Institute of International Studies, observed "The Chinese president's visit is very important to regularized and instruct the development of bilateral relationships in the future."[16] Gong Li, professor of international relations at the International Strategic Research Center of the Central Party School of the Chinese Communist Party, said, "Hu's trip was a benchmark of bilateral ties indicating the Sino-Japanese relationship is entering a new stage of stability."[17]

Unfortunately, like former PM Abe, Prime Minster Fukuda also fell from grace very quickly due to domestic politics. Infighting amongst LDP colleagues over policy direction and unrelenting attacks from political opponents finally took its toll on the elder PM. His solid work on improving relations with their key rivals—China and South Korea—did not save him from experiencing the same fate as Abe a year earlier. There were other issues, however, such as the inability of the government to identify all the holders of the 50 million unattributed public pension accounts, intense fighting over whether Japan should continue its presence in the Indian Ocean region supporting the U.S.-backed anti-terror mission, and the re-implementation of a petrol-tax that was badly needed for budgetary reasons.[18] Altogether, the domestic situation and the toxic political environment in The Diet swallowed up Fukuda's political future like a group of orca whales immersed in a feeding frenzy in the north Pacific. In September 2008, Fukuda was a spent man. *The Economist* newsmagazine described the Japanese Prime Minister as "bruised, bothered and bewildered."[19]

As of this writing, in late-September 2008, the new prime minister is Taro Aso, a 68-year old conservative nationalist. He finally achieved his longtime goal in becoming the prime minister of Japan. He became the nation's 92nd prime minister when he received 351 votes (67%) out of 527 cast in The Diet. As expected, in country with a society still based upon a formidable hierarchical system, Aso, like Fukuda, also has direct bloodlines leading to the office of prime minister. He is the grandson of former Prime Minister Shigeru Yo-shida—who was the 45th prime minister of Japan from 1946 to 1947.[20] The post-WWII period was very difficult for a proud nation like Japan. Most the country's major cities lay in ashes from relentless U.S. bombing raids, including the dropping of atomic bombs on Hiroshima and Nagasaki, respectively. It was a time of simple survival.

Now, Yoshida's grandson, Taro, faces a different Japan with different challenges. Yet, Aso also knows that his time to accomplish his political agenda is quite limited due to the corrosive nature of Japanese domestic politics. They say the road to hell is paved with good intentions. Shinzo Abe lasted one year as PM. Yasuo Fukuda survived 11 months in the PM office. Aso, a savvy politician from the old school of Japanese politics must know the road ahead, politically speaking, is full of dangerous and daunting twists and turns. How long will he survive? Based upon the recent occupiers of the PM office in Japan, Aso better move very quickly to achieve anything in the current state of Japanese politics. He who waits is lost.

ALLIANCES AND RELATIONSHIPS

In 1999, *Time* magazine had a cover story titled, *Japan Returns to Nationalism*. The cover story, written by Tim Larimer, told of a Japan that was witnessing an increasing level of patriotism due to perceived external threats to the nation's security. Larimer writes, "Japan periodically experiences outbreaks of nationalistic fervor, but this time the backlash from pacifist and liberals has been unusually quiet . . . A general feeling of insecurity—over the economy, over North Korea's missile-rattling, over Japan's lost place in the world—shields the Obuchi government from criticism and gives it a lot of leeway to push an aggressive agenda."[21] Former Japanese Prime Minister Yasuhiro Nakasone commented that these demonstrations of patriotism are "part of an effort to re-establish Japan's identity."[22]

Ten years later, Japan is still struggling with its identity, and in trying to find its place in the world. The post-WWII paradigm continues to dominate its key relations. In terms of its security, its alliance and relationship with the U.S. remains the foundational stone upon which its foreign policy is built, particularly in relation to its activities within the Asia-Pacific region. Japan's second most important relationship is with the People's Republic of China. Though, China has replaced the U.S. as its number one trading partner, there is still great tensions and periodic bitterness between these regional rivals. It is a complex relationship fraught with danger and shows signs of hope, simultaneously.

At the beginning of the 21st century, the U.S.-Japan Security Treaty, originally signed in 1951, remains relevant and functioning. Chalmers Johnson, president of the Japan Policy Institute, has written that the security treaty is indeed still important but he finds it odd that after several decades the treaty has not been significantly amended despite major economic and geopolitical changes within the Asia-Pacific region. Johnson, a former chairman of the Center for Chinese Studies and professor of political science at the University of California at Berkeley, writes, "The important thing to understand is not that Japan might be on the verge of change, but why nothing fundamental has changed since the U.S.-Japan Security Treaty came into effect 47 years ago . . . In short, why do both the United States and Japan continue to shore up the old Cold War system rather than dismantle it?"[23] It is a question that is increasingly asked in Japan as well.

In November 2007, the U.S. Council on Foreign Relations and the Japanese Keizai Koho Center held a symposium in Tokyo, Japan to talk about the changing elements and factors in Asia-Pacific and how it will affect the U.S.-Japan alliance. Richard Haass, president of the Council on Foreign Relations stated from the outset that Japan is an "underachiever" that needs to perform at a higher level within the international arena.[24] Haass, a former special assistant to U.S. President George H.W. Bush from 1989 to 1993, followed up that opening salvo by further stating, "A more internationally active Japan is essential given that the world today is a mixed bag of historically rare opportunity coupled with new sets of daunting challenges, to which there can be no unilateral solutions."[25] At the end of the day, Haass observed "it is time that experts and academics across the Pacific to rethink the purpose of the U.S.-Japan relationship . . . What worked during one era of history will not automatically be relevant in a very different era of history."[26]

In March 2008, Brad Glosserman and Katsu Furukawa produced a joint-analysis titled, "*A New U.S.-Japan Agenda*", at the Pacific Forum CSIS in Honolulu, Hawaii. Glosserman, the executive director for the Pacific Forum CSIS in Honolulu, and Furukawa, a Research Fellow of the Research Institute of Science and Technology for Society in Japan Science and Technology Agency, proposed a nine-point agenda for further cooperation by the U.S and Japan during the 21st century. Both individuals believe that the U.S. and Japan will play extremely important roles not just regionally, but also globally. Glosserman and Furukawa assert that "The U.S.-Japan relationship remains central to regional and global security. The bilateral alliance is a cornerstone of U.S. engagement with Asia. The extended nuclear deterrent provides stability and assurance for Japan. Most significantly, however, the coordinated application of the two countries' resources to international problems is a force multiplier: working together, Japan and the U.S. can do far more than they can by themselves."[27]

At the end of Glosserman and Furukawa's detailed analysis, they sum up why these two major Pacific powers must remain allies and work together in Asia-Pacific. Simply, combined, they have the resources and strength to ensure peace and stability in a region, and, perhaps, the world, which is experiencing an historic economic and power shift at the beginning of the 21st century. Both scholars agree that "Japan aspires to enhance its diplomatic standing in the world. This is driven, in part, by a consideration to balance against and simultaneously engage with a rising China. Indeed, the changing geopolitical landscape in Asia is prompting Japan to embrace "value-oriented diplomacy," emphasizing the adoption of universal values and disciplines as major diplomatic instruments, such as democracy, freedom, the rule of law, and the market economy."[28]

Yet, there are those observers, such as Joseph Nye, Sultan of Oman Professor of International Relations at Harvard University's John F. Kennedy School of Government, who believes that many analysts perceive a "malaise" in Japan about its alliance with the United States.[29] The disgruntled Japanese point to issues such as the rise of China, the moving of U.S. marines off the island of Okinawa, North Korea's nuclear program, and that China simply has received more attention than Japan in the 2008 presidential election season. Professor Nye recognizes the importance of these issues to the Japanese people. He also acknowledges that there are factions within Japan who wish to see their nation become a "normal" country in terms of its foreign policy and military capabilities—including nuclear weapons. However, Nye believes that this type of policy evolution, right now, would cause greater problems than solutions within Asia-Pacific.[30]

Professor Nye takes a longer view of the current geopolitical situation in the Asia-Pacific region. He wrote, in an op-ed piece that was published in *The Korea Times*, about how he sees the future situation in northeast Asia, "The U.S. regards a triangular Japan-China-U.S. relationship as the basis of stability in East Asia, and wants good relations between all three of its legs. But the triangle is not equilateral, because the U.S. allied with Japan, and China need not become a threat to either country if they maintain that alliance."[31]

Unsurprisingly, the second most important relationship for Japan in Asia-Pacific is the one it has with the People's Republic of China. This relationship for Japan is much more complex and dangerous due to historic events extending back to the late-19th century. The first Sino-Japanese War (1894–1895), the invasion of Manchuria (1931), the second Sino-Japanese War (1937–1945) and several issues and incidents since WWII have contributed a tremendous amount of tension between the two countries. It is a relationship fraught with visceral anger (and hatred) and deep mistrust. Former General of the Australian Army, Peter Abigail, believes that the China-Japan relationship holds the key for sustaining future peace and stability in the region.[32]

Yet, when one looks at the multitude of newspaper and magazine articles, academic journal articles and books written on China-Japan relations, you come away with an overwhelming sense that no one truly knows how this volatile situation is going to turn out. Indeed, in terms of Sino-Japanese relations, the 21st century is just one big question mark. Without doubt, this relationship is crucial in keeping northeast Asia and the Asia-Pacific region peaceful and prosperous. But, China's rise is not only challenging the U.S. position in Asia, but Japan's as well. Thus, some believe that the U.S. and Japan must remain allies to thwart or neutralize the Chinese hegemonic emergence in the Pacific region.

Milton Ezrati, a Senior Economist and Strategist for Lord, Abbett, & Co., wrote, in an article for *Harvard International Review*, "Asia first glimpsed its future in 1997 when Japan and the United States renegotiated their long standing defense arrangements and China tried to sway Taiwan's elections by lobbing missiles into the Taiwan Strait."[33] Ezrati also wrote that the U.S. Pacific Fleet positioned themselves between China and Taiwan due to this missile exercise. The message, according to Ezrati, was quite clear on two counts for the Chinese: First, the U.S.-Japan alliance which allowed American bases in Japan were a major geopolitical problem for their future intentions within the region. Secondly, the U.S.-Japan alliance, in 1997, had stood between them (China) and Taiwan. And, it appeared that these two major powers were committed to protecting Taiwan's sovereignty.[34] In essence, Japan was increasingly a problem for China because it could potentially exercised greater influence and power in northeast Asia due to its American connection. Ezrati, author of the book, *Kawari: How Japan's Economic and Cultural Transformation Will Alter the Balance of Power Among Nations*, surmised that "this incident, in 1997, demonstrated a Sino-Japanese rivalry has been building, and it will surely intensify in coming years."[35]

In 2005 and 2006, it appears that Japanese Prime Minister Junichiro Koizumi did much to provoke anger amongst the Chinese on a regular basis. Koizumi, periodically, visiting the Yasukuni Shrine where Japan's WWII dead were interned (including war criminals) in Tokyo and the alteration of historic content in Japanese history books used in their schools had created a firestorm of protest from China's government and citizens. The Japanese appeared to be indifferent to the Chinese complaints and discontent.[36] Kent Calder, Director of the Reischauer Center for East Asian Studies at (SAIS) Johns Hopkins University, wrote, "Although Japan and China have close economics ties, their diplomatic relations have been strained by clashing interests and cultural friction."[37] Calder also noted that both countries "account for nearly three-quarters of the region's economic activity and more than half of the region's military spending. Despite their deep economic ties and a doubling of their bilateral trade in the past five years, their relationship is increasingly strained, with dangerous implications for the United States and the world at large."[38]

Hopes were raised with the emergence of a new Japanese prime minister, Shinzo Abe, elected in September 2006. Abe immediately pushed for a new summit with China, and he indicated that there would be no visits to the Yasukuni Shrine in the near future. Abe's Chief Cabinet Secretary, Yasuhisa Shiozaki, called for a new bilateral summit. Shiozaki decleared, "We should make use of this occasion to improve relations between Japan and China, and Japan and South Korea. It is important for all sides to work toward enabling bilateral summits to take place like they used to."[39] Victor Mallet, an observer of Asian affairs for the *Financial Times*, wrote, "Shinzo Abe's appointment this week as Japanese prime minister has been welcomed in Asian capitals as the possible dawn of a new era of co-operation between Japan and China, the two economic giants and traditional rivals in East Asia."[40]

Yet, within a few months, China became increasingly uncomfortable with Japanese Prime Minister Abe's aggressive foreign policy initiatives to put Japan back onto the world stage. Abe supported the following policies concerning Japanese foreign policy: First, he proposed new sanctions against North Korea due to their missile testing in late-September 2006. Secondly, he increased Japanese support for U.S. interventions in Iraq and Afghanistan. Third, he believed Japan should participate in the promotion of "universal values", "value-oriented democracy" and "freedom". Fourth, and finally, Abe strongly supported Japan's participation in the East Asian Summit. Altogether, this re-energized foreign policy struck the Chinese leadership as being too U.S.-oriented and simply too aggressive regionally.[41]

However, in April 2007, Feng Zhaokui, a journalist for the *Beijing Review*, wrote an article about the importance of China and Japan being able to cooperate in the future. Feng quotes the late Chinese leader Deng Xiaoping stating, "Maintaining friendly cooperation between the two countries is a mission not only endowed by history, but also by reality...From a strategic point of view, any differences or difficulties in bilateral ties are temporary, insubstantial and not insurmountable."[42] Feng, attempts to define the bigger picture for the two powerful nations in Asia and the world, by writing, "The bilateral relations are not to fulfill the global ambition of any big power, or to win votes for any political party, but to benefit the peoples in the two countries, as well as the people in Asia and the world."[43]

In February 2008, Seiichiro Takagi, a Professor at the School of International Politics, Economics and Business at Aoyama Gakuin University in Tokyo, wrote a commentary that stated, "The term "strategic relationship of mutual benefit" has come to symbolize the improved relations between Japan and China in the past year or so."[44] Professor Takagi did indeed identify these "common strategic interests" for Japan and China within his commentary. He divided these "interests" into two types: reciprocal and identical. For the former, Takagi mentions peaceful development, establishing mutual trust, understanding and simple friendship between the two peoples. The latter category consisted of foreign policy commonalities such as denuclearization of the Korean Peninsula, the reform of the National Security Council and the United Nations, and the promotion of ASEAN toward achieving greater regional cooperation throughout East Asia."[45]

China and Japan are presently immersed in serious talks concerning their respective futures, and the future of Asia-Pacific in the 21st century. And, the U.S. will certainly be part of their regional calculations. Gone are the days when the U.S. could secretly negotiate the movement of nuclear weapons through Japanese ports and waters with the approval of Japan.[46] In fact, documents discovered by Yasuko Kono, a professor of Japanese political and diplomatic history at Hosei University in Tokyo, at the U.S. National Archives established that the governments of South Korea and Taiwan wanted America to have nuclear weapons on the island of Okinawa to protect them from potential aggression by China, North Korea and the Soviet Union.[47]

At the end of the first decade in the 21st century, the security environment in Asia-Pacific has changed considerably. The Soviet Union now rests upon the ash heap of history—dissolving in December 1991. China, now communist and capitalist, is now seen as having a positive influence over North Korea and its difficult and enigmatic leadership. And, China-Japan relations are making progress—though history continues to impede its overall development. In May 2008, Michael Green, a scholar at The Center For Strategic and International Studies (CSIS) in Washington, DC, spoke at The Center For National Policy, about the future role of Japan in Asia and about the U.S.-Japan relationship. Professor Green stated at the very beginning of his talk that "there is a healthy bipartisanship, I think, to U.S.-Japan relations these days, which is encouraging. We have, I think, come out of basically a decade of bipartisan efforts to strengthen the alliance."[48] Green singled out U.S. critics of Japan's role in the U.S. security network in Asia-Pacific. He believes they are simply ignorant of what the Japanese have provided Americans over the past decades. That is, the ability to project U.S. power in this volatile but vital region.[49]

Green, an East Asian analyst at CSIS, told his audience, "For the U.S., I think it's worth briefly remembering what it is that Japan brings us strategically. It begins—certainly, it began five decades ago with our bases, Article Six of the Security Treaty. Without Japan's association and support, without U.S. bases, we wouldn't be able to project power the way we do, anywhere near the way we do in East Asia or West Asia."[50]

Finally, Professor Green reminded his listeners that Japan remains a major financial powerhouse and it is deeply involved in many of the world's most important financial institutions, "Remember, it's (Japan) the second largest contributor to most of the major international financial institutions, whether it's the World Bank or the IMF, the Asian Development Bank, the United Nations (UN). Japan has soft power."[51]

In concluding this chapter, it should be noted that Japan indeed plays an important strategic role—geopolitically and economically—in regional and global affairs. I might take this moment to inform readers that Japan, as of 16 September 2008, possesses $593.4 billion of U.S. Treasury Securities.[52] In other words, America's ability to project its influence throughout Asia-Pacific, and beyond, is fundamentally and irrefutably being financed by the generosity of Japanese banks. Therefore, not only is Japan the 'unsinkable aircraft carrier' in terms of U.S. security strategy for the Asia-Pacific region, but it also appears that the Land of the Rising Sun is also the 'unsinkable bank' in terms of financing the American Empire and its voracious regional and global agendas.

NOTES

1. Richard J. Samuels, *Securing Japan: Tokyo's Grand Strategy and The Future of East Asia* (Ithaca: Cornell University Press, 2007), p. 205.

2. Ibid.

3. Patrick Smith, *Japan: A Reinterpretation* (New York: Pantheon Books, 1997), p. 16.

4. Ibid., pp. 16–17.

5. Norimitsu Onishi, "Japan's Likely Next Premier in Hawkish Stand", *The New York Times*, 2 September 2006.

6. Ibid.

7. Ibid.

8. Ibid.

9. Akio Morita and Shintaro Ishihara, *"The Japan That Can Say No"*, was published in 1989. This famous essay represented a new dialogue within Japan concerning its future as a nation-state. Shintaro Ishihara later expanded this essay into a book,

The Japan That Can Say No: Why Japan Will Be First Among Equals (New York: Simon & Schuster, 1991)

10. *China Daily*, "Japan Takes First Step in Revising Pacifist Charter", 15 May 2007, p. 1.

11. *The Economist*, "Keeping His Head Just Above Water", 2 August 2007. The article was sub-titled: "Humiliation For The LDP, but Shinzo Abe Pretends It's a Mandate"

12. Richard Katz and Peter Ennis, "What Next For Japan?", *foreignaffairs.org*, 1 August 2007.

13. Ibid.

14. The Yomiuri Shimbun, "Fukuda Triumphs in LDP Race/New Leader Eyes 'Revival' of Party After Winning 63% of Vote", *Daily Yomiuri Online*, 24 September 2007.

15. Ding Ying, "The Season of Regeneration", *Beijing Review*, 15 May 2008, p. 10.

16. Ibid.

17. Ibid.

18. I used three different sources for this section of the book:

The Yomiuri Shimbun, "Fukuda May Admit Pledge Can't Be Met/Apology For Broken Pension Promise Eyed", *Daily Yomiuri Online*, 18 December 2007.

Hiroko Tabuchi, "Japan's Parliament Passes Anti-Terror Bill to Revive Indian Ocean Mission", *Daily Yomiuri Online*, 11 January 2008.

Peter Alford, "Japanese PM Faces a Mutiny", *The Australian*, 26 April 2008. Alford is the Tokyo correspondent for *The Australian*.

19. *The Economist*, "Another Grey Man Bites the Dust", 4 September 2008.

20. The Yomiuri Shimbun, "Aso Elected LDP Head", *Daily Yomiuri Online*, 22 September 2008.

21. Tim Larimer, "National Colors", *Time*, 16 August 1999, p. 15.

22. Ibid.

23. Chalmers Johnson, "Why the U.S.-Japan Security Treaty is in Trouble", *Pacific Rim Report*,

February 2000.

24. Takashi Kitazume, "Changing World Asks More of Japan", *The Japan Times*, 24 November 2007, p. 15.

25. Ibid.

26. Ibid.

27. Brad Glosserman and Katsu Furukawa, "*A New U.S.-Japan Agenda*", Pacific Forum CSIS, Volume 8, Number 4, Honolulu, Hawaii, March 2008.

28. Ibid.

29. Joseph S. Nye, "Future of Japan-U.S. Alliance", *The Korea Times*, 12 May 2008.

30. Ibid.

31. Ibid.

32. Interview with Peter Abigail, Australian Strategic Policy Institute, Canberra, Australia, 22 May 2006.

33. Milton Ezrati, "On the Horizon: The Dawn of a New Sino-Japanese Rivalry", *Harvard International Review*, Volume 24 (1), Spring 2002.

34. Ibid.

35. Ibid.

36. Matthew Forney, "Why China Loves to Hate Japan", *Time*, 10 December 2005.

37. Kent E. Calder, "China and Japan's Simmering Rivalry", *Foreign Affairs*, in the March/April issue, 2006.

38. Ibid.

39. David Pilling and Mure Dickie, "Japan's New PM Pushes for Summit with China", *Financial Times*, 28 September 2006, p. 4.

40. Victor Mallet, "Japan's Best Chance to Strike a Deal with China", *Financial Times*, 28 September 2006, p. 19.

41. Zhou Yongsheng, "Rising Sun? Japan Tries to Establish Itself on the International Stage with its Assertive Foreign Policy", *Beijing Review*, 1 February 2007, pp. 10–11.

42. Feng Zhaokui, "Clearing Away the Ice: China and Japan are on the Right Path to Developing a "Culture of Trust"", Beijing Review, 12 April 2007, p. 10.

43. Ibid.

44. Seiichiro Takagi, "Japan-China Relations: How to Build a "Strategic Relationship of Mutual "Benefit", The Japan Institute of International Affairs, 13 February 2008.

45. Ibid.

46. Kyodo News, "U.S. Envoys Involved in '60s Secret Nuke Arms Pact", *The Japan Times*, 21 November 2007, p. 3.

47. Kyodo News, "Seoul, Taipei Wanted Nukes in Okinawa: Return Islands to Japan But Stay Strong for Cold War, They Told U.S.", *The Japan Times*, 22 November 2007, p. 2.

48. Michael Green, "The Role of Japan in Securing Stability in Asia", The Center For National Policy, 28 May 2008.

49. Ibid.

50. Ibid.

51. Ibid.

52. Department of the U.S. Treasury/Federal Reserve Board, Major Foreign Holders of Treasury Securities, 16 September 2008.

Chapter Five

South Korea:
Caught between Giant Elephants

As the 21st century unfolds and the world is experiencing a greater degree of globalization in terms of communications, finance, labor and technology, the Korean Peninsula remains a geographical and historical anachronism. Since WWII, this large finger of territory that extends into the Pacific Ocean from northeast Asia has yet to unify economically, militarily and politically, and take its proper place amongst its powerful neighbors—China, Japan and Russia. Ironically, based upon my ten years of living in the Asia-Pacific region, it is exactly these same powerful neighbors who are rather reluctant to see the Korean Peninsula unified in the relatively near future.

China views communist North Korea as a buffer between themselves and a democratic and powerful South Korea who remains allied with the United States. Japan, another U.S. ally, is also unnerved by the prospect of a unified Korea due to its unapologetic half-century of dominance and brutalization of the peninsula from 1895 to 1945. Finally, Russia is not thrilled by the fact that a powerful Korea would be another strong competitor for them to have to deal with in the northeast Asian region. Finally, what role would the U.S. play on the Korean peninsula if such a unification occurred in the near future?

In my opinion, the U.S. will play an inestimable role in maintaining a 'balance of power' amongst these East Asian 'elephants'. Hopefully, America can prevent an unexpected stampede amongst these powerful pachyderms toward achieving greater glory and stature within this vital region of the world. One South Korean official spoke about why its U.S. alliance is so important to its future in this volatile area, "We picked you (U.S.) as allies because we're caught between giant elephants."[1] Michael Auslin, a resident scholar in Asian Studies at the American Enterprise Institute, writes, "Faced with this unchangeable situation, and with a hostile dictatorship to their north, South

Koreans are doggedly realistic about their choices. Washington should be just as realistic about the value of this key U.S. ally."[2]

NEW LEADERSHIP—DIFFICULT CHALLENGES

On 25 February 2008, Lee Myung-bak was inaugurated as the tenth president of the Republic of Korea. His ascendance to the presidency was seen by many observers of Korean politics as a return to a more conservative agenda for the nation after a decade of reform-oriented policies sought by former presidents Kim Dae-jung (1998-2003) and Roh Moo-hyun (2003-2008). Lee was able to convince the Korean voters that his strong business background was just the tonic needed to provide the necessary leadership for revitalizing the nation's economy.

During his presidential campaign, Lee, a conservative from the Grand National Party, declared that the following issues would be the primary focus of his administration:

1) Re-energizing the Korean economy
2) Strengthening relations with the U.S. and with other foreign powers
3) Inter-Korean engagement[3]

Lee's economic plan was bold and visionary. He called it the "747" economic plan that was designed to promote 7% annual economic growth, lift South Korea's per capita GDP to $40,000 (U.S. dollars) and make South Korea the seventh largest economy in the world.[4] A bold plan, indeed, and the Korean people were ready for such a plan due to their declining financial fortunes during the last few years of the Roh Moo-hyun administration.

Throughout South Korea, there was no argument or debate that the South Korean economy was struggling. According to a report produced by the Bank of Korea (BOK) and the World Bank, in 2007, South Korea's gross national income (GNI) had slipped a bit. South Korea was now ranked 13th among the 209 economies evaluated in 2007, after having been ranked 12th position in 2005. Its trade deficit had expanded to $1.6 billion during July 2008, and the country's inflation rate rose to its highest levels in ten years by reaching 5.9% during the same month.[5] Without a doubt, the recent domestic economic figures were heading in the wrong direction.

However, in 2007, this same report from the Bank of Korea and the World Bank had also shown that South Korea's per-capita GNI ($19,690) rose two notches and they now ranked 49th in the world; In 2005, they had ranked 51st in the world. Yet, when compared to their primary Asian economic rivals, South Korea still paled in comparison:

1) Japan ($37,670)
2) Singapore ($32,470)
3) Hong Kong ($31, 610)[6]

Again, though, in 2007, statistics indicate that South Korea continues to exist in a rather strange economic situation overall. For instance, their nominal gross domestic product (GDP), the total value of goods and services produced in the country, actually rose to $970 billion from $888 billion from the year before, and their exports rose a substantial 37.1% ($41.4 billion) as well. However, as expected, the increased cost for oil and the need for other commodities saw a dramatic rise in imports, 47.3% ($43 billion)—the highest in eight years.[7]

These are serious financial trends that need to be reversed if South Korea is to remain one of the dynamic economic forces in Asia-Pacific. Nevertheless, the economic story of South Korea is one of breath-taking dimensions when you think of where they came from after the economic and social devastation related to the Korean War (1950-1953). South Korea's per capita GNP was under $100 until 1963![8] Despite recent setbacks, and a global economy that is standing at the cusp of a potentially severe and long-term recession (perhaps, even a depression) in 2009, South Korea's current GNI ranking of 13th in the world represents nothing short of a miracle.

I believe, at this point, it is appropriated to provide some historical perspective concerning the stunning dimensions of South Korea's economic growth. This economic development occurred in South Korea, from 1961 to 1979, during the dynamic but controversial reign of General Park Chung Hee who was an authoritarian without apologies. As mentioned earlier in this chapter, the recent financial setbacks, in 2008-2009, notwithstanding, it is important to provide a brief snapshot of the South Korean economic story that continues to demand our admiration and respect:

1) Poverty (households) was over 40% in 1965; Below 10% in 1980;
2) Per Capita—$87 (1962); $9,511 (1997); $10,000+ (2006)
3) South Korean economy (GNP) grew almost 9% annually for over three decades
4) South Korean GNP: $2.3 billion (1962); $442 billion (1997)
5) Automobiles: 30,800 (1962); 10,413,427 (1997)
6) By the 1990s, South Korea had the 11th largest economy in the world;

7) 13th largest trading nation in the world; Major producer of ships, cars, electronics and steel;[9]

REGIONAL DIPLOMACY

South Korea, in recent years, has displayed an aggressive agenda with concern to establishing good relations with its regional neighbors, including North Korea. However, its overall effectiveness will be somewhat limited due to the internal and intense ideologically-based debate and verbal sparring that is occurring between conservatives and progressives. Though, obviously, this topic can represent a book unto itself, nevertheless, the main point to be made here is that the Korean body politic is badly split about which direction is best for South Korea. It is true that the presidencies of Kim Dae-jung and Roh Moo-hyun had represented progressive ideas and polices. It can be said, to a large degree, that these two presidents certainly represented the type of beliefs and politics that were aggressively embraced by the younger generations within Korean society.

Yet, in 2008, the political pendulum had obviously swung the other way with the election of conservative Lee Myung-bak. However, since his election to the presidency, Lee has struggled with the decision concerning which ideological path is best for South Korea? This is the political question that looms over the nation on every decision and issue. Hahm Chaibong, a professor in the department of political science at Yonsei University in Seoul, wrote, in 2005, "South Korea today is a bitterly divided country. Clashes between conservatives (posu) and progressives (chinbo) over everything from the direction of economic and political reforms to the location of the nation's capital have created a deep domestic fissure."[10] I believe it is important to acknowledge and understand this deep division within the Korean body politic because it also affects the development and direction of the nation's foreign policy as well.

Despite the present turmoil within South Korea's domestic politics, Scott Snyder, a senior associate at the Asia Foundation and Pacific Forum CSIS, believes that South Korean foreign policy remains fundamentally unaltered, he writes, "A perennial South Korean foreign policy objective has been the successful management of ties with each of the four major powers surrounding the Korean peninsula: Japan, Russia, China, and the United States. Although Lee has also prioritized good relations with China and Russia by sending special envoys to Beijing and Moscow, there are early signs that Lee's emphasis on the United States and Japan is making China uneasy while South Korea's relationship with Russia continues to underperform its potential."[11]

John Feffer, co-director of Foreign Policy in Focus, believes that Korean peninsula represents the key geographical heart of future peace in East Asia. If the issues concerning the future status of the Korean peninsula remain unresolved then the chances of achieving long-term peace and stability in the region are dubious at best. Feffer mentions within an article he wrote that there are those who believe that the current six-party talks concerning the status of the North Korean nuclear program can possibly lead to a collective security alliance amongst the primary participants. However, he remains rather skeptical about this future endeavor. Feffer believes the U.S. and North Korea, for their own reasons, would shy away from such a commitment or organization, while China, Russia and South Korea would embrace it—for their own reasons.[12]

Feffer provides a simple but irrefutable geopolitical reason for U.S. reluctance to join such an association relating to East Asian security in the near future. He writes, "Washington will likely maneuver to weaken any such multilateral structure so that it doesn't threaten existing bilateral alliances, hamper strategic flexibility, or reduce what the Chinese like to call great power "hegemonism," namely the preponderant U.S. military presence in the region."[13] Feffer goes on to say that North Korea would also turn away from this type of agreement in fear that it would eventually undermine the communist party's leadership within the country. Any potential 'Helsinki model' which many North Koreans believe was the beginning of the end for the communist governments in Eastern Europe and the Soviet Union is to be avoided at all costs.[14]

In September 2008, Han Seung-Soo, Prime Minister of the Republic of Korea, spoke at a forum that was recognizing the 50th anniversary of the International Institute For Strategic Studies (IISS), and the Asian Institute inauguration. The topic theme of the forum was "Korea in the Emerging Asian Power Balance."[15] Prime Minister Han provided an expansive and visionary talk related to this theme entitled, "Global Korea in the 21st Century." He believes that this period of history is critical for South Korea. It must create a foreign policy that addresses the critical regional and global challenges of the 21st century. Han also envisions South Korea playing a key role in both geopolitical realms. Yet, he sees the unprecedented rise, for the first time in regional history, of the (3) major powers in Asia: China, Japan and India.[16] Thus, no one really knows how this new regional 'hegemonic' dynamic is going to pan out.

Accordingly, the recently elected South Korean Prime Minister stated in his speech at the IISS conference that there are emerging security risks and increased geopolitical competition within East Asia. Prime Minister Han stated, "East Asia is arguably the new fulcrum of global strategic competition. Three of the world's five declared nuclear powers have direct strategic interests and presences in Northeast Asia. The world's newest nuclear proliferator, namely North Korea, continues to test strategic stability on the Korean Peninsula and Northeast Asia. Five of the world's largest standing armies all reside in Asia. Many of the regional actors are investing in new power projection capabilities."[17]

Han also mentions that "(South Korean) President Lee Myung-bak assumed the presidency at a historical turning point for Korea and Asia. For the most part, although Korea continued to prosper over the past decade, it was also evident that business-as-usual could not prevail . . . Over the course of the next four and a half years, however, this government remains committed to a range of critical reforms and new approaches including the all-important foreign policy arena and inter-Korean relations . . . ensuring the formation of a 'Global Korea'."[18] At the end of his talk, Han outlines the primary objectives of President Lee's agenda for South Korea:

1) Restoring confidence and outlining a new rationale for the critical ROK-U.S. alliance
2) Expanding Korea's "Asian Diplomacy" is a critical component of our government's regional initiatives
3) We remain fully committed to the peaceful and diplomatic resolution of the North Korean nuclear crisis through the Six-Party talks and excavating new opportunities in South-North relations.
4) A 'Global Korea' cannot be truly global without assuming our fair share of the common burden[19]

This new and bold visionary plan representing South Korea's future involvement in regional and global affairs is not a total surprise to me. In June 2005, I was invited by former president Kim Dae-jung's office to attend the conference commemorating the fifth anniversary of the North-South Summit that brought together South Korean President Kim Dae-jung and North Korean leader Kim Jong-il. President Kim Dae-jung was subsequently awarded the Nobel Peace Prize (2000) that year for his courageous and historic efforts to begin a new dialogue between the two countries—with the hope of eventually unifying the Korean Peninsula.

The North-South summit itself represented the first time the leaders of both North and South Korea had met since the post-WWII partitioning of Korea in 1948. Needless to say, Korean politics, in both countries, has not been the same since this historic summit. I noticed immediately a new and confident attitude amongst South Koreans. The nervous and hyperactive behavior often shown by South Korean officials that disguised their insecurities about themselves and their geopolitical situation in the region was no longer evident, at least to me.

I even asked Bruce Cumings, a history professor at the University of Chicago and one of the most prominent historians concerning Korea, who was also invited to this festive gathering that had prominent world leaders and individuals attending, if my impression of the Koreans was not simply a figment of my imagination. Cumings immediately agreed with my observation and he told me that we were perhaps witnessing a whole new chapter in the political development between the two Korean nations. He also noted that this new evolution of Korean relations was certainly going to have an affect upon the role of the U.S. on the Korean peninsula. I completely agreed with his analysis.

I lived in South Korea for six months in 1994, and I have been back several times—the last visit being in May 2009. The recent foreign policies activities and initiatives taken by the South Korean government during the last few years did not surprise me at all. I have felt during my last visits to South Korea, within the period 2005-2009, a new nation was emerging within a dynamic and powerful East Asian region. Yet, a question keeps emerging in the back of my mind—can South Korea establish its own identity and purpose in East Asia?

If the last couple of years are any indication of South Korea's intentions for themselves and their future role within Asia-Pacific, I believe the answer to my question is yes. The emergence of South Korea is remarkable on so many levels but its recent initiatives within East Asia have shown a sense of national confidence that just wasn't evident in the 1990s. In 2008, South Korea, like their brethren in North Korea, is duly noting its 60th anniversary as a nation-state. But it is a rather uncomfortable historic moment for these nationalistic and proud people. The Republic of Korea (ROK) was created due to the partitioning of the Korean peninsula after WWII by the major superpowers—the U.S. and Soviet Union. There was no referendum or plebiscite held concerning the future political destiny of Korea. It was a deal done by those who were not born there or lived there. It was a geopolitical decision that has had serious ramifications for the country and northeast Asia ever since. The Korean War (1950-1953) and the post-war military build-up along the two and an half mile-wide DMZ at the 38th parallel came to represent one of the most dangerous places on earth.[20] Tensions were real and surreal.

I remember teaching an American History course for the University of Maryland at a base located very near the DMZ, and having the feeling I was the Martin Sheen character in a remake of Francis Coppola's movie, *Apocalypse Now*, where South Korea had now replaced South Vietnam as the narrative. Simply put, I was living and working in a very dangerous neighborhood and, eventually, I learned to just ignore or at least rationalize my fears and the daily tensions that I felt while living close to Camp Red Cloud—located north of Seoul.

Yet, every time I tell my students a few of my stories about my experiences living in South Korea, during the spring, summer and fall of 1994, I feel a certain sense of gratitude to having earned the knowledge of what it was like to live in Korea during a very tense time in its history. In fact, I was there when former U.S. president Jimmy Carter traveled to Pyongyang through the area where I lived and worked to sign an agreement with North Korea and its former leader Kim Il-sung to dismantle their nuclear program.

Ironically, about a month later, I was visiting the newly opened Korean War Memorial, located near Yongsan Army Base in Seoul, with three of my University of Maryland history classes, when an American walked up to me to inform me that North Korean leader King Il-sung had died of a massive heart attack. To say the least, the summer of 1994 was quite an experience for a guy who had just arrived from the University of Idaho.

In the year 2008, South Korea initiated a diplomatic blitz throughout the East Asian region. In March 2008, South Korean president Lee Myung-bak spoke of implementing a "future-oriented attitude" toward Japan and the issues that divide them.[21] Lee's diplomatic approach was viewed by several Korean scholars as being more pragmatic and less nationalistic toward Japan than his predecessor, Roh Moo-hyun. This diplomatic perspective was expressed by Ko Seung-kyun, a professor of political science at Hawaii Pacific University, who commented, "I am very optimistic about (Japan-South Korea) relations."[22]

In retrospect, Professor Ko believed that former president Roh had overemphasized his "kinship" with North Korea at the expense of obtaining better relations with Japan. He stated, "Roh didn't know how to conduct South Korea's relations with Japan...The internal politics can't be separated from external relations."[23] In the end, Ko believes that President Roh's domestic politics were simply too tinged with nationalism when it came to relations with Japan.[24]

Yet, despite the improved tone in relations between Japan and South Korea due to the election of Lee Myung-bak, there remain some serious disagreements between these two powerful neighbors. To be specific, the ownership of the islets of Dokdo (known as Takeshima in Japan) continues to be an historic and territorial bone stuck in the throat of the South Korean government. Both Japan and South Korea claim these small islets for themselves, and no one is backing down. As expected, the tension concerning this territory has once again consumed the dialogue between these powerful neighbors.

In July 2008, South Korean President Lee ordered his ambassador to Japan to return to South Korea due to this sensitive issue. President Lee stated, "It is deeply regrettable and disappointing that Tokyo has once again laid claim to Dokdo, which is part of South Korea's territory, historically, geographically and under international law."[25] If South Korea's claim to Dokdo is not recognized by Japan, President Lee has issued a subtle threat by saying, "I will deal sternly with any attempts to ignore Korea's sovereignty over Dokdo."[26] Thus, the beat goes on between the Koreans and the Japanese over issues that have continued to haunt their relations since the 19th century.

Conversely, the South Korea-China relationship has improved markedly. On 25 August 2008, the third summit between President Lee Myung-bak and his Chinese counterpart Hu Jintao represented a new phase of cooperation and joint efforts to stabilize the Korean peninsula. The two leaders agreed upon a new course of action that included a "strategic cooperative partnership and it reconfirmed their commitment to the peaceful settlement of the North Korean nuclear weapons dispute."[27] A defense expert, speaking anonymously, stated "The Lee-Hu agreement is expected to pave the way for advancing bilateral military relations in conformity with the strategic cooperative partnership. Regardless of the development of the South Korea-U.S. alliance, the Chinese government seems determined to enhance the security posture for the entire Korean Peninsula and China through the strengthening of bilateral defense cooperation with South Korea."[28]

President Hu affirmed that "China wants the two Koreas to maintain momentum for reconciliation and cooperation, indicating that China will be ready to more actively play a mediating role in the nuclear dispute following its successful hosting of the Summer Olympics."[29] It should be mentioned here that China does possess some leverage with both Koreas because, at this time, it is the number one trade partner of both the North and the South. Two months later, in October 2008, President Lee proposed that China, Japan and South Korea hold a tripartite meeting between their respective finance ministers to "discuss close policy coordination in the face of global financial turmoil."[30]

President Lee, according to an article published in the *Yonhap News Agency*, also "instructed his Cabinet ministers to immediately push to hold a bilateral finance ministerial meeting with Russia, which was agreed to during his summit talks with Russian President Dmitry Medvedev in Moscow on Monday."[31]

It is quite apparent to an outside observer that South Korea is becoming increasingly active and forceful in its foreign policy endeavors. As expected, South Korea wants to be, and will be, a major player during the complex deliberations concerning the future decisions, direction and dynamics that will determine the destiny of the Asia-Pacific region in the 21st century.

THE KOREAN PENINSULA IN THE 21ST CENTURY:
THE GREAT UNKNOWN

In 2009, the Korean Peninsula remains artificially divided at the 38th parallel and a symbol of a bygone era—the Cold War. Its buffered border—symbolized by the DMZ—between North Korea and South Korea, remains one of the most heavily armed regions in the world. This potentially apocalyptic Cold War anachronism is clearly beginning to recede in importance militarily, and in terms of ideological distinctiveness.

In June 2000, South Korean President Kim Dae-jung and North Korean leader, Kim Jong-il, met at Pyongyang (North Korea's capital) International Airport. Their dramatic meeting represented the first public dialogue between the leaders of these two nations since the partitioning of the peninsula which occurred after WWII. In 2000, South Korean President Kim became convinced that North Korea did not completely oppose the existence of U.S. troops upon the Korean peninsula. In point of fact, the North Korean leadership simply wanted the U.S. to engage them in a policy discussion rather than constantly threatening them with some type of military retaliation such as regime change.[32] In 2000, the world was taken aback to see the North and South Korean athletes marching together at the Sydney Olympics. It was the first presentation of a unified Korea in a public forum since the end of World War II.[33]

As mentioned earlier in this chapter, in June 2005, I was invited to attend the fifth anniversary of the North-South Joint Declaration at the Shilla Hotel in Seoul, South Korea. During this high profile international conference, I had the opportunity to meet the former president and the 2000 Nobel Peace Prize winner, Kim Dae-jung, for a second time. The first time I met Kim was in September 1994 at his Asia-Pacific Peace Institute. The former South Korean president gave the keynote address, and that was followed by then president, Roh Moo-hyun, who had made an unannounced appearance. President Roh gave a passionate speech that fully supported future efforts to bring peace and unity to the Korean peninsula.

I must admit I was a bit stunned by the energized atmosphere and spirit that existed at this conference because when I first came to South Korea in May 1994, the political mood of the country and people was profoundly different and much more cautious in their attitudes toward North Korea. Within a decade, South Korea appeared to be a country in the midst of change and transition. This perception was not just a brief historical aberration but, indeed, it represented a true indication for where the country was heading at the beginning of the 21st century. Put succinctly, Korea has experienced a seismic and fundamental shift in its economic and foreign policies, especially during the George W. Bush administration. During the first years of the Bush administration (2001-2009), it became quite obvious to the South Korean leadership, during the Roh administration (2003-2008), that the U.S. was lukewarm, if not indifferent, toward further exploration and implementation of Kim Dae-jung's '*Sunshine*' policies.

Nevertheless, despite U.S. intransigence on these reform-oriented geopolitical policies, the two Koreas have continued to achieve an enlargement of the common ground that exists between these two adversaries. Tragically, this division of a people unified by common blood and culture has been separated by a brutal history and war. Yet, there are signs of hope. Trade and investment continues between the two Koreas and though a breakthrough in terms of unification remains years away, solid progress is clearly being made on this contentious peninsula in northeast Asia.

A prime example of progress is the 'six-party' talks concerning the dismantling of North Korea's nuclear program. In 2007, the primary participants—the U.S., China, Japan, North and South Korea and Russia—agreed in principle to provide North Korea with humanitarian aid and oil, and these nations also promised not to seek regime change in the near future. These negotiated agreements actually represented two geopolitical truths.

First, the U.S. possessed diminishing leverage with the North Koreans due to its two wars in the Middle East (Iraq and Afghanistan). The American military was shown to be badly 'overstretched' logistically, and lacking a coherent strategy to win either war. Second, China's role in getting North Korea back to the negotiating table, and to get them to accept this complicated agreement was crucial and grudgingly noted by the Bush administration. For many observers, this important 'six-party' agreement with the North Koreans showed that China was 'coming of age' in terms of participating and providing critical leadership in important international negotiations—and succeeding.

China's diplomatic efforts will probably continue to play an increasingly important role in keeping North Korea and its volatile and unpredictable leadership (read: Kim Jong-il) on a short leash. The Chinese certainly have a dog in this fight because their economic growth needs to continue unabated, producing jobs and wealth, without unwanted turbulence from their immediate neighbors, causing instability within the Middle Kingdom. Former diplomatic correspondent for The Washington Post and longtime observer of Asia, Don Oberdorfer, stated, "China played a major role in the 'six-party' talks with concern to North Korea's nuclear weapons program. This is the first time that China is on the world stage since 1949. Its actions, so far, have been positive."[34]

Thus, though quite subtly, a new geopolitical dynamic is taking shape within Asia-Pacific. China represents a new and powerful diplomatic and economic force in the affairs of the region. What this shift in power and influence truly means for the U.S. in a region it has dominated since the end of WWII remains unclear. As expected, this geopolitical evolution is presently consuming the energies and minds of the foreign policy establishment in America.

In 2007, China became the number one trade partner of both North and South Korea.[35] However, this economic shift should not be seen as a geopolitical shift away from the U.S., or seen as an anti-U.S. movement - especially within South Korea. Instead, one might want to acknowledge the re-assertion of culture and history upon the Korean peninsula. On the surface, this historic and regional shift appears to be natural in its manifestation.

Yet, many scholars have discovered that this common history has been a mixed blessing—at best. Analysts of this region can attest that the potentially bright future that many have predicted for Asia-Pacific during the past quarter-century, particularly for northeast Asia, can go terribly wrong. The recent global financial meltdown is a good example of an unexpected event jeopardizing the future prosperity and stability in the Asia-Pacific region. Thus, since the 19th century, predicted greatness for the region has often been undermined by bloody wars, regional upheaval and economic collapses. Therefore, the Korean peninsula remains a geographical, geopolitical and historical question mark. Its ultimate fate continues to remain outside the grasp of its leaders and the people who live upon this contentious land.

Yet, according to Ban Ki-Moon, the former South Korean Foreign Minister and now the General-Secretary of the United Nations, stated, in 2006, that there is real hope for the Korean peninsula in the 21st century, "Beyond the remnants of the Cold War and the North Korean nuclear challenge, the most important preconditions for achieving permanent peace on the Korean peninsula and in northeast Asia are a coherent strategic vision and the willingness of regional members to work together through a multilateral framework."[36] It appears that good fortune has smiled upon Mr. Ban because he will have a golden opportunity to create that new strategic vision for northeast Asia, including the Korean peninsula. In late-2006, he was chosen to be the Secretary-General of the United Nations. Thus, Ban became the first Asian to hold this vaunted position in 35 years. His appointment, in the minds of many Asian analysts, could not have come at better time because the dramatic rise of Asia, during the past quarter-century, has made it increasingly the axis and fulcrum of global affairs in the 21st century.

Ban Ki-Moon's elevation to the top spot at the U.N. will also neutralize some of the deep-rooted skepticism directed toward an organization that many Asians continue to see as a Western entity designed to dominate the affairs of Asia-Pacific. Journalist Michael Fullilove writes that the U.N., though it intervened in the Korean War in the early 1950s and also helped to relocate three million Indo-Chinese refugees in the 1970s, remains an institution that provokes a significant degree of mistrust and suspicion within the region. This jaundiced view of all Western-created institutions is related to issues such as state sovereignty and the region's relatively recent colonial history. These critical factors, among others, continue to influence and overshadow the region's perspectives and decision-making processes.

Within the last decade, again, a heightened degree of mistrust was publicly displayed toward international institutions such as the International Monetary Fund, due to its decisions concerning loans and reform policies that many Asia-Pacific nations felt were forced upon them while they were struggling to remain financially solvent during the 1997–1998 financial meltdown. Those difficult memories have not faded at all over the past decade.[37]

In 2009, the U.S. and the world are experiencing the worst economic collapse since the 1930s. South Korea, and the other Asian nations, may now decide to create their own financial apparatus. In fact, there are voices within the region which are inquiring whether or not Asia-Pacific needs to put some 'financial daylight' between themselves and the periodically turbulent West. Fullilove, however, does not perceive any kind of separation occurring in the near future between Asia-Pacific and the West due to irrefutable security threats (disease, resource scarcity and environmental catastrophes) within the region, he writes, ". . . these interconnected security threats in the region has demonstrated the advantages of international cooperation."[38]

Kim Dae-jung, sometimes referred to as the 'Nelson Mandela of Asia' has spent his adult life working toward bringing democracy to South Korea. In June 2000, he courageously stepped forward to begin a new dialogue with North Korea and its leader, Kim Jong-il. After almost a decade since the historic meeting between the two Kim(s) a new spirit has emerged in South Korea, and North Korea has made fewer and fewer threats of impending attack upon the South. Both leaders have recently fallen upon difficult times with concern to their personal health. Kim Dae-jung has retired from national politics and Kim Jong-il suffered a stroke in the fall of 2008.

Hence, the question needs to be asked, 'who will be the future leader(s) to push a bold and visionary North/South unity agenda in the 21st century?' Right now, for both countries, the answer remains speculative and undefined.

When that leader(s) emerges on the Korean peninsula, the 'democratic' South and the 'hermit kingdom' North will no longer represent a geopolitical situation that is sadly nothing more than an outdated relic from the days of the Cold War. In 2009, the Korean peninsula remains divided by the 38th parallel, nevertheless, the day of unification will come for this tormented land. And, when that day arrives, the geopolitical impact of a unified Korea will undoubtedly be felt throughout the Asia-Pacific region, but particularly in northeast Asia.

I think all Koreans need to remind themselves what can happen when dangerous forces are unleashed upon the peninsula, along with the intervention of foreign powers. The Korean War (1950-1953) can not be repeated in an age that possesses and produces weapons of mass destruction; of which, both sides possess great quantities. Therefore, it might be appropriate and pertinent to provide a brief overview of the final conditions and numbers associated with a war that occurred almost 60 years ago.

The following statistics, related to the Korean War, should be a sobering reminder to both the North and South Korean leadership that another war, especially one where modern weaponry will be massively utilized by both sides, will result in producing a level of death and destruction beyond one's comprehension:

KOREAN WAR (1950–1953)

-An estimated 3 million Koreans died from war related causes
-900,000 Chinese dead and wounded
-33,000 Americans died; 1,000 British died; 4,000 other nationalities died;
-129,000 civilians killed in the South—during the North's brief occupation;
-84,000 kidnapped
-200,000 South Koreans press-ganged into the northern territory
-Economic systems destroyed (North and South)
-South Korea: 5 million homeless; 300,000 women widowed; 100,000 children orphaned
-Millions of families separated; Tens of thousands of schools and buildings destroyed
-$3 billion in damages; 43% of manufacturing facilities destroyed; 50% o mines wrecked
-Inflation skyrocketed[39]

In 2009, South Korea exists cautiously between, and survives amongst, the large and powerful elephants within northeast Asia. South Koreans know instinctively that the stakes are high and potentially costly. If they make the wrong decisions or draw the incorrect conclusions, especially concerning issues of vital national importance such as economic policy and the nation's security, the 21st century could be very threatening and volatile. Geography, hegemony and politics have not always been kind to the 'Hermit Kingdom'. Therefore, history has taught all Koreans that Asia-Pacific can indeed be a very dangerous and foreboding region. To prevent the brutality and exploitation experienced in the 20th century, primarily due to the Japanese and the Korean War, the Korean peninsula will need courageous and visionary leadership to survive in what is steadily becoming the most competitive region in the world.

NOTES

1. Michael Auslin, "Caught Between Giant Elephants", *The American* (A Magazine of Ideas), 11 December 2007.

2. Ibid.

3. Scott Snyder, "Inauguration of Lee Myung-bak: Grappling with Korea's Future Challenges, Brookings Northeast Asia Commentary, Brookings Institute, 27 February 2008.

4. Ibid.

5. Lee Hyo-sik, "Economic Trouble Deepens", *The Korean Times*, 1 August 2008.

6. Ibid.

7. Ibid.

8. Ezra Vogel, *The Four Little Dragons: The Spread of Industrialization in East Asia* (Cambridge: Harvard University Press, 1991), p. 43.

9. Michael Breen, *The Koreans: Who They Are, What They Want, Where Their Future Lies (*New York: St. martin's Griffin, 2004), p. 134. Don Oberdorfer, *The Two Koreans: A Contemporary History* (New York: Basic Books, 2001), p. 37.

10. Hahm Chaibong, "The Two South Koreas: A House Divided", *The Washington Quarterly*, Summer 2005, p. 57.

11. Synder, "Inauguration of Lee Myung-bak", Brookings Institute, 27 February 2008.

12. John Feffer, "The Paradox of East Asian Peace", *Foreign Policy In Focus*, 13 December 2007.

13. Ibid.

14. Ibid.

15. Dr. Han Seung-Soo, Prime Minister of the Republic of Korea, "Global Korea in the 21st Century", 50th Anniversary and the Asian Institute Inauguration", 26 September 2008.

16. Ibid.

17. Ibid.

18. Ibid.

19. Ibid.

20. Gavan McCormick, "Korea at 60", www.zmag.org, 8 September 2008.

21. Jason Miks, "New Optimism for Japan-South Korea Relations, but Sources of Tension Remain", www.worldpoliticsreview.com, 3 March 2008.

22. Ibid.

23. Ibid.

24. Ibid.

25. Na Jeong-ju, "Seoul maps Out countermeasures to Tokyo's Claim Over Dokdo", *The Korean Times*, 14 July 2008.

26. Ibid.

27. Yoo Cheong-mo, "Lee, Hu Set New Milestone in South Korea-China Relations, *Yonhap News Agency*, 25 August 2008.

28. Ibid.

29. Ibid.

30. Yoo Cheong-mo, "Lee Proposes Ministerial Talks With Japan, China over Global Turmoil", *Yonhap News Agency*, 3 October 2008.

31. Ibid.

32. Bruce Cumings, *Korea's Place In The Sun*, p. 503.

33. Don Oberdorfer, *The Two Koreas*, p. 434.

34. Interview with Don Oberdorfer, 28 December 2006.

35. C. Fred Bergsten, et al., China's Rise: Challenges and Opportunities (Washington, DC: Peterson Institute For International Economics and the Center For Strategic and International Studies, 2008), p. 221.

36. Ban Ki-Moon, "For Permanent Peace: Beyond the Nuclear Challenge and the Cold War", *Harvard International Review*, Summer 2006.

37. Michael Fullilove, "Ban's Debut is Chance for Asia to Step in to Spotlight", *Financial Times*, 19 December 2006, p. 11.

38. Ibid.

39. Breen, *The Koreans*, p. 124.

Chapter Six

China: Revolution and Power

In 2009, the primary topic concerning China's future role - is raging throughout various associations, institutions, think-tanks and universities throughout America and Asia. There is no established consensus on this topic—right now. But, the intensity of the debate will heighten as China's *economic* revolution and *military* development translates into possessing stronger influence within Asia-Pacific. Former U.S. Secretary of State Henry Kissinger wrote in an article for *The Australian*, in June 2005,

> The rise of China, and of Asia, will, over the next decades, bring about a substantial reordering of the international system. The centre of gravity of world affairs is shifting from the Atlantic, where it was lodged for the past three centuries to the Pacific. The most rapidly developing countries are located in Asia, with a growing means to vindicate their perception of the national interest.[1]

As expected, the publication of articles and books related to China's future has shifted into overdrive within America and Asia-Pacific. This chapter will provide numerous economic and political observations and geo-political views concerning the future relevance of China in the 21st century: First, simply put, will China become America's geo-political adversary, strategic competitor, or regional partner in Asia-Pacific? Second, how will the world react to the continued growth of the Chinese economic juggernaut in the 21st century? Third, will China's financial prowess be ultimately directed toward global dominance? Fourth, can China avoid a domestic upheaval from significant challenges, such as unemployment, pollution, corruption and wealth disparities? Finally, what will be the geopolitical affect of China's revolutionary in Asia-Pacific?

This chapter will address these critical questions and present recent evidence that China is indeed already emerging as a regional and global power. However, its long-term prospects as an emerging superpower and challenger to U.S. global hegemony remain speculative, though history strongly indicates potential trouble ahead for America and the West.

RISE OF CHINA: THE ASIA-PACIFIC DILEMMA

The current debate of whether China should be considered a geo-political adversary, a strategic competitor or a regional partner concerning the U.S. in Asia-Pacific will be the primary focus of debate amongst foreign policy analysts for the next generation. Yet, what is unnerving to many observers of the region is the accelerating speed in which the geo-political dynamics have been altered. Yet, no one anticipates, or desires, the United States to withdraw from Asia-Pacific, including China. Nevertheless, the transformation of the East Asian hemispheric landscape, due to the recent economic trends and military modernization occurring throughout the region, is simply shocking to even the most seasoned or skeptical Western observer.

Jonathan Spence, globally renowned historian from Yale University and long-time and eminent China chronicler, puts this debate and its inherent complexities, I believe, in their proper perspective:

> The prospect of China's rise has become a source of endless speculation and debate. To speak of China's "rise" is to suggest its reemergence. It can also imply a recovery from some kind of slump or period of quietude. But "rise" can also mean that a change is being made at someone else's expense. Must a fall always accompany a rise? If so, then a conflict will occur almost by definition. These are difficult questions made all the more so by the fact that a country as vast and complex as China makes up at least half of the equation.[2]

David Shambaugh, director of the China Policy Program at the Elliot School of International Affairs at George Washington University, agrees with Professor Spence's trenchant observation concerning China's current status in Asia. In January 2006, Shambaugh spoke at the Chicago Council on World Affairs—his topic was *"The Changing Nature of the Regional Systems in Asia-Pacific."*[3] Professor Shambaugh emphasized that China represents a complex challenge for the U.S. and the Asia-Pacific region. Thus, China's new economic prowess and military development is a bit troubling for its regional neighbors. Yet, over 70% of China's foreign direct investment (FDI) originates in Asia-Pacific.[4] As a consequence, China has emerged as the financial engine that drives the region's economy forward. Shambaugh makes a subtle but substantive point when he analyzes China's current intentions for itself and the region, "China is not attempting to dominate *ASEAN* (Association of Southeast Asian Nations) or *APEC* (Asia-Pacific Economic Cooperative), the region's two most important organizations at the present time, but how much longer will China allow itself to be a 'backseat' partner?"[5] That is the key question that the region wants answered, but it is an answer some dread with equal trepidation.

Natalia Rigol, an associate editor for the *Harvard International Review*, believes there is little cause for alarm, right now, for those who fear a U.S.-China showdown in the near future.[6] Rigol presents a rational argument on the current nature of relations between these two global hegemons. First, from a geo-political standpoint, China, presently, accepts the *status quo* condition of U.S. hegemonic power in Asia-Pacific. And, there is currently no major issue, or primary reason, for China to challenge the U.S. position. Secondly, within the Asia-Pacific region, the Chinese have not *directly* challenged American leadership, or any of its key alliances.[7]

Yet, China is determined to establish itself as a dominant power in Asia and a significant player around the world by further integrating itself into the international business community. Merle Goldman, Professor of History, Emeritus, at Boston University, stated, "China has integrated itself into the world system by becoming a member of such global institutions such as the WTO, IMF and the United Nations. Thus, the economic transformation of China has occurred very fast."[8]

This concerted economic behavior can be described as the Chinese version of '*dollar diplomacy*' that was energetically pursued and imposed by the American government and its business interests in the Caribbean region, and in Central and South America, during the 19th century. This economic-based interventionist philosophy remains a powerful reality within these regions today. In truth, the U.S. utilized intimidating tactics, including military intervention, to obtain the type of business agreements desired by its powerful corporations. And, the U.S. Congress, throughout its history, has played its traditional role as the obedient mid-wife in such capitalistic endeavors.

In the case of China, this time-honored economic strategy is once again paying off handsomely for this new Asian juggernaut in the Asian-Pacific region. However, the Chinese are well aware, and sensitive to the fact, that not all their regional neighbors are comfortable with the Middle Kingdom's growing economic strength, due to its relentless double-digit growth over the past three decades.

According to recent global trade statistics, China now represents over 13% of total world trade—second only to the U.S. Therefore, to avoid what Rigol calls "sociopolitical instability" in the region, China has negotiated mutually beneficial economic partnerships with most of them.[9] In short, China's diplomatic efforts to date have been subtle and '*under the radar*' in terms of acquiring and projecting influence throughout Asia-Pacific. Nevertheless, almost everyone acknowledges that China and the region's destiny will change dramatically in the upcoming years and decades.

Of course, the ultimate outcome in the Asia-Pacific region will certainly depend on the U.S. response to China's economic and military rise in the 21st century. If mishandled (i.e. war), the financial and security structures built and cultivated, within the region since the end of WWII, would suffer irreparable harm. In view of this truth, a regional catastrophe must be avoided—if at all possible. If such an event did occur, it would absolutely and fundamentally alter the direction of Asia-Pacific's economic, political and security development for the rest of the 21st century.

Therefore, the omnipresent question confronting both America and China, if not East Asia at-large, is what will be the ultimate outcome from the stresses and strains associated with the expected financial, military and technologically-driven changes? At the present time, the *answer* to this crucial question remains speculative at best. The regional implications would be are huge. Nevertheless, the answer to the question mentioned above remains the key for America, China and the Asia-Pacific region. Historically speaking, I believe U.S.-China relations in the 21st century will be as important to the future prosperity and stability of the Asia-Pacific region, as German-French relations have been for European growth and harmony since the end of WWII.

Eric Heginbotham and Christopher Twomey believe America is exercising an Asian policy that is poorly designed for the realities confronting the region and the interests of the U.S. in the 21st century. They believe U.S. President George W. Bush is currently exercising the *realpolitik* philosophy utilized in the late-1800s by German Chancellor, Otto von Bismarck. Yet, unfortunately, they also think that this particular policy is ill-suited for the challenges and demands confronting the U.S. in Asia, at this point in time. First, this Bismarckian (i.e. 'realist') approach dilutes America's ability to shape and define Asia's security framework, and, secondly, its implementation will result in increased nationalist sentiments that will trigger regional tensions—leading to unrest and unpredictable results.[10]

Thus, America should support Asia's multilateral institutions, such as ASEAN, APEC, ASEAN Regional Forum, and, perhaps, a formalized version of the Northeast Asian Cooperation Dialogue. This path, in their opinion, would go a long way toward stabilizing the region and enhancing America's voice in regional affairs. Secondly, support the development of democracy and its relevant institutions, but do not support "nationalist agitation" because the outcome is almost always unpredictable, and the perceived potential of U.S. intervention could lead to an unwanted war.[11] Death and destruction are not the kind of factors that usually lead a nation, or a people, toward democracy.

Perhaps, the implementation of 'soft power', as defined by Harvard University government professor, Joseph Nye, can be much more advantageous and influential for the U.S. in Asia than the use of overwhelming military power to achieve its goals. American culture consisting of our schools, music, books, movies and our way of life, remain powerful forces and extremely influential for hundreds of millions of global citizens seeking a better existence. In short, Professor Nye believes that 'soft power' is a very attractive alternative for individuals, and governments, who desire to transform their respective societies, and enhance their ability to bring new ideas to challenging problems.[12]

Finally, the recently updated analysis of China-U.S. relations by the Congressional Research Service uses the word 'competition' to describe the present-day relationship between the two major powers in Asia-Pacific. Kerry Dumbaugh, specialist in Asian Affairs within the Congressional Services' Foreign Affairs, Defense, and Trade Division, writes that both nations are in "competition for resources, power, and influence around the world."[13] Dumbaugh points out that China's relations with its regional neighbors have improved significantly since the mid-1990s. Issues such as "territorial disputes, diplomatic deadlocks, and deep ASEAN concerns about China's military ambitions and its regional economic competitiveness" represented a plethora of troubles for the Chinese government within the region.[14]

However, this sense of foreboding and mistrust of China has receded over the past decade. The Chinese have reached out to the members of ASEAN—with the signing of a Free Trade Agreement in 2004. In the same year, the Chinese signed major trade deals purchasing iron ore and energy from Australia. And, in 2005, China initiated a "strategic dialogue" with India concerning terrorism, resource competition and America's role in Asia.[15]

Though, America's role in Asia continues to consume many Chinese officials, and the definition of U.S.-China relations remains frustratingly elusive, there are scholars and observers of U.S.-China relations who feel both countries need each other to create regional and global stability. Professor Patrick Shan, born and raised in China, who currently teaches Chinese History at Grand Valley State University, stated matter-of-factly that "China and the U.S. will not go to war because they need each other to stabilize the global economy."[16] Professor Shan also mentioned, "I simply do not believe that China will ever attempt a pre-emptive attack on America. And, China has worked very hard during the past decade to improve its relations with its neighbors."[17]

Perhaps, the best example of China reaching out to its neighbors, and attempting to be seen as a constructive leader and stabilizing force in the northeastern region of Asia, is their founding, in June 2001, of the Shanghai Cooperation Organization (SCO). The primary focuses of the SCO is to establish economic and security agreements with Russia and the Central Asian nations formerly of the Soviet Union. Within this dual-policy framework, there is a consensus to build gas/oil pipelines, initiate rail-link development, and participate in joint military activities. The activities of the SCO have certainly caught the attention of policymakers in the U.S. and Asia. However, no one is interpreting this relatively new organization as a direct threat to America's dominant position in Asia-Pacific.[18]

Unsurprisingly, it is not hard to find informed opinions or voices of alarm in America or Asia-Pacific, that interpret China's emergence as a *real* power in the region as a threatening development—that will *probably* lead to some level of military conflict. The most candid of these voices is the University of Chicago Professor John Mearsheimer, who states unequivocally that "If China continues its impressive economic growth over the next few decades that the U.S. and China are likely to engage in an intense security competition with considerable potential for war."[19] Professor Mearsheimer, a self-described great power 'realist', also believes that if China becomes a threatening force in Asia, America's key allies and friends in the region will join the U.S. in containing China's hegemonic intentions.[20]

However, there are skeptics who believe that the anti-China mentality gripping the (President George W.) Bush Administration is a by-product of the neo-conservative elements within the policymaking structures of the U.S. government. Professor Michael Klare points to the Defense Planning Guidance (DPG) for fiscal years 1994-1999—as the "master blueprint for U.S. dominance in the post-Cold War era."[21] Professor Klare, director of the Five College Program in Peace and World Security Studies at Hampshire College, identified (3) events, in 2005, that reflected a new (manufactured?) hostility toward China.

First, in February 2005, the announcement that the U.S.-Japan alliance was to be strengthened—the U.S. knew that China would react in a hostile manner to this new agenda; Second, Secretary of Defense Donald Rumsfeld's speech at a strategic conference held in Singapore, in June 2005, singled out the Chinese and its military buildup as a real threat to stability in East Asia; Third, in July 2005, the Pentagon released a report, *The Military Power of the People's Republic of China*, that once again focused upon the potential danger of China's military development. Klare writes, "the main thrust of the report is that China is expanding its capacity to fight wars beyond its own territory and that this effort constitutes a dangerous challenge to global order."[22]

Yet, amongst our allies in Asia-Pacific, there appears to be a vociferous and volatile debate concerning the nature of the Chinese threat to the region. Two Australian writers and longtime observers of China's development since the 1960s, Gregory Clark and Ross Terrill, perceive China's emergence in Asia, and the world, through different prisms of interpretation. Clark, vice-president of Akita International University and a former Australian diplomat, sees the 'bogey-man' thesis, once again, being applied to China by its detractors.[23] Terrill, an associate researcher at Harvard University's John K. Fairbank Center, interprets China as a country in transition and burdened with indecision by whether to become a fully functional nation-state, or a new Chinese empire. This dual-internal struggle has reached a midpoint, and China's final determination of its future will have tremendous regional and global ramifications, according to Professor Terrill, the author of *The New Chinese Empire.*[24]

Clark, however, believes the current hysteria over China's dramatic economic and military growth is a manifestation of the "China Threat" lobby which has been constantly in motion since the Korean War, 1950-1953. *Every* political or military struggle in East Asia is always traced back to some subliminal plot hatched up by the Chinese government. In both Australia and America, the 'China Threat' crowd is constantly linking China with any, if not all, events in Asia that are considered a threat to the Yank-Aussie interests in the region.[25] Clark sees all this nonsense as 'smoke and mirrors' to protect the real interests involved in these contrived moments of frantic Chinese xenophobia—the military-industrial-intelligence complex, he observes that "when it is all over and the alleged threat has proved to be quite imaginary, the threat merchants move on to find another target. But not before billions have been spent. And millions have died."[26]

Professor Terrill, in disagreement, perceives sees a more savvy, ambitious and dangerous Chinese empire emerging in the 21st century. By contrast, the American empire is seen by the author as a tripod of global interests: technology and investment, popular culture and a non-imperialistic military that intervenes and then leaves. In short, America represents a 'soft empire' in its overt handling of international affairs. However, Terrill believes that the Chinese see themselves, and their *new* empire, in a very different light. China's leaders perceive themselves as the "guardians of truth".[27] According to Professor Terrill, the new Chinese empire does indeed represent a *real* threat to America's global preeminence and its hegemonic system—both of which are based upon its economic, political and social values:

> The new Chinese empire is different. At once more modest and more arrogant, it is an empire of theater and presumption. It is a construct both of domestic repression and of international aspiration. Its arsenal of weapons includes secrecy,

deception, and a sense of history that enables it to take a long view of China's interests and ambitions.[28]

When you look at the raw numbers, the Chinese are indeed putting together a rather formidable force that appears to could the potential to project Chinese power well beyond their shores. In an increasingly transparent world, any nation's military build-up does not go unnoticed—especially by America. Therefore, the lack of clarity on the issue of military expenditures by the Chinese government is emerging as an unsettling issue between the U.S. and China.

This thesis, concerning the potentiality of a 'China threat' and the lack of accurate information on their overall military spending, are detailed in the Department of Defense's (DoD) annual report to the U.S. Congress from the Office of the Secretary of Defense, titled, *"The Military Power of the People's Republic of China"*. This well-structured report contained numerical figures representing China's troop levels, budgetary and expenditure figures, missile capabilities and present military priorities and strengths within the East Asian theatre, and what it will mean for future U.S. military strategists and regional policymakers.[29]

One of the primary focuses of the report was its analysis of China's capabilities in dealing with Taiwan, and with those nations who might potentially come to the island's defense, if a military conflagration erupted between them. It is not a secret to U.S. regional analysts that the most important regional matter for China is to re-assimilate Taiwan into the Chinese nation-state family. This is a *red-button* issue for the People's Republic of China's (PRC) leadership in Beijing. The DoD's report also provides credible evidence that China's massive re-modernization of its military also represents the potential capability of disturbing the *'power balance'*, or status quo, within East Asia.[30] This disturbing fact has certainly the caught the attention of China's neighbors who are increasingly unsettled about such a development. Here are some of the basic figures presented in the DoD report on China's *overall* military situation:

Ground Troops: 1.6 million;
Tanks: 6,500
Artillery Pieces: 11,000
Air Force: 1,500 fighters; 780 bombers
Naval Forces:
Destroyers/Frigates—64
Landing Ships—43
Submarines—57
Ballistic Missile Capability:

Short Range—650–730;
Medium Range—29–37;
Intermediate Range—14–18
Intercontinental Range—20 to 24 (5,500 km)
20 (8,500 km)
Submarine Launched—20 to 24[31]

Initially, China's responded angrily to the DoD's report and its analysis concerning the threatening situation involving China and Taiwan. In a fit of nationalistic frustration, Zhu Chenghu, a PLA (People's Liberation Army) major-general and professor at China's National Defense University, stated that China might have to resort to using nuclear weapons against America, if the U.S. interfered on the behalf of Taiwan during a war with China. This remark certainly caught the attention of the Bush administration and the Pentagon. However, the Beijing government dismissed the remark as an individual making a "personal opinion" about a sensitive matter. Interestingly, General Zhu was not reprimanded publicly for his impolitic and provocative comment.[32] Many China-watchers were not surprised by the lack of zeal shown by Beijing to denounce Professor Zhu's inflammatory remark. Many believe that Zhu's position is widely supported within the upper ranks of the PLA. Therefore, the CCP (Chinese Communist Party) is reluctant to rebuke the general publicly. Jing Huang, a foreign policy analyst at the Brookings Institution, believes "Mr. Zhu would never have been able to make such comments unless he was backed by powerful forces within the PLA."[33]

So, what is the future outcome, economically and militarily, between these two Pacific powers—America and China? In an attempt not to be ambiguous or evasive on this serious question, the *actual* consensus concerning U.S.-China relations remains deeply divided. Robert Kaplan and Richard Haass are perfect examples of the intellectual division existing in American policy circles today. Both are greatly respected and have done excellent work on global issues, especially concerning U.S. security matters. Kaplan, a renowned global analyst, interprets the American position in the Pacific as the defining epic that will determine the U.S.'s future role as a global power in the 21st century.

According to Kaplan, the keys to America's future hegemonic presence in the Pacific will be its capacity to project naval power (re: Alfred T. Mahan's 1890 thesis[34]), and to possess the technological capabilities to match similar advances made by China in its land-based missile systems, and within its naval surface and submarine fleets as well. Kaplan writes, "In the coming decades, China will play an asymmetric back-and-forth game with us in the Pacific, taking advantage not only of its vast coastline but also of its rear base—stretching far back into Central Asia—from which it may eventually be able to lob missiles accurately at moving ships in the Pacific."[35] At the end of his article, Kaplan states that the U.S Navy must redefine itself to meet the military challenges represented by China, and take special note of the significant geographical factors confronting our regional strategists with concern to China and East Asia.[36]

Haass, currently the President of the Council on Foreign Affairs, America's most prestigious foreign policy organization, states that both America and China simply can not let things get out of control in East Asia, because both nations have too much to lose—economically, militarily and in terms of global influence. However, he also emphatically believes it's futile to attempt to control, or manage, the overall development of any nation-state,

> The rise and fall of countries (like China) is largely beyond the ability of the United States or any other outsider to control. The performance of states is mostly the result of demographics, culture, natural resources, educational systems, economic policy, political stability, and foreign policy.[37]

Haass admits that a great deal of history is determined by relations between and amongst the great powers, at any particular point in time, and the key relationship that demands watching in the 21st century is the one between China and the U.S. Presently, the recent rise of Chinese nationalism presents a degree of difficulty for America and China to reach an understanding on many significant issues.[38] However, Haass asserts with absolute certainty that "a U.S.-China cold war would be costly, dangerous, and distracting, robbing attention and resources from pressing internal and global challenges. Both countries have a stake in avoiding this outcome."[39]

I think it is appropriate and proper to end this section of the chapter with a survey that was completed by David Rothkopf, a visiting scholar at the Carnegie Endowment for International Peace and a widely respected national security analyst. In 2005, Rothkopf conducted an extensive survey at the Carnegie Endowment for International Peace on a number of issues, priorities and topics concerning U.S. foreign policy.

Overall, almost 180 individuals participated in answering Rothkopf's multiple questions. I will only focus on a few of the answers obtained by Rothkopf and his team of researchers. These experts were asked twice a double-fold question: The first was which countries and/or entities are most likely to be important allies, friends, or otherwise important to the support of U.S. initiatives over the next (5) and the next (20) years? The second question was the flip side of the first question. Which countries and/or entities would most likely be America's potential adversaries, rivals, or challengers to our interests in the world over the next (5) years and the next (20) years? The answer for *all* four categories was China.[40]

Hence, it is not an understatement to say that the American foreign policy establishment is quite divided over the *proper* response to China's rise in global affairs. Therefore, should we be surprised that our national policies emanating from the White House and the U.S. Congress toward China are just a mirror of the varied opinions within the ranks of academics, journalists, think-tanks and other policymakers within the U.S. government? Almost all the "experts" mentioned in this chapter basically agree that the moment of truth is coming relatively soon for America and China. Yet, we are not even close to having achieved a consensus concerning the development of a coherent and operational strategy concerning the rise of China, and East Asia, in the 21st century.

ADAM SMITH'S ECONOMICS WITH CHINESE CHARACTERISTICS

Napoleon is alleged to have stated, "When China wakes up, it will shake the world."[41] This famous and prophetic quote remains shrouded by a degree of doubt concerning its authenticity, but its essential truth has come to pass in the 21st century. However, what is not in doubt is the present-day rumblings emanating from China's dynamic and evolving economy. Indeed, the world's focus is shifting irrefutably toward the Asia-Pacific Rim. Specifically, it is the steadily growing Asian economies, with China performing as the region's locomotive that is turning the global economic crankshaft away from a North Atlantic (i.e. America and the European Union) perspective to one now comprising of the United States and the East Asian Hemisphere.

Henceforth, this specific section of the chapter will focus on two primary topics of vital concern: First, an overview of China's current and future economic prowess and the ramifications for America and the West. For whom, most see as the main victims of the economic *collateral damage*, such as massive unemployment and the relocation of millions of lives, taking place within their local communities and throughout their native countries?

Secondly, the potential for conflict in East Asia over the issue of having access to the available natural resources in the global marketplace, especially oil. Specifically, if the advanced economies of the world continue their pace of growth and the volume of natural resources begin to diminish, who gets the resources? This is *the* key question that needs an answer from the major economic powers in the very near future.

According to Gilbert Achcar, Professor of Politics and International Relations at the University of Paris-VIII, "China plays a key role in the world capitalist market, and the more this market becomes dependent on the state of the Chinese economy, the more global capitalism will have a stake in the stability of China."[42] In short, China's economic growth has created a mutual need between itself and the outside world. Neither can prosper without the other. It's an international version of a shotgun wedding—East and West brought together despite misgivings by both partners. For example, America needs the Chinese to purchase billions of dollars of our Treasury notes to pay for our record national deficits, and China needs access to our domestic market to sell their exports—which in turn keeps the economic engines running in the Middle Kingdom and helps to maintain employment for millions.

The West, though, is finding out that this new economic gambit called globalization has a serious downside. In America and Australia, their respective automobile industries are increasingly confronting unrelenting Asian competition, primarily from Japan and South Korea. The production of cars and steel represent middle-class wages and it also provides a certain degree of self-respect for workers in these industries. In short, making automobiles and steel personifies a certain dignity and strength reflected by its owners and workers in their local communities and countries.

This sector of the American economy is under threat, and its painful transition due to international competition is tearing communities apart—as witnessed in my adopted home-state of Michigan. General Motors (GM), once the kingpin of American corporations, is now in freefall in terms of its U.S. market share, and overall car sells, in North America. However, this American corporate icon now possesses the largest market share (11.2%)—for a foreign automaker—*in* China. It now possesses a *workforce* of over 15,000 in the 'Middle Kingdom'. Conversely, its U.S. market share (26.2%) continues to slump, falling another 1.3% during 2005. Thus, unsurprisingly, GM's highly profitable auto plants in China are now paying the bills in its ever-shrinking North American operations and market share.[43] It should be noted that, in January 2007, GM publicly announced that it had achieved record car sales in China. Its overall sales in the Chinese market improved 32% during 2006. Overall, GM sold 876,747 vehicles in China in 2006.[44] Many of them were assembled at GM's production plants which are now situated in China—not Michigan.

Yet, GM's surge in profits in China was a distant second place to Ford's own eye-popping 89% increase in car sales (155,404) in China for 2006.[45] Both Michigan-based car companies have drastically reduced their hourly and salaried work forces in their North American operations over the past few years. In 2007, no one really knows when the U.S. auto industry will hit rock bottom, but *most* recognize that it will probably go the way of the American steel industry during the 1980s, where approximately 70% of the industry's employment was terminated due to more efficient and cheaper steel from it international competitors. In short, in 2007, the cold-blooded realities of the modern-day marketplace, and the raw power of globalization, possess an irrefutable omnipresence throughout the automotive industry in America. Hence, it appears for now, only a fraction of the U.S. auto industry will remain profitable and viable during the 21st century.

Yet, this profitable situation for GM appears to be a short-term panacea, because Chinese automakers are now in the process of building cars for their own domestic market, and for the international market as well. The Lifan Group, led by visionary Yin Mingshan, is planning to export cars to Europe and America by 2009. In 2006, the Lifan Group took a bold step in this direction by purchasing one of the world's most sophisticated engine plants in Brazil from the DaimlerChrysler and BMW auto company. They will dismantle it and transport it 8,300 miles to Chongqing in western China. In the end, the Lifan Group wants to produce a competitive sedan with leather seats, dual air bags and a DVD system for only $9,700.[46]

America and Europe are not the only targeted markets for these Chinese autos in the near future. Australia is now being seriously considered as a new market for their cars. Of course, the (much) less costly Chinese models will completely undermine the price structure for cars in the Land Down-under. If allowed to penetrate the Australian market with any degree of significance, the Aussie auto companies will almost certainly become a victim of collateral damage and perish from their local communities, because they will almost certainly be forced out of business due to a price war they can't win.

Australian Greens Federal Senator Christine Milne stated, "If China obtains total access to the Australia's car market, the nation's auto plants will soon be closed. It would be suicidal for the Australian car industry to give China a full-go at its domestic market."[47] John Wormald, a senior analyst for Autopolis—a major automotive consultancy firm, confirms Senator Milne's assertion that Australia's car industry would be drastically damaged by unrestricted trade, "The effect of Chinese car makers entering the Australian market would be dramatic. The effect will be to pull the whole price structure (for cars) down. Even if the local industry isn't directly competing against Chinese vehicles the effect of their coming will be severe."[48]

This same scenario is repeating itself in industry after industry in America, Australia and the rest of the world. Growing market shares, trade surpluses and an ever-expanding Chinese economy is indeed shaking the economic world as we know it. Therefore, again, not unexpectedly, demands for government intervention on behalf of struggling industries in America are becoming a common occurrence in Washington DC. Nucor's CEO, Daniel R. DiMicco, in charge of the largest steelmaker facility in America (in Charlotte, North Carolina) is concerned about the future ability of the U.S. to produce competitive steel in a global market being shaped by Chinese industrial policies. DiMicco states that China is exporting steel despite absorbing most of it for domestic use. He claims more steel mills are being built in China, and they are "massively subsidized" by government supported interest-free loans, an undervalued currency, and generous export tax breaks.[49] Thus, according to the embattled Nucor CEO, "If China decides to export significant amounts of steel, there will be no such thing as competition."[50] The American and Australian auto industries and the U.S. steel industries are concrete examples of the degree of market penetration associated with China's new economic presence in terms of global production and trade.

Already, China has a dominating global production presence in several categories involving labor-intensive goods, such as toys (70%), bicycles (60%), shoes (50%) and luggage (33%).[51] The Chinese are now making serious and successful global inroads in product production requiring low-tech capabilities, such as microwave ovens (50%), television sets and air conditioners (33%) and refrigerators (20%).[52] Oded Shenkar, author of *The Chinese Century*, writes that as China "moves up the ladder" in terms of product sophistication and technology, unlike Japan and Korea before them, they are not allowing these lower rung economic production systems to be moved (outsourced) to other countries. The profits from these low-level manufacturing sources of production continue to finance China's move toward "knowledge-intensive areas" such as products associated with the information age.[53] The primary reason for China's reluctance to outsource these lower-tech positions is because the Chinese government must maintain stable levels of employment for its 1.3 billion citizens. This challenge is unrelenting for the Communist leadership in Beijing.

The only reasons keeping China from even further domination of the products mentioned above, and gaining an even larger market share in the West, is the agreed upon quotas and tariffs which are insisted upon by the national governments throughout the developed world (i.e. the U.S., Japan, Australia and the European Union). There is a good reason for these economic protections for America—massive job losses. Scott Robert, a researcher at the Economic Policy Institute in Washington DC, provided disturbing and frightening evidence concerning the employment ramifications of America's trade policies with China since 1992. Robert's analysis determined that almost 700,000 jobs were lost between 1992 and 1999. And, he projects even greater job losses (almost 900,000) for the American economy in the near future, if trade policies and trends remain the same with China.[54] In short, if everything remains the same in terms of trade policies and economic trends between the U.S. and China, the potential job losses for America's economy will be approximately 1.6 million.[55]

Though, the U.S. economy will gain some jobs during this period of global readjustment and transition, the message remains quite clear and disturbing. Presently, and during the next decade or so, China will represent a monumental threat to those who earn their livings in the manufacturing sector of the American economy. Again, Robert indicates that states in the Upper-Midwest and the Mid-Atlantic like Michigan, Wisconsin, Minnesota, Ohio, Indiana, Pennsylvania, New Jersey and New York, have been, and will continue to be, hit hard by the Chinese economic juggernaut.[56]

China's voracious appetite for the world's natural resources has grown almost exponentially. Thus, unsurprisingly, the global prices for various commodities (oil, gas, iron ore, copper, cement mix, etc.) have risen dramatically as a result. The end results, in terms of global distribution, are not equitable, nor just. In short, the diminishing volume and/or availability of various resources represent a real danger for *future* global stability on several levels: economically, politically, socially, and, especially, militarily.

An editorial in the *Asian Times* declared that China now possesses the 4th largest economy in the world—having catapulted themselves over Great Britain, France and Italy in 2005. Economist Jim O'Neill at Goldman Sachs, in London, stated that China immense growth during 2005—without a revised Gross Domestic Product (GDP) completed—"China could squeak in ahead of Britain even without a revision. It just goes to show how much it's contributing to the world economy."[57]

Lester Brown, founder of World Watch Institute in 1974, and currently president of the Earth Policy Institute, wrote, in spring 2005, "Although the United States has long consumed the lion's share of the world's resources, this situation is changing fast as the Chinese economy surges ahead, overtaking the U.S. in the consumption of one resource after another."[58] Brown points to China's importation of grain, meat, coal and steel consumption as examples of the 'Middle Kingdom' surpassing American levels of consumption—except for oil.[59] However, in his latest book, *Plan B 2.0*, Brown states unequivocally, that "the inevitable conclusion to be drawn from these projections (concerning China's future resource needs) is that there are not enough resources for China to reach U.S. consumption levels."[60] China, from the standpoint of consuming the earth's resources, is increasingly interpreted by its neighbors and global competitors as a threatening element to their own survival in the 21st century.

Though, I have focused primarily on the effects upon the American economy, the same scenario is playing out in national economies around the world. Therefore, the question that is increasingly asked amongst the *devel-*

oped world, *developing* nations and even amongst *Third-World* countries is how does a nation maintain its competitiveness against an economic Goliath who possesses an immense work force and an extremely low-wage economy? Will Hutton, the former editor of the London *Observer* and economic editor of *The Guardian*, utilizes within his book, *The Writing on the Wall*, the research of Suzanne Berger at MIT, and her team of researchers, who interviewed 500 companies in America, Europe and Asia. Their collective efforts produced an irrefutable conclusion concerning the variables of globalization, and that was "wage costs are not the be-all and end-all of economics."[61]

However, Berger's own book, *How We Compete*, indicates that a Chinese worker earns only 4 percent of the wage of an American worker, though she quickly points out that the Chinese worker is only 4 percent as productive as an American worker.[62] Hutton, presently the chief executive of The Work Foundation, again, uses Berger's work to provide evidence, and dilute the ever-growing myth, that not all the low-skilled and low paying jobs will disappear from western economies and Japan. Berger's research showed that companies often found it necessary, physically and culturally, to have production facilities close to their respective markets.[63] Nevertheless, the recent out-sourcing of millions of jobs from the U.S., and from other developed economies in the world, has accelerated without question. Without question, indeed, it certainly appears that hiring Chinese workers, at a fraction of the labor costs encountered in developed economies, has proven extremely tempting and profitable for hydra-headed multi-nationals.

THE CHINESE REVOLUTION AND THE ASIA-PACIFIC RIM

What is China to America? What is China to the Asia-Pacific Rim? In truth, the answers to these questions remain frustratingly beyond the grasp of most analysts and experts who studied the region. As a result, it comes as no surprise that the range of opinions throughout Asia-Pacific represents a vast spectrum of interpretations. Often though probably too simplistically, the main arguments are divided into two camps: The first group is those who see China's emergence in Asia as a *threat* to U.S. leadership. The opposing viewpoint is represented by those individuals who interpret China's recent rise as *non-threatening*—for now. The one perspective that there seems to be a general consensus upon is that China *is* changing the 'dynamics' of the region, and the American response to this transition holds the key to the region's future.

Specifically, this section will focus on (3) thematic questions concerning Asia-Pacific and the 21st century: *First*, how will America respond to

China's rise in Asia-Pacific? Some perceive the 'China challenge' as the defining determinant for the U.S. position, in the Pacific region, during the 21st century. *Secondly*, how are America's key allies—Australia, Japan and South Korea—adjusting to China's new economic prowess and military influence in the region? And, *finally*, can America maintain the fundamental framework that has created and ensured unity and understanding, in terms of collective security, between itself and its key regional allies since 1950?

To answer the first thematic question, I believe America will respond to China's rise with policies and a strategy consisting of passive/aggressive characteristics. This is a typical response by those (America, in this case) who are internally threatened but do not want a specific individual, or nation (China, case in point), to think they are vulnerable due to their emerging presence in their day-to-day lives. In short, the U.S. is still figuring out what to do about this emerging economic and military powerhouse in East Asia.

In the last five years, America and China have taken turns criticizing and assisting each other on a number of issues confronting Asia-Pacific. For instance, the North Korean situation is a perfect example where both sides have had to compromise to find a workable solution. Since 2001, the U.S. has been distracted by the 'war on terror' in Afghanistan and Iraq. Both wars have absorbed an enormous amounts of American financial and human resources. Not unexpectedly, when the North Korean leader, Kim Jong-il, announced, in 2005, that his country was re-instituting its nuclear weapons program, the Bush Administration reluctantly looked to China for diplomatic assistance with this dangerous regime. In truth, the U.S. is stretched dangerously thin, diplomatically and militarily, particularly since its ill-founded invasion of Iraq. And, the Bush Administration has acknowledged that China has maintained a strong relationship with North Korea since the end of WWII.

Of course, the neo-conservatives within the Bush White House disliked this admission of diplomatic inadequacy which exposed the inherent weaknesses within their overall plan toward achieving global dominance. Nevertheless, the U.S. government urgently asked and received assistance from President Hu Jintao, and the Chinese Communist government, when North Korea stunned Asia and America with its first ever nuclear test in October 2006. As a result, after direct Chinese intervention, the North Korean leader, Kim Jong-il, agreed to return to the six-party talks involving China, North & South Korea, Japan, U.S. and Russia.[64]

It is important to remember that China is not doing this out of ideological altruism, but, in truth, it has huge financial interests at stake within this geopolitical crisis. If northeast Asia is engulfed by a regional war, those 9–10% annual economic growth figures enjoyed by China for the last twenty-five years will become a sweet memory for President Hu's government. And, such a war's collateral damage may include the termination of the Chinese Communist party's leadership in China as well.

However, China is not permitting American hegemonic unilateralism to be the only game, in terms of future economic and energy policies, in the region. China, as mentioned earlier in the book, created the Shanghai Cooperation Organization (SCO), and was a strong supporter of the East Asian Summit (EAS) that was convened for the first time in December 2005. In both cases, it is correct to perceive these two developments as future harbingers toward challenging American economic dominance in Asia-Pacific. China, though cautiously and subtly, is giving the U.S. prior notice that the future economic policies concerning the region will not be predominately created and designed to benefit U.S. interests. This reality alone is revolutionary in its ramifications for the American establishment.

Finally, the Americans and Chinese need each other - much more than their respective publics realize or understand. Simply put, America depends on China buying U.S. treasury notes every day to pay for our overindulgent capitalistic lifestyle. Laura Tyson, a former economic adviser on President Bill Clinton's Council of Economic Advisors, once commented rather poignantly, "America spends, Asia lends."[65] U.S. politicians don't have the political nerve, or the personal integrity, to inform their constituents about the uncomfortable and budgetary truth that America is now approximately ten trillion dollars in debt. In short, the national economy is not producing enough wealth to pay for all the things that Americans believe they are entitled to in life. As a consequence, the Chinese government was persuaded to purchase hundreds of billions of dollars of U.S. treasury notes to prop up America's increasingly overweight society and its ever-growing debt from mindless consumerism and out of control governmental spending.

Conversely, China can not force the U.S. to change its domestic spending habits because much of the present-day credit and trade debt is due to buying cheap Chinese goods at stores, such as Wal-Mart, K-Mart, Target, etc. China's mind-boggling economic expansion over the last thirty years, and relative social stability, would evaporate overnight if the U.S. market plunged into financial chaos. Both nations would wake up to high unemployment and social upheaval. In an almost Shakespearean sense, America and China are like two scorpions in a bottle. Each possesses the capacity to cripple the other, if not the ability to mutually destroy the other—financially. Thus, it is in the interest of both countries to maintain this Catch-22 financial charade parading as sound economics.

Point of fact, war is to be avoided at all costs. Issues such as Taiwanese sovereignty, North Korea's nuclear missile program, oil and gas deposits amongst the Spratly Islands which are located within the South China Sea, and Japan's future military role in East Asia, are extremely sensitive for the governments of the U.S. and China. These issues occasionally flare-up in the course of doing regional business, but, thus far, have been resolved quietly and efficiently. A U.S.-China war would be an utter catastrophe for both nations and their geopolitical objectives for Asia-Pacific. But, can they co-exist in the long run? No one is certain on this vital question.

Therein, a sense of 'mutually assured destruction' hangs over everyone's heads in Asia-Pacific. To put a finer point on this volatile situation, the U.S. and China are increasingly seen by most citizens in this region as the 'dual-caretakers' of it for the 21st century. This acknowledged reality is also why many will also be on edge during the coming years and decades. Can this *partnership* produce the type of peace and prosperity desired by the people and nations within the Asia-Pacific region? America, being the only superpower at this time, carries the brunt of the responsibility for creating a productive relationship with China. Rest assured, the people in this region are watching intensely the actions of both very carefully.

The second thematic question concerning how America's key allies will react to the growing economic and military presence of China in Asia-Pacific is already taking shape. I visited South Korea in 2005, Australia in 2006, China, South Korea and Japan in 2007, and China and Vietnam in 2008, and China, South Korea and Japan in 2009, during the last five years. Therefore, I will answer this particular question with some personal observations concerning each nation related to their current, and probable, relations with America and China.

As expected, I will provide a brief analysis for each situation, some of which is based upon my travels and professional activities involving these nations and the region at-large. Also, I will present a few of my own opinions about America's key allies: Australia, South Korea and Japan. And, the U.S.-China relationship will be addressed as well.

First, I will examine Australia. My last visit to this island continent was in May-June 2006, and I still can't get the impression out of my mind of Australia being so small and vulnerable. It is true that their overall territorial sovereignty is huge—essentially equal to the U.S., but its miniscule population (20 million—1/15 of the U.S.) is dangerously small, in terms of national defense. Even if Australia acquired top-shelf technological military weaponry, their tiny military forces (approximately 55,000) is basically equal to the size of the New York City Police Department. In truth, Australian forces would be no match for a massive invasion force from one of its Asian neighbors.

Australia continues to live precariously on the southern cusp of the East Asian Hemisphere. Its national defense is tied to a nation (America) that is dangerously in debt (over $10 trillion) and an overextended military (Afghanistan and Iraq). And, its current and future economic prosperity is increasingly tied to the financial whims of a communist nation—China. Yet, I kept hearing from academics, politicians, writers, and regional observers that everything is fine and that the future will continue to be bright and prosperous.

Upon reflection, I remember the tone and lilt of their voices possessing a shrillness which indicated to me the degree of doubt existing within their statements of hopefulness. In short, they appeared to be determined to convince themselves, more than me, about the future of Australia. It is this interpretational impression that I took away from my last trip to Australia. Yes, they are a wealthier society. Yes, Australia has signed numerous trade (primarily for its natural resources) deals that will continue to deposit billions into its national treasury. Yes, Australia is playing a larger and more influential role in the South Pacific region, and, to some degree, internationally.

Yet, something wasn't quite right. I think, despite their increased wealth and increased influence regionally and globally, there was a sense that this situation was fraught with danger. China's influence in Australian domestic and foreign affairs was acknowledged by all, but everyone also reiterated that Australia could maintain its '*balanced diplomacy*' between America and China. Like America, Australia's economic future is increasingly tied to China's own expansion. A *Catch-22* situation is evolving for Australia with the two major powers, America and China, are pulling on the opposite ends of the rope—with Australia in the middle.

For Australians to say that this *realpolitik* dilemma does not exist or that they will not have to make a choice, between the U.S. and China, somewhere down the road is simply delusional. There is no doubt in *my* mind, the moment of truth will arrive for Australia, and their *decision* could very well determine its destiny for the rest of the 21st century. The unsettling truth for Australia, though they consider themselves a 'middle power', is that they are simply too small to survive, as a neutral entity, the wake that would result from a U.S.-China confrontation—a situation that would engender a massive geo-political tsunami sweeping over the region.

South Korea is, of course, in a very different situation. Though, like Australia, it greatly depends upon America and China for its national security and economic prosperity, respectively. However, it is these same two countries who are delaying the eventual unification of the Korean peninsula. At least this was the perception communicated at the 5th anniversary of the North-South Summit that took place, in June 2005, at the Shilla Hotel in Seoul, South Korea. In June 2000, South Korean President Kim Dae-jung and North Korean leader Kim Jong-il met at Pyongyang International Airport, shook hands, smiled before the world media and, more importantly, for the first time since the end of the Korean War (1953) brought hope to this troubled peninsula.

I thought South Korea, during the period 2005–2009, had a noticeably different nationalistic feel to it. The people and their society appeared confident and much more willing to assert themselves in their own lives, and in their relations with other countries. This was quite evident to me at the internationally attended conference commemorating the historic meeting between the North and the South. And, there is no doubt in my mind that the Korean peninsula will unify, though I remain uncommitted in terms of determining a specific timetable suitable for this prognosis; but if you force me to—I think within the next 10 years the Korean peninsula will be unified.

However, as stated earlier, I also believe that the countries surrounding the Korean peninsula are less than enthusiastic about the eventuality of a reconciliation taking place between these two Cold War adversaries. And, I believe that most Koreans understand that their primary neighbors, China and Japan, feel this way. Therefore, the future progress toward this territorial consolidation will probably be a slow and sluggish process. Why?

First, in 2009, Japan is fearful of having a strong and unified Korea as its neighbor because their recent collective history is one of Japanese occupation, repression and violence toward the Koreans since the late-19th century. Unlike America, history to Koreans is not considered inconsequential, irrelevant or unimportant. They are proud of their recent accomplishments as a society—meaning their newfound economic and military strength. And, Koreans perceive, not China, but Japan as their greatest threat—geopolitically. All you have to do is watch a sporting event between these two nations, even on television, and the hairs on your arms will stiffen from the intense kinetic energy produced by the rabid and nationalistic fans of both nations.

Without a doubt, Korean-Japanese relations are a long way from achieving a high level of confidence and trust on both sides. Plus, it is important to understand that Japan has never looked across (120 miles) the Tsushima Straits and witnessed a strong Korea. This fact alone has had a sobering affect upon the Japanese leadership. Finally, from a geopolitical standpoint, Japan is currently confronted with the reality of having a strong (South) Korea and China in close proximity. This situation has never happened in the region's prior history. Nevertheless, this modern historical truth is acknowledged and respected by the Japanese.

Second, China is concerned about a unified Korea for other reasons. First, the Chinese Communists are worried about the potential of having a strong and unified Korea with western values, a modern military and an established democracy on its northeastern border. This does not bode well for the Beijing leadership which is trying desperately to keep the communist system of government in power, despite an annually growing number of public disturbances throughout the country. The Middle Kingdom, historically, has looked upon the 'Hermit Kingdom' as an inferior and subservient entity.

However, in 2009, South Korea, a former tributary state during the dynastic period of Chinese history, is much wealthier in per capita terms and is much more advanced technologically than China. Also, if you combined both Korean militaries on the peninsula, there would be approximately 1.6 million in uniform. This force is essentially equal to China's own forces. If you also consider the advanced weaponry that the North and South possess, then you can see why China is a bit ambiguous about promoting Korean unity. Though, North Korea is recognized internationally as an economic basket case, South Korea's economy currently ranks 13th in the world (as stated in Chapter 5). South Korea, along with Singapore and Taiwan, is considered one of Asian economic 'tigers'. Interestingly, though, North and South Korea have both stated that they would be willing to accept the presence of U.S. military bases upon the peninsula even after unification. Why?

Well, simply put, both Korean nations are wary about China's future intentions in northeast Asia. With the presence of U.S. troops on the peninsula, this would mitigate, to some degree, China's desire to dominate the Korean peninsula as it did in prior centuries. Presently, despite serious misgivings by many Koreans concerning America's presence on the peninsula, it is still perceived as being much more benign, militarily and politically, than the potential of having a concerted Chinese, or Japanese, influence exerted upon them. You can make a credible argument by stating the 'balance of power' theory remains a real part of the Korean reality on this volatile piece of real estate. In the coming years, I am certain that the last vestige of the Cold War era will finally come to an end on the Korean peninsula.

However, I am equally convinced that a new 'power equation' will emerge in northeast Asia. In the future, the Korean nation will find itself constantly seeking the middle ground within a geo-political struggle between its two powerful benefactors—China and America. Though, there is considerable opinion that a Sino-Japanese confrontation is never far from the realm of possibility, and such an event would very easily replace the issue of China-U.S. regional competition within the Korean foreign ministry.

But, in the meantime, the brewing hegemonic competition for leadership within the Asia-Pacific region between the Americans and Chinese will certainly tax and fully test the dexterity of Korea's diplomatic skills during the first decades of the 21st century. Koreans know what happens when politics fails (Korean War, 1950–1953), because it took over fifty years for them to get to this point of actually discussing the possibility of unification and, eventually, achieving a significant degree of self-autonomy. Observers of the region are quite cognizant of the fact that there is a lot on the line for both North Korea and South Korea.

In concluding this chapter, I want to express a few thoughts on the '*inevitability*' of war occurring in northeast Asia, due to the accepted premise that a titanic struggle between China and America will develop because both are determined to exercise hegemonic dominance over Asia-Pacific during the 21st century. Those who perpetuate and support this thesis can, indeed, make a credible and historically-based argument that can clearly lead one to agree that such a fate is inevitable.

Yet, I remember what my old friend and historian Howard Zinn, professor emeritus at Boston University, has told me on numerous occasions during conversations, and from listening to him deliver lectures at colleges and universities in the Midwest, that the only thing predictable about history is its unpredictability. The 20th century is clearly evidence of that truism. In truth, there are no absolutes about the future, based on what has happened in the past. However, you can learn certain lessons, and truths, from history and apply them to the present and future, but it's never a perfect fit.[66]

I believe Professor Zinn's basic assumption and judgment concerning the potential use and understanding of history to be sound and wise. Everyone has a different take on the importance of history, and our media has often distorted or manipulated it to fit their ratings-driven agendas. Unfortunately, much of today's news, throughout the world, is owned and influenced by corporate interests or government censors. The end product is often diluted of its informational importance or relevance. It lacks the nutritional intellectual value to feed a starved and ignorant citizenry who depend on these news outlets for its understanding of the world.

In short, the more we know about different individuals and unfamiliar cultures, the better off we are in understanding what makes them tick as a society. Without this critical and crucial knowledge, we are simply operating in the dark, leaving ourselves completely at the mercy of reactionary demagogues and warmongers, whose collective paranoia interprets all alien cultures and people as enemies of the state. The recent debacles in Afghanistan and Iraq are sad examples of this irrefutable truth.

Therefore, the *key* and *vital* question remains unaltered and unanswered: Can America and China avoid a military conflagration during the 21st century, due to their *perceived* hegemonic self-interests within Asia-Pacific? The real answer is that no one truthfully knows. Yet, history does provide a sterling example for both countries to consider—The Shanghai Communiqué—created in February 1972.

It was this publicly announced 'joint statement', agreed to by U.S. President Richard Nixon and China's Chairman Mao Zedong at the end of their historic meeting, which ushered in a new era of relations between these two major Asia-Pacific powers. It helped to end the U.S. involvement in the Vietnam War, and it also marked the end of the overtly hostile Cold War diplomacy that existed between the most powerful democracy in the world, and the most populated communist nation on earth. This diplomatic breakthrough, though originally viewed with hostility and skepticism by hard-line conservatives in America, in 1972, was later judged by almost all foreign policy analysts and historians to be a tremendous diplomatic achievement for U.S. President Richard Nixon, National Security Adviser Henry Kissinger, and, most importantly, for America.

Zhang Yuping, who is Vice-Dean in the College of Humanities and Law at North China University of Technology, was a visiting scholar at Central Michigan University during the academic year 2005-2006. Professor Zhang stated in an interview that "Mao greatly influenced my generation. He did everything for the people. The Cultural Revolution was right at the beginning, but later on things went badly."[67]

Though, in the West, a number of present-day scholars—concerning Chinese history since 1949—have described Mao as a rigid doctrinal tyrant, or as an egomaniacal dictator without a conscience. Despite these recent works of scholarship describing Mao in rather brutal and unflattering terms, Professor Zhang continues to see Mao in a favorable light, "Mao was probably 80% good and 20% bad in my opinion. He gave China and the Chinese people strong leadership during his life, but, it is true, he did have some weaknesses."[68]

Perhaps, Professor Zinn's analysis is essentially correct, that our current situation with China touches upon different issues, in a different time. All of which represents an unquestioned degree of unpredictability. Yet, can we not learn something from the courageous and visionary events that occurred, in 1972, within the pages of American diplomatic history? I believe so. President Nixon, Chairman Mao, National Security Adviser Henry Kissinger and Chinese Premier Zhao Enlai went beyond the realm of commonly held wisdom, and geo-political dogma, and changed the course of history between the U.S. and China. Can it be done again?

Former National Security Advisor Zbigniew Brzezinski, during the Carter Presidency (1977-1981), believes China has shown great wisdom in running its affairs since the fall of the Berlin Wall in 1989, and that they have not made the same mistakes committed by Soviet leader, Mikhail Gorbachev, during the shocking collapse of the Soviet state in 1991.[69] Brzezinski, author of *The Grand Failure: The Birth and Death of Communism in the Twentieth Century*, presciently predicated the rapid downfall of the Soviet Union due to its serious internal and philosophical contradictions that simply undermined the structural integrity of the most powerful communist state in the world.

Since 1978, Chinese leaders such as Deng Xiaoping and Jiang Zemin, and current president Hu Jintao, have avoided the dangerous pitfalls that brought down the communist party apparatus in the Soviet Union in December 1991. However, in 2009, China is sailing in uncharted political waters. Professor Brzezinski believes "the Chinese are moving fairly fast from their revolutionary roots."[70] He also believes their current economic policies irrefutably show that "China is simply not following communist doctrine."[71] If this is so, and it certainly appears it is, then perhaps this moment represents another opportunity in history for bold thinkers and visionaries, in American and China, to construct and design a new geo-political paradigm in which both countries can co-exist and thrive simultaneously.

In 1972, the U.S. and China found acceptable common ground from which both nations could mutually benefit. Two countries with brave and visionary leaders broke down the ideological barriers separating them from their desired geo-political destinies. Smart and wise people, in both countries, began the de-escalation of Cold War tensions between themselves and those who depended on them for power and influence within their respective governments. In effect, Nixon and Mao began the incremental process of dismantling the intense and rigid ideological artifice that was constructed to separate these two societies since 1949.

In 2009, is it beyond the pale, that perhaps our current political leaders, or future leaders, representing the American government can create a new version of the Nixon–Kissinger stratagem which will result in a new 'communiqué' concerning America, China and Asia-Pacific in the 21st century? Put directly, can America once again, boldly seek and achieve another groundbreaking act of diplomacy with China. I believe the ball is in *America's* court. History has shown, irrefutably, that we did it once. Can we accomplish it again? Do we have the vision and the will to achieve it again?

According to MIT Professor Noam Chomsky, the brilliant and often controversial linguist and U.S. foreign policy critic, the U.S. may have no other alternative but to build a new and constructive relationship with China during the 21st century. Chomsky, a globally renowned analyst of American foreign policy, believes the current cacophony of voices attempting to define U.S.-China future relations are "purely speculative and there is no way, that I can see, to guess which is more plausible."[72]

However, Professor Chomsky does see China becoming increasingly proactive in its foreign relations with other parts of the world. He believes that President Bush and his neo-conservatives are confronted with a situation they can do little about in the short-term,

Unlike Europe, it (China) can't be intimidated . . . Another factor is America's huge financial resources (investments) in Northeast Asia . . . Its (China) trade and diplomatic inroads into regions that the U.S. has assumed it controlled, like Latin America and even Saudi Arabia . . .

On the other hand, the Chinese export economy is an enormous gift to U.S. corporations. American manufacturers can produce with extremely cheap and brutally exploited labor, with few regulatory conditions or environmental concerns, and it can export cheap goods at huge profits, undermining their major domestic enemies—unions and American working-class wages. And importers, like Wal-Mart, benefit from these conditions in China. (American) financial institutions are itching to get into the act. So, it's a growing and disturbing dilemma for both the American political establishment and U.S. workers as well.[73]

Presently, I refuse to succumb to the darker impulses and the bombastic rhetoric that are often heard and presented in the current debates concerning the future challenges confronting U.S.-China relations. However, with history as my advisor and guide for the 21st century, I believe there *are* individuals with the necessary courage, knowledge and wisdom, in both America and China, to help their respective countries find new common ground, and to recognize their mutual agendas—regionally and globally. This pragmatic, rational and interests-based stratagem has the potential to transform a possible adversarial relationship into a new partnership that could fundamentally transform the Asia-Pacific region and redirect its destiny.

Perhaps, the 'Asia-Pacific Century', as many observers have predicted to be the fate of the 21st century, will indeed emerge as the new geopolitical reality. Its meaning will represent a definitive and fundamental transfer of global power. The rise of China and the economic prowess of Asia at-large, represent the foundational stones of this stunning geopolitical transformation. In essence, during the 21st century, the world will witness an historic epoch of monumental significance.

However, the ramifications from such a momentous shift in global economic (and I presume military power as well) power remain unknown. Nevertheless, once again, geography, hegemony and politics will mold and shape the history of the present century as they have of the previous ones. China has been around for approximately four thousand years. Thus, for the Chinese, the current situation, at the beginning of the 21st century, is just another chapter in the Middle Kingdom's long and storied past.

NOTES

1. Henry Kissinger, "China Shifts Centre of Gravity", *The Australian*, 13 June 2005. This article was published in Australia's only nationally published newspaper.

2. Jonathan D. Spence, "The Once and Future China", *Foreign Policy*, January/February 2005.

3. David Shambaugh lecture, "The Changing Nature of the Regional Systems in Asia-Pacific", Chicago Council of Foreign Affairs, 26 January 2006.

4. Ibid.

5. Ibid.

6. Natalia Rigol, "A Game of Giants: The Future of Sino-U.S. Relations", *Harvard International Review*, Spring 2005.

7. Ibid.

8. Merle Goldman lecture at Alma College (Michigan), 16 October 2006; Professor Goldman focused upon China's future and its economic reforms.

9. Rigol, "A Game of Giants", 2005.

10. Eric Heginbotham and Christopher P. Twomey, "America's Bismarckian Asia Policy", *Current History*, September 2005, pp. 243–250.

11. Ibid.

12. Joseph S. Nye, Jr., *Soft Power: The Means to Succeed in World Politics* (New York: Public Affairs, 2004).

13. Kerry Dumbaugh, "China-U.S. Relations: Current Issues and Implications for U.S. Policy", *CRS Report for Congress*, Congressional Research Service—The Library of Congress, 20 January 2006.

14. Ibid.

15. Ibid.

16. Interview with Professor Patrick Shan, 20 October 2006.

17. Ibid.

18. Lionel Beehner, "The Rise of the Shanghai Cooperation Organization", *Council on Foreign Relations*, 12 June 2006.

19. John Mearsheimer, "The Rise of China Will Not Be Peaceful at All", *The Australian*, 18 November 2005.

20. Ibid.

21. Michael T. Klare, "Revving Up the China Threat", *The Nation*, 24 October 2005.

22. Ibid.

23. Gregory Clark, "No Rest for 'China Threat' Lobby", *Japan Times*, 7 January 2006.

24. Ross Terrill, *The New Chinese Empire: And What It Means For The United States* (Cambridge, MA: Perseus Books Group, 2003), p. 28.

25. Clark, "No Rest for 'China Threat Lobby", 7 January 2006.

26. Ibid.

27. Terrill, *The New Chinese Empire*, p. 26.

28. Ibid.

29. Office of the Secretary of Defense, "The Military Power of the People's Republic of China", *Annual Report to Congress*, 2005.

30. Ibid.

31. Ibid.

32. Mure Dickie, Kathrin Hille and Demetri Sevastopulo, "Report Strikes Beijing Nerve at Politically Sensitive Time", *Financial Times*, 21 July 2005.

33. Ibid.

34. Alfred Thayer Mahan, *The Influence of Sea Power Upon History* (originally published in 1890). It represents one of the most influential military essays ever written concerning the use of naval power on the global stage. In short, a nation uses its naval power to protect its vital interests throughout the world.

35. Robert D. Kaplan, "How We Would Fight China", *The Atlantic Monthly*, June 2005, p. 49.

36. Ibid., p. 64.

37. Richard N. Haass, "What to Do About China", *U.S. News and World Report*, 20 June 2005, p. 52.

38. Ibid.

39. Ibid.

40. David Rothkopf, *Running The World: The Inside Story of the National Security Council and the Architects of American Power* (New York: Public Affairs, 2005), pp. 452-453.

41. Bruce Cumings, "The World Shakes China", *The National Interest*, Spring 1996. Cumings uses this famous Napoleon quote in his article, but he also mentions that he is not sure if the quote is 100% accurate. Nevertheless, I have used it in this chapter on China.

42. Gilbert Achcar, "Assessing China", *www.zmag.org*, 25 June 2005.

43. Joe Guy Collier, "Growth in China Gives GM a Boost", *Detroit Free Press*, 6 January 2006.

44. *News Brief*, "GM, Ford See Sales in China Jump", *The Detroit News*, 9 January 2007, p. 2C. This was just a small news article tucked away on page 2 of the newspaper's business section. You got the impression that they didn't want too many of their readers finding it.

45. Ibid.

46. Keith Bradsher, "China Seeking Auto Industry, Piece by Piece", *The New York Times*, 17 February 2006.

47. Interview with Christine Milne, 5 June 2006.

48. Robert Wilson, "China Exports Take Aim at Australia", *The Australian*, 29 March 2006.

49. I found an article by Ameet Sachdev—"Trade, China and Steel"—published in the Chicago Tribune—in August 2005—on the website of Daniel W. Drezner (*www.danieldrezner.com*); The article focused upon Nucor CEO Daniel R. DiMicco and the problems confronting the U.S. steel industry in the global marketplace.

50. Ibid.

51. Oded Shenkar, *The Chinese Century: The Rising Chinese Economy and Its Impact on The Global Economy, The Balance of Power, and Your Job* (Upper Saddle River, New Jersy: Wharton School Publishing, 2006), p. 2.

52. Ibid., p. 3.

53. Ibid.

54. Ibid., p. 136.

55. Ibid.

56. Ibid., p. 138.

57. Editorial, "China, the World's 4th Largest Economy?", *Asia Times*, 14 December 2005.

58. Lester R. Brown, "China is Replacing U.S. as World's Leading Consumer", *New Perspectives Quarterly*, Spring 2005.

59. Ibid.

60. Lester R. Brown, *Plan B 2.0: Rescuing a Planet Under Stress and a Civilization in Trouble* (New York: W.W. Norton & Company, 2006), pp. 10–11.

61. Will Hutton, *The Writing on the Wall: Why We Must Embrace China as a Partner or Face It as an Enemy* (New York: Free Press, 2006), pp. 303-304. I believe it is appropriate to list Suzanne Berger's book since it was the basis of Hutton's argument concerning the myth of the outsourcing of low-wage jobs.

Suzanne Berger, *How We Compete: What Companies Around the World Are Doing to Make It Today's Global Economy* (New York: Currency—a division of Random House, 2005).

62. Ibid., p. 304.

63. Ibid.

64. Journalist Andrea Mitchell did a story for NBC news, and an article on the *MSNBC* website reflected that story under the title, "Report: Kim 'sorry' About North Korea Nuclear Test", 20 October 2006. The story on the MSNBC website was a collective effort with information provided by Reuters, NBC, MSNBC and the Associated Press.

65. I retrieved this attributed quote to Professor Laura Tyson from a 'blog' concerning Professor Noam Chomsky's views on subjects dealing with the American Empire from the 1940s to today. This quote showed up in Chomsky's brief overview concerning the current situation between the U.S. and Asia.

66. Based upon numerous conversations and lectures involving Professor Howard Zinn from 1994 to 2009;

67. Interview with Zhang Yuping, 25 April 2006. Afterwards, Professor Zhang invited me to speak to the students at North China University of Technology in the spring of 2007. I accepted.

68. Ibid.

69. Interview with Professor Zbigniew Brzezinski, 8 January 2007.

70. Ibid.

71. Ibid.

72. Noam Chomsky—Randall Doyle E-Mail Correspondence, 2 January 2006.

73. Ibid.

Chapter Seven

America: The Fragile Empire

It is my belief that America's footprint, or hegemonic capabilities, will diminish, to some degree, for a number of reasons during the 21st century. Part of my analysis is based upon the current economic developments and political trends emerging in the Pacific Rim region, and in America. Another factor in my evaluation is founded upon the *shifting* of power or the *perception* by our regional allies that U.S. *hegemonic* power is slowly devolving in the Asia-Pacific region. Thus, a growing consensus within the U.S. foreign policy establishment believes that the *source* of America's incremental descent, within the western Pacific region, is China. It is a nation that does not hide or obfuscate the fact that it has indeed both a regional and a global agenda for the 21st century.

Yet, there exists institutional confusion, within America and even China, on what the Middle Kingdom actually wants to accomplish in the near and distant future. Tim Shorrock reported in *Asia Times*, in 2002, "the country's (China) government and intellectual elite are deeply split about how to deal with the world's only superpower and (how to) handle relations with the global community."[1] Hence, the *real* question remains unanswered for many Americans and for the Asia-Pacific community at-large, on whether China's rise will be peaceful, or will it represent the beginning of a period of contention and conflict. As a result, it is my belief that the Asia-Pacific region will become the world's primary geo-political focus during the 21st century.

William Overholt, Director of RAND's Center for Asia-Pacific Policy and is also the Asia Policy Research Chair at the Center, writes that the U.S. will certainly play a major role into the foreseeable future within the Asia-Pacific region, but America must also understand that an historic shift and transformation is also occurring as well. Professor Overholt, a former Joint Senior Fellow at Harvard's Kennedy School and Asia Center, writes, ". . . the overwhelming majority of Asian countries view the United States as the "least distrusted" of the big powers. At the same time, U.S. foreign policy must adapt to a number of crucial changes that have occurred. The Soviet threat has disappeared, and Russian influence in East and South Asia is now quite limited. Japan has lost its economic dynamism, its regional economic dominance, and most of its regional leadership role. China has become the region's most dynamic economy and has shifted from a policy of destabilization to a policy of joining the system."[2]

THE CHINA DILEMMA

As mentioned in the introduction, both America and China are wrestling with the question of future responses to each other over known and unknown questions that will arise during the course of the 21st century in the Pacific Rim. Henry Kissinger, former U.S. Secretary of State and Director of the National Security Council during the Presidential administrations of Richard Nixon and Gerald Ford, addressed this future dilemma in his book, *Does America Need a Foreign Policy?*, by emphasizing that America and China need to find common ground and work together to keep Asia-Pacific stable and prosperous. Dr. Kissinger does acknowledge that there are those, in both countries, who see evitable conflict between these two major powers. Yet, he reiterates that this 'conflict' scenario will not produce the type of long-term results, concerning peace and stability in East Asia, sought after by these hawkish proponents.[3]

Kissinger, the former Harvard government professor, has been directly involved with the Chinese government since his secret mission to China, in 1971, on the behalf of President Nixon, to re-establish diplomatic relations between the two nations. Therefore, based upon almost four decades of experience negotiating with various Chinese leaders, Dr. Kissinger sees a different course of action as being the most constructive and productive for future relations between America and China:

> China policy should be liberated from familiar slogans. The issue is not how to label the relationship but what content it can be given. Cooperative relations are not a favor either country bestows on the other. They are in the common interests of both countries. There are enough issues to test the seriousness of both sides . . . A permanent dialogue is needed as the best means to create a more stable world or, at a minimum, to demonstrate to the American people and America's allies why it is not possible.[4]

It should be noted that Dr. Kissinger has significant financial interests in China, and has maintained strong political ties to the Chinese government since his departure from the U.S. State Department in 1977. To be specific, he receives large consultancy fees from China's government and business hierarchies for his analysis concerning global affairs, while representing Kissinger Associates. Nevertheless, it is also true that every president since Nixon has requested his advice on China and its future intentions for the Pacific Rim. In short, Kissinger sees a grudging, but respectful, relationship between these two powers. He sees a tense but constructive geo-political equilibrium developing in East Asia, because he is absolutely convinced that there is simply too much at stake for both countries to be dragged into a devastating conflagration that would bring down the whole region.[5]

However, there are analysts and scholars who say that mankind has no choice on this matter, because history presents an irrefutable counter-argument on this 'balance of power' subject. In short, it is strongly believed by these students of world history that conflict between an established hegemonic power and one that is rising to hegemonic status, especially in the same region, will occur with a large degree of certainty. Why? Their argument is based upon the historical fact that aspiring hegemonic powers almost always collide due to having the same agenda - to dominate world affairs. And, as in politics and sports, you can only have one champion, or winner, after the competition is over. History has shown that there is an unwritten law concerning human affairs—there is a never-ending process of one individual, or nation, seeking to stand above the rest. There is a certain stability and understanding amongst competitors—of all stripes—that respects this cosmic truth concerning universal competition.

In the first decade of the 21st century, many American foreign policy analysts, concerning the Pacific Rim, perceive China as the new enemy to confront (and contain) because the Chinese have not denied their desire to become a hegemonic force in East Asia. These same 'experts' will often say that America represents the *'indispensable nation'* throughout the region, and the world, in terms of establishing and maintaining peace and stability. In truth, though, these true believers of America's global mission actually interpret the U.S. being much more than a *'balancing force'* or an exemplary *'shining city on the hill'* for East Asians to respect or emulate. They, in fact, really desire America to remain *the* unquestioned power in the region, and the world.

In short, these individuals interpret the rise of China as a *very* negative development. Many Asian analysts and regional observers of power-politics in East Asia are convinced that the potential for conflict between the U.S. and China is heightened because history has repeatedly shown that an emerging hegemonic power—regionally or globally—is often perceived immediately as a direct threat to the *existing* force structure developed by the recognized hegemonic power.

Derek McDougall, associate professor in politics at the University of Melbourne, writes about the geopolitical complexities and questions facing the U.S. and the West with the re-emergence of China, and its future role concerning regional and global affairs in the 21st century. McDougall, author of *Asia Pacific in World Politics*, observes, "Part of the answer to this question depends on what happens with China. "Rising China" is a key feature of Asia Pacific international politics in the post-9/11 era. At one level this is simply recognition of the economic growth occurring in China and the impact this is having on the political and economic landscape of the region. The success of its strategy of economic modernization means that China will carry greater political clout within the region. However, there are various possibilities as to how China will use this weight. A confrontationist course on some issues could lead to clashes with other powers. At the very least China will insist on having a major influence on the issues that are its most direct concern."[6]

John Mearsheimer, the R. Wendell Harrison Distinguished Service Professor of Political Science at the University of Chicago, states quite confidently in his book, *The Tragedy of Great Power Politics*, that history has shown that two competitive hegemonic powers, regionally or globally, will experience conflict because that is the nature of global powers exercising their economic and military influence upon the world stage.[7]

The counter-argument is that we (America) can not jump to immediate conclusions, even if history indicates that hegemonic powers have a strong tendency to collide due to their regional, or global expansionist (economic or military, or both) agendas. However, students of history also know that there are few absolutes in human history, except for the unpredictability of human endeavors. Thus, critics of Mearsheimer's thesis, concerning the almost certainty of 'great power' conflict, remain unconvinced that the U.S. and China are cosmically destined to go to war.

Zbigniew Brzezinski, the former national security advisor to President Jimmy Carter, and currently a Counselor at the Center for Strategic and International Studies, believes that China's future aggression against America is exaggerated and overdone by great-power advocates. Brzezinski, who is also a professor of foreign policy at Johns Hopkins University, strongly believes that China's major priority is to develop its economy. Their military buildup does not alarm him because he does not see any unusual trends emerging that would indicate that China is becoming a significant threat to U.S. interests, regionally or globally, in the relatively near future. And, any analysis concerning long-term threats is purely speculative.[8]

Brzezinski, though relatively optimistic about future U.S. relations with China, remains ever the voice of cautious in his analysis of the situation, he writes, "First of all, the United States' concerns about some aspects of the Chinese rivalry, for example, in trade, in business, or potentially in the military area, are quite legitimate. (Yet), there is a bipartisan desire to assimilate China into the international system...Secondly, part of my reason for optimism is my sense that the Chinese leadership is not guided by some Manichaean ideology in which their future depends on the imposition of their value system on the world like, for example, Stalinist Russia or Hitler's Germany."[9]

Brent Scowcroft, the former national security adviser to Presidents George H.W. Bush and Gerald Ford, also believes that U.S.-China relations—for now—are positive and going in the right direction. In 2009, his outlook is primarily based upon recent and ancient Chinese history, Scowcroft writes, "I, too, am optimistic. From the U.S. side, the process started back in the early 70s when we reached out to China at the heart of the Cold War—and we reached an understanding with China that we would join together to oppose Soviet hegemony. That put a different coloration, in the eyes of the American people, on China and what is was about . . . But I think one of the least likely directions for any instability is outward aggression. Chinese history indicates that the Han Chinese have not been unusually aggressive. When China has been aggressive, it's usually after they've been conquered from the outside and are run by "outsiders."[10]

Yet, the basis of this intense argument of whether China is a short-term or long-term threat might be moot, due to a looming and potential financial crisis emerging in America. Today, a total meltdown (i.e. circa 1929) is highly possible and it appears that the fiscal integrity of the national budget is now in jeopardy. Most point to shockingly bad financial management and corruption on Wall Street, and an indifferent U.S. Congress as the main culprits. The national debt is now over 10 trillion dollars and it continues to grow at an alarming rate. The country's global trade deficit also spirals upward, though the contacting economy and higher unemployment will probably reduce demand for foreign goods for the next couple of years. To be precise, President Bush's lassiez-faire economic policies have put America's financial house in a dangerous and precarious situation. This frightening prospect of possessing massive debt—domestically and internationally—represents a direct threat to America's future capacity to project—economic and military—power throughout the world.

Paul Krugman, the recipient of the 2008 Nobel Prize for economics, believes the U.S. is in great financial danger and that America must relearn some basic and fundamental economic lessons concerning its national economy. Krugman, who is a influential columnist for *The New York Times*, writes, "Then things got interesting and dangerous again. Growing international capital flows set the stage for devastating currency crises in the 1990s and for a globalized financial crisis in 2008...What we're going to have to do, clearly, is relearn the lessons our grandfathers were taught by the Great Depression. I won't try to lay out the details of a new regulatory regime, but the basic principle should be clear: anything that has to be rescued during a financial crisis, because it plays an essential role in the financial mechanism, should be regulated when there *isn't* a crisis so that it doesn't take excessive risks."[11]

Krugman, a professor of economics and international affairs at Princeton University, remains somewhat hopeful and he believes the financial crisis that is currently enveloping the U.S. and global economies and markets can be rectified if individuals are only willing to be creative and purposeful in their endeavors. He states in his bestselling book, *The Return of Depression Economics and the Crisis of 2008*, "We will not achieve the understanding we need, however, unless we are willing to think clearly about our problems and to follow those thoughts wherever they lead. Some people say that our economic problems are structural, with no quick cure available; but I believe that the only important structural obstacles to world prosperity are the obsolete doctrines that clutter the minds of men."

Essentially, America's capacity to project global power—even protecting the nation's vital interests—could be compromised if the recent U.S. financial collapse is not reversed in the near future. Presently, however, there is irrefutable evidence that America's global financial stature is slowly deteriorating. As expected, the present-day financial tsunami is slowly but steadily crippling U.S. capacity to influence or shape global events. Investigative financial reporter for the International Press Service, Emad Mekay, wrote that the Geneva-based World Economic Forum (WEF) issued its 2006–2007 Global Competitiveness Index (GCI). The U.S. has dropped from the number one ranking in the world, to now being ranked 6th.[12] Mekay, who has written major exposes on the World Bank, the Asian Development Bank and on the International Monetary Fund, states that America's sudden decline is due, according to this highly respected international economic institution, to its high spending on the 'war on terrorism', homeland security and the lowering of taxes. All of these factors represent a serious potential for triggering a fiscal crisis in the U.S.[13]

Paul Kennedy, a prominent history professor at Yale University, provided in his epic work, in 1987, *The Rise and Fall of the Great Powers*, a vivid description on how the 'great powers' of the past fell apart, and quickly, primarily due to financial reasons and a military 'over-stretched' by global obligations. Quite often the great powers of the past fought one too many wars that eventually compromised the financial capabilities of these hegemonic states. Once a great power's financial/industrial base is fundamentally compromised, their sphere of influence contracts, regionally and internationally.[14]

Many readers, in the late-1980s, interpreted Kennedy's work as a prophetic warning to America's government and society. Twenty years later, the U.S. is facing a massive and growing national debt, alarming domestic budget deficits, and exploding international trade imbalances, especially with China. When the economic good times returned in the mid-1990s with the dot.com explosion, many critics, such as foreign policy scholars Joseph Nye and Niall Ferguson, chastised Kennedy for his negative predictions concerning America's future.[15]

However, in 2009, Professor Kennedy's economic/power thesis, published in 1987, toward the end of the Reagan Administration (1981–1989), is making an unexpected comeback in American thinking. Kennedy's critics are now lying low. Why? Well, it doesn't take a MIT economist to tell Americans that the U.S. financial situation is increasingly shaky. The value of the U.S. dollar is weakening throughout the world. America's national debt and the nation's trade deficits are rising to frightening levels. And, the U.S. continues to pay for two expensive and ill-fated wars in Afghanistan and Iraq. Oil prices, from 2006 to the fall of 2008, had spiked to record highs, and a gallon of gas cost over $5.00 in some parts of America.

However, in early 2009, gas prices have plummeted due to the global recession, nevertheless, American consumers continue to struggle with rising cost-of-living expenses at a time when most U.S. workers are currently experiencing a decline in their purchasing power. Also, rising unemployment and diminishing employment prospects are becoming commonplace in the US. Thus, fear and vulnerability lay just beneath the surface for millions of American workers.

According to Forrester Research, in 2003, U.S. companies were expected to transfer 3.3 million jobs in the next 12 years (2003–2015) overseas.[16] These job loss estimates, from six years ago, have tragically become an ugly reality for millions of American workers. Martin Crutsinger, Associated Press economic reporter, wrote, in April 2007, that 3.2 million factory jobs *have* disappeared; essentially *1* in *6* factory jobs in the America is now gone. And, Crutsinger writes that most of the unemployed workers believe that their jobs will never return to their local communities.[17]

Since 2000, manufacturing industries such as auto, furniture, textiles and household goods, produced in states such as Michigan, Ohio, Indiana, Illinois and Wisconsin, have been devastated by globalization and foreign competition. My adopted home-state, Michigan, has suffered the most from the recent economic earthquake that has struck the American heartland. In October 2008, Frank Bentayou, a reporter for *The Plain Dealer* (Cleveland), wrote an article that provided shocking statistics concerning the recent economic decline in Michigan and Ohio. However, Michigan, by far, has been hit the hardest by the recent "depression-level" economic events. Since 2000, the Wolverine State has lost 496,900 jobs—a 10.5% reduction of its entire work force. The Buckeye State was the second hardest hit with 213,300 jobs being lost—a 3.8% decline in its workforce.[18] It is not overblown hyperbole to say that America's heartland, indeed, is currently experiencing from an acute economic version of cardiac arrest on a scale not seen since the days of The Great Depression in the 1930s.

Most of these solid-paying 'blue collar' jobs are now being relocated to Asia. The de-industrialization of the post-WWII American heartland is accelerating and, thus, as a result, the workers themselves are experiencing a dramatic and fundamental re-transformation of their existence and identification as workers throughout the region. For many, this historic epoch has hit them like a tsunami and the wreckage from this financial storm will be devastating for the millions who are watching their way of life slowly vanish before their eyes.

Though, Richard Longworth writes in his insightful and excellent book, *Caught In The Middle*, that many of the small cities and towns in the Midwest chose to disregard or ignore the economic storm clouds that were increasingly appearing on the horizon since the 1970s. According to Longworth, a senior fellow at The Chicago Council on Global Affairs, after several decades of U.S. industrial dominance, since the end of World War II, globalization and foreign competition were steadily eroding the industrial base within the American heartland; this erosion during the last eight years has accelerated significantly. The American heartland is now confronting an uncertain future.[19]

However, Longworth, in January 2008, published an article in the *Chicago Tribune*, states the Midwest will once again play an important role in America's future economic prosperity—like it always has in the nation's history. But, for this economic reinvention to occur, the region's business and political leaders must develop a 'common strategy'.[20] Longworth, a former award-winning foreign correspondent and senior writer for the *Chicago Tribune*, remains a firm believer in the region's future and its resiliency in the face of difficult economic times,

"The Midwest is the traditional spear-point of the American economy. It was the frontier when the first pioneers moved west. Its mills and factories powered America's Industrial Revolution. Here, commerce boomed and labor wars first raged. The Great Depression began on Midwestern farms; when the nation recovered, the Midwest recovered first. Two decades later, the Midwest felt the first ravages of the Rust Belt and the first sting of Japanese competition. What happens to America happens first to the Midwest."[21]

Hopefully, whatever does happen in the Midwest will occur in Michigan—soon! The auto industry continues to represent the heart of the Michigan economy—even in 2009. According to Associated Press writer Kathy Barks Hoffman, in May 2008, the auto industry will continue to slide during 2009. Though, some analysts, such as Dana Johnson, an economist at Comerica Bank, believes there will be better days for the industry in 2010. However, during the meantime, Hoffman writes that the state of Michigan will continue to divest itself from being too dependent on the auto industry and will seek to diversify and expand its development base and business formations.[22]

Hoffman also wrote that Michigan's auto assembly and parts manufacturing, in 2000, accounted for about 7% of Michigan payroll jobs—now it's 4%. Though, Michigan depends upon the auto industry more than any other state, since 2000, the state's auto industry has seen a loss of over 159,000 jobs.[23] In another article on Michigan's auto industry, published by the *Kalamazoo Gazette*, in October 2007, it stated that Michigan had lost 34% of its auto jobs since 2002.[24]

Of course, in 2009, the percentage of auto jobs lost permanently in Michigan has grown significantly since 2007. Perhaps, Richard Longworth may very well be right about the future prospects of an economic resurgence occurring throughout the Midwest, I just hope it happens in Michigan *real* soon. In January 2009, it was announced that Toyota became the world's biggest carmaker by selling more vehicles (8.97 million) than General Motors (8.35 million) during 2008. The dethroning of GM's 77-year reign as the world's largest producer of automobiles did not come as a surprise to industry insiders. However, many see it as representing an historic shift and as a sign of things to come for the U.S. auto industry. And, GM is already predicting that its sales in the U.S. market will decline again in 2009.[25] No American industry has experienced a more profound epiphany during the past few years than the U.S. auto industry. Nevertheless, there remains a general feeling that things can be turned around in the U.S. auto industry, but I believe the window of opportunity is closing faster than many realize.

It is my belief that the American car industry will suffer the same fate as that of the nation's steel industry in the 1970s & 1980s. The majority of U.S. jobs (over 70%) in the steel industry were lost forever. Can the American auto industry escape the same fate? Maybe, but doubtful. Globalization and international competition are cold-blooded and relentless, and the Big Three in Detroit are finding out just how brutal the global marketplace can be when you are trying to survive with products that nobody wants to purchase.

In the fall of 2008, the Democratic Party nominee, Barack Obama, the junior senator from Illinois, campaigned heavily in the industrial Midwest, and swept the region on the election night. Some Midwestern states, such as Ohio and Indiana, which have voted Republican in recent presidential elections, now casted their votes for the Democratic candidate. In fact, Indiana which had not voted for a Democratic presidential nominee since 1964, voted for the Democratic nominee due to his economic message emphasizing hope and the creation of new jobs—especially green jobs. The Democratic Party swept the entire 'Rust Belt' for the first time in many years. Obama's speeches concerning job creation, not political ideology, was the primary reason for the Democratic Party's victory throughout the industrial Midwest on election night. However, Obama's victory may not produce the kind of economic results as some desire. If President Obama keeps his campaign promises, the new economy will emphasize the creation of 'green jobs' and 'smart jobs' and not those representing fossil-fueled smokestack industries of a bygone era. In 1965, manufacturing represented 53% of the U.S. economy, but, in 2004, it accounted for only 9%.[26] Enough said.

As mentioned earlier in this chapter, the post-WWII Baby Boomers are on the verge of retirement en masse. Thus, they represent a terrifying financial tsunami in terms of potential costs for the U.S. government. The astronomical budgetary numbers associated with this generational eventuality are sobering and very threatening. Of course, very few American politicians have the courage to tell their constituents the truth about the oncoming fiscal train wreck that awaits them as the moment of truth draws closer. Harvard University historian, Niall Ferguson, author of *Colossus: The Price of America's Empire*, believes the U.S. is heading for a 'day of reckoning' in terms of the financial costs related to the post-WWII retirees. When the Baby Boomers deluge begins in a few years, some economists believe that income taxes, or payroll taxes, will have to be increased 69% and 95%, respectively, to meet the government's obligations.[27]

Therefore, no matter how you spin these economic issues, the employment and retirement challenges, and obligations, confronting America and its governmental institutions are going to be incredibly daunting as the 21st century matures.

Finally, there are those observers who believe that America is in the process of 'containing' China. These individuals do not believe America wants war immediately, but they also do not think that the U.S. will *share* its hegemonic status with the Middle Kingdom. Hence, they believe that America has chosen a *third* path in dealing with China. In short, these analysts, scholars and 'experts' (consumers beware) see the U.S. utilizing various means to '*manage*' China's development, subtly and strategically.

Henceforth, America is actively creating a new web of acknowledgements, alliances, agreements, and understandings with countries throughout the Pacific Rim and Central Asia. This process can be accurately described as 'soft containment' with a hard objective—keep China's influence minimized if possible. *I* am one of those who believe this is the *real* policy toward China today.

In the next section, I will briefly examine the new developments in the Asia-Pacific Rim region. Though, collectively, these new developments are not totally understood by the American public, due to the paltry amount of foreign news presented on the major television networks in the U.S. Yet, it is becoming increasingly apparent to many observers, in America and Asia, that U.S. diplomatic and military activities in this strategic arena of the world, represents nothing more than the concentrated exercise of balance-of-power strategies directed toward a rising regional power; in this specific case, China.

NEW GEOPOLITICAL LANDSCAPE

The United States instituted a Cold War strategy called *containment* in the late-1940s against the Soviet Union. One of my foreign policy heroes, George F. Kennan, created a detailed summation of post-WWII Soviet intentions in his famous 8,000 word 'Long Telegram' sent to the U.S. State Department in 1946. In short, the Soviet Union was seen as a challenger to the U.S. hege-monic position after World War II. The U.S. government needed a coherent and comprehensive plan to deal with future Soviet aggressions in the world, but especially for Western Europe.

Kennan became a foreign policy star after the implementation of his post-WWII stratagem, but he later attempted to distance himself from his geopolitical masterpiece when it was invoked and re-directed toward every geopolitical situation throughout the world, especially in Asia (Korea and Vietnam). Despite, what Kennan considered its misapplication, this vision-ary blueprint to prevent Russian dominance in Western Europe was the *philosophical* backbone of U.S. deterrence throughout the world until the collapse of the Soviet Union in December 1991. Ironically, unlike most of his contemporaries, Kennan outlived the Cold War itself. The Soviet Union dissolved in late-1991, and George F. Kennan (Mr. X) passed away at the age of 101 in 2004.

Like Professor Kennedy's '*Rise and Fall*' thesis, it appears that Kennan's sixty-year old '*containment*' blueprint is making a quasi-comeback and being re-implemented in the 21st century, but this time it's directed toward East, Central, South and Southeast Asia—with China in mind. If we go clock-wise from the top of Northeast Asia to the Central Asian republics, formerly of the Soviet Union, you will find a common thread connecting this vastly diverse and disparate group of countries—all have negotiated stronger relations or ties to the U.S. due to China's stunning rise in Asia.

Yet, in 2009, does America possess the global leadership—economically and militarily—to succeed in achieving another grand strategy directed toward a potential adversary (China) as it did after WWII with the Soviet Union? The voices of doubt and skepticism are growing louder within the U.S. foreign policy establishment. A growing consensus believes that America can indeed lead but it is absolutely necessary that we receive assistance from our friends and allies. Our geopolitical footprint is simply not as large as it used to be. I am a member of this geopolitical camp. But, the real question is whether the American foreign policy establishment, in its many forms, is ready to accept the increasingly noticeable limits with concern to our *actual* capabilities in achieving the goals and objectives of any future foreign endeavor and initiative taken upon by the U.S. government?

According to Parag Khanna, Director of the Global Governance Initiative in the American Strategy Program of the New America Foundation, in 2009, this recent geopolitical maneuverings in Asia may be the last breath of U.S. global hegemony. The world is simply becoming too complex and daunting for America to dominate or coerce into accepting its global agenda. The costly and failing wars in Iraq and Afghanistan are clear examples of the inability of the U.S. to force its political ideas and global agenda upon their allies, enemies, or even weaker nations within the global community. Khanna writes, "With neither its hard power nor its soft power functioning effectively, the United States is learning that history happens to everyone—even Americans. Much as rubber bands snap far more quickly than they stretch, empires collapse not long after they reach their fullest extent. America would like to remain safely distant from—but able to dictate to—the European and Asian powers on either end of the Eurasian "world island," much as it did nearly a century ago at the Paris Peace Conference (in 1919) . . . But detached geography is an advantage only if allies will share the burdens."

Clearly, Professors Kennan, Kennedy and Khanna have all put forward provocative ideas and analyses concerning global affairs at various stages of the post-WWII world. At this time, I will provide my own thoughts concerning present-day Asia-Pacific. These observations are based upon living and working within the region for approximately ten years of my life. Thus, I will now provide brief overviews of a few of the countries within the Asia-Pacific region that I believe will play significant roles in the first decades of the 21st century:

Russia: Former Russian President Vladimir Putin continues to run Russian politics and its foreign affairs, even though he left office in 2007. The new

Russian president Alexander Medvevdev appears to be extremely limited in his authority to make decisions concerning Russia's future. In the summer of 2008, Russia invaded the nation of Georgia over the sovereignty and future status of a province (South Ossetia) within Georgia. The province sought to separate from Georgia. If it is finally successful in this endeavor, the geopolitical landscape of Europe could become quite unsettled in the upcoming years. Though, the circumstances of the war remain controversial, the reassertion of Russian power startled NATO and the European Union, particularly those nations in Eastern Europe.

Yet, Russia remains on relatively good terms with the U.S. However, Putin and Medvevdev will encounter a new U.S. president, Barack Obama, after 20 January 2009. There is no indication, so far, what the new president's policy toward Russia will be. However, it is a safe bet that President Obama will not be peering into Putin's soul, like his predecessor, to figure out Russia's next move(s) within the Eurasian region.

Despite the shortcomings associated with Russia, the U.S. needs its support in combating Islamic fundamentalism terrorism in the Middle East region. Also, Russian assistance is required in preventing Iran and North Korea from becoming permanent nuclear powers. Of course, the Russians are not pleased with the U.S. presence in Central Asia. Nevertheless, it has provided diplomatic support on various American proposals and resolutions concerning Iran, Afghanistan and Pakistan. All of which are crucial factors within the U.S. 'grand strategy' for the Eurasian region.

One of the better books written about the deteriorating political and social conditions within Russia is titled, *Kremlin Rising*, by Peter Baker and Susan Glasser.[28] They present a rather grim analysis of modern-day Russia, of which, few Americans comprehend or understand. As of this writing, January 2009, global oil prices have collapsed below $40 per barrel, down from the peak of $147 in mid-2008. Obviously, the global recession (perhaps, a depression in the near future) has reduced the global demand for oil significantly.

Yet, it is also acknowledged by global energy experts and observers that the current low price for a barrel of oil will not become a permanent condition. China, India and the East Asian hemisphere—overall—continues to grow and their thirst for oil and gas remains a universal constant. As a result, Russia's recent petro-dollar funded military resurgence and regional muscle-flexing may be just the beginning of a new geopolitical reality. The U.S. will not be confronted by another Cold War, but the weak and humiliated Russia of the 1990s has recovered. The hundreds of billions of petro-dollars it receives today, and into the future for its mammoth gas and oil holdings, will fuel-inject its reappearance as a major power involving global affairs during the 21st century.

Japan: This nation continues to be burdened by domestic and international indecision. It is a nation that desires 'normalcy' which includes having a stronger voice in its own foreign policy. Yet, this proud and successful nation refuses to comprehend, recognize and properly apologize for its atrocious actions and behavior during the pre-WWII (1930s) period and WWII itself. This period in Japanese history continues to haunt the nation's psyche and it limits its geopolitical influence in Asia-Pacific and the world.

Yet, Japan remains the second most productive economy in the world, and its military prowess, though self-contained due to a U.S.-created constitution (Article 9) and by the presence of U.S. military bases throughout the country, is greatly respected throughout Asia-Pacific. But, in truth, Japan's potential effectiveness and influence within Asia-Pacific is significantly diminished by the Japanese themselves. In 2009, the vast majority of Japanese since maintain strong reservations concerning the possibility of their country enlarging its military and role in global affairs.

Another problem is the recent fragility of its elected government. Leadership is simply non-existent in Japanese politics. Japan appears to be a country badly divided over its future direction. I believe the main reason for the atrophic nature of Japanese politics is the fact that the Liberal Democratic Party (LDP) has almost controlled the House of Representatives, within the Japanese Diet, continually since the mid-1950s.

Since the end of Junichiro Kazumi's reign as prime minister, in 2005, Japan has had (3) different prime ministers in the last four years. Shinzo Abe and Yasuda Fukuda only lasted approximately one year in office. In September 2008, Taro Aso, chosen by the LDP caucus to be its new prime minister, has already run into difficulties and his future appears limited—just like his previous two predecessors. Obviously, the greatest problem confronting the Japanese government is that it cannot sustain any kind of reform program or create any long-term planning. The elected governments simply collapse too quickly from infighting before any kind of real work is accomplished.

In 2007, two excellent books were published by prominent Japanese scholars concerning the present and future domestic and international challenges confronting Japan in the 21st century. Richard Samuels, Director of the Center for International Studies at MIT, wrote *Securing Japan*, and Kenneth Pyle, the Henry M. Jackson Professor of History and Asian Studies at the University of Washington, wrote *Japan Rising*; both books are excellent works describing modern Japan and its excruciating dilemma in its attempt to becoming a "normal nation."

I lived in Japan for over three years. I witnessed the bizarre nature of Japanese politics. The 'Land of the Rising Sun' remains an enigma even for those, like myself, who love and have studied this nation's history for years. Thus, I don't see any major breakthroughs in terms of Japan fundamentally changing its domestic or international behavior. This is good and bad.

South Korea: U.S. relations with South Korea remain the most complicated and difficult at the beginning of the 21st century. Like Japan, South Korea also seeks greater autonomy for itself. And, in recent years, particularly on the issue of North Korea, a deep chasm has emerged between these two longtime allies.

In 2009, President Lee Myung-bak has appeared to be more supportive of the U.S. objectives for northeast Asia than his previous predecessors, Kim Dae-jung and Roh Moo-hyun, respectively. Both of his predecessors sought warmer relations with North Korea. In fact, in 2000, Kim Dae-jung won the Noble Peace Prize for his bold and historic attempt to introduce his visionary 'Sunshine Policies' by traveling to Pyongyang, North Korea and meeting with Kim Jong-il. It was the first time the two leaders of Korea met since the country was partitioned. The U.S. was very chilly in its reaction to this groundbreaking diplomacy.

However, despite periodic tensions within their relationship, the U.S. has promised to maintain at least 25,000 troops, or more, in South Korea. And, the existing troops located in Seoul will be soon relocated down the peninsula about 40 miles south of Seoul - the nation's capital. This fact clearly indicates that the South Korean government desires a U.S. military presence in northeast Asia until the North Korean situation is finally resolved.

I also believe the South Koreans want us to stick around because of the emergence of China. Though, China has become South Korea's number one trading partner, the Koreans do not want to be engulfed by the Middle Kingdom's hegemonic shadow. South Korea is not interested in becoming a quasi-tributary state like in the days of dynastic China. Therefore, a U.S. military presence, though intensely disliked by the political life in South Korea, will remain upon the Korean peninsula into the foreseeable future. The American presence essentially allows South Korea some breathing room in a region that is already tense and getting tighter geographically due to three primary reasons: the rise of China, growing nationalism within Japan and the reemergence of Russia due to its gas and oil riches.

The best of the recent books describing the changing domestic political environment and the geopolitical trends affecting the Korean peninsula are entitled, *The Two Koreas*, and *The Koreans*, authored by Don Oberdorfer and Michael Breen, respectively. Though, the best historian on modern Korea, in my opinion, is Professor Bruce Cumings at the University of Chicago.

Vietnam: In May 2008, I visited Vietnam for the first time. I did not know what to expect, but I was pleasantly surprised throughout my entire stay. I visited Hanoi, Ho Chi Minh City and a few places in the vicinity of these two cities. What I discovered was a vibrant society that has embraced capitalism with great energy and purpose. I also found that Vietnamese society was more open and raucous than China. I mention this because the Vietnamese are modeling their economic development based upon the Chinese model—except with Vietnamese characteristics.

The people were very kind and always smiling. There appeared to be no residue of bitterness associated with the Vietnam War. That chapter of their history had been closed. I did, however, witness a middle-aged woman being arrested by the police for selling pineapple within the Hanoi business district which is forbidden. Nevertheless, the 'mom n' pop' businesses were flourishing.

Also, when I traveled to beautiful Ha Long Bay, outside of Hanoi, I saw a couple of industrial parks that had numerous foreign companies within them. Put simply, Vietnam is the new economic Asian tiger. Yet, it feels a bit uncomfortable with China's emerging prowess on its northern border. Thus, it is not surprising that Vietnam has made various gestures of friendship and cooperation with the U.S.

In fact, a few years ago, Vietnam floated the idea of having America return to Cam Rahn Bay. The U.S. government politely but firmly stated it had no such desire—for now. However, Asia is transforming so quickly that perhaps a U.S. presence in Vietnam, again, might not seem such a bad idea if relations with China sour in the near future. Therefore, expect more entreaties from the Vietnamese for U.S. business investment and, perhaps, the re-establishment of the American military in-country—creating a South Korea-like presence.

I think the U.S. might have given greater consideration to Vietnam's original offer but the Vietnam War is still a little too close to the American psyche. And, of course, China would definitely be displeased to find U.S. military forces, once again, near its southern border. Also, cries of 'containment', and maybe even 'imperialism', would echo within the halls of power in Beijing. To be honest, Chinese complaints would have some legitimacy and veracity. Nevertheless, as China grows in stature in Southeast Asia, expect other small nations in the region to quietly request closer ties to America.

India: In 2006, President George W. Bush negotiated a deal with India to supply them with advanced nuclear technologies. This deal remains in limbo. Critics, in the U.S. and in Europe, are unhappy that India has never signed the Non-Proliferation Treaty (NPT); concerning the eventual removal of all nuclear weapons in the world. Most analysts perceive President Bush's agreement with India as representing a classic case of diplomatic hypocrisy. In short, America is rewarding India for its past defiance. Yet, at the same time, the U.S. is punishing North Korea for ignoring the very same international standards. In essence, Bush had fundamentally undermined America's own moral arguments with concern to the proliferation of nuclear weapons.

However, I believe the *real* agenda for the U.S. was to seek India's assistance toward creating a new 'triangular diplomacy' in Asia, as a counterbalance to China's growing power within the region. Historically, this is not the first time this geopolitical strategem has been utilized by the U.S. in East Asia. In 1972, during the Cold War, the United States (read: President Richard Nixon and National Security Adviser Henry Kissinger) visited and negotiated with Communist China (read: Chairman Mao Zedong and Premier Chou Enlai), to create 'triangular diplomacy' as a counter-weight against potential expansionism by the then Soviet Union, because the U.S. was on the verge of losing the Vietnam War.

Put succinctly, President Bush is simply reconstructing 'triangular diplomacy', thirty-five years later, by recruiting India to assist the U.S. in counterbalancing the emergence of a powerful China in East Asia. Why? Well, it appears that the U.S. is, once again, on the verge of losing another ill-advised military adventure—Iraq. In fact, this time we are on the verge of experiencing (2) major setbacks in Iraq and Afghanistan, respectively.

Therefore, as expected, U.S. foreign policy *realists* (read: Henry Kissinger) believe that a U.S. defeat in Iraq and Afghanistan will certainly result in a loss of American prestige and stature around the world. Henceforth, this potential outcome may embolden the terrorists, but more importantly, the Chinese may seek to fill the global power vacuum created by another U.S. foreign policy blunder.

Central Asia: The U.S. is in the process of developing stronger relations with these former Soviet states: Kyrgyzstan, Tajikistan and Turkmenistan and Uzbekistan.

Strategically, Central Asia lies at the heart of the historic 'grand chessboard'. Geographically, it is situated between the Middle East and China. Today, several of these newly established states, created after the Cold War, have U.S. military facilities situated inside their borders. Their presence is understood to assist these nations in a volatile region against a resurgent Russia, or to contain a suddenly powerful and expansionist China. And, let's not fool ourselves with false altruism, the U.S. also want to maintain its interests and oversight of the oil and gas that exists in the Caspian Sea region. In a world with diminishing access to fossil fuels, the Caspian Sea will become one of the vital battlegrounds in the global struggle for energy.

Therefore, the control of the Eurasian landmass is seen by some regional analysts, based upon prior historical interpretation, as being absolutely vital to a nation's ability to exert global influence and power and have access to the area's energy riches. It is essentially Halford Mackinder's theory of Eurasia being "the geographical pivot of history."[29] In 1904, Mackinder expounded upon his theory to an audience at the Royal Geographical Society in London, England. This theory lost favor during WWII, due to Adolf Hitler's adoption of it, but it is making a major comeback in the first decade of the 21st century. It appears that most of the world's remaining oil and gas deposits are located within the Eurasian region. Stay tuned.

SOFT CONTAINMENT: WILL IT WORK AGAINST CHINA?

After reading numerous articles and books, listening to many lectures on various perspectives concerning China and its future, and having visited China for the last three years (2007–2009), I fundamentally believe that the U.S. is quietly and stealthily constructing a 'soft containment' of China during the first decade of the 21st century. If one does an honest appraisal of U.S. interests in Asia, it is quite apparent that China's emergence as a major power has not only caught the attention of the U.S. government, but has inspired a series of American political and military activities to subtly encircle the Middle Kingdom in an attempt to limit its future influence in East Asia. *Containment*, as a geopolitical philosophy, has been a very effective stratagem throughout American history.

Upon historical hindsight, it can be stated, to a degree of truth, that containment represents a fundamental strategic philosophy that has been implemented since the early 19th century. George F. Kennan, though a renowned U.S. foreign policy analyst in the latter-half of the 20th century, was also a great admirer of John Quincy Adams' diplomatic accomplishments and philosophy in the early 19th century. In point of fact, it can be strongly argued that it was Adams who created the first version of 'containment' with the penning of the Monroe Doctrine in 1823. And, perhaps, elements of Adams's work can be seen in parts of the philosophical foundation, and strategic vision, that Kennan later created in the mid-20th century toward curbing the global influence of the Soviet Union after World War II.

Adams, then Secretary of State under President James Monroe, defined the U.S. position in the Western Hemisphere, in the early 1820s, concerning those European nations seeking an opportunity to re-colonize several Latin American states after Spain's demise. In fact, what Secretary Adams, whom many historians consider America's greatest Secretary of State, was actually doing was 'containing' European territorial ambitions within the Western Hemisphere. Upon hindsight, the U.S. was successful in its bold diplomatic efforts to keep Europe out of the region, due to a strong British naval presence in the Atlantic and Caribbean. However, I believe, it can also be effectively argued that the Monroe Doctrine was the first usage of this strategic '*containment*' philosophy—designed to confront great-power *expansionism* without the immediate threat of war.

It is also believed by a growing list of prominent U.S. scholars that a new doctrine of anti-expansionism is now being reapplied toward China in the opening decade of the 21st century. Its successful implementation against European powers in the 19th century, with concern to the Western Hemisphere, and the Soviet Union during the latter-half of the 20th century in Western Europe, is clear evidence of its potential effectiveness. Yet, its successful implementation against China, at the beginning of the 21st century, remains questionable at best.

Historically, China has not looked fondly upon intrusive and threatening outsiders. In fact, China has looked upon the outside world with a considerable amount of skepticism and scorn. First, the Chinese are very proud of their ancient culture and numerous historical achievements in the fields of education, philosophy, literature and science. Secondly, the dark chapter of Chinese history represented by Europe's (including Japan and America as well) successful attempts to implement exploitive colonialism within China, beginning in the 1830s until WWII, has left the Chinese hypersensitive to any pressure or threats from external sources. Therefore, it would not surprise this author to see China take calculated steps in limiting U.S. efforts toward achieving this new containment objective in East Asia. The American encirclement of the Middle Kingdom could very well bring out the worst in the Chinese Dragon.

Michael T. Klare, Director of Peace and World Security Studies at Hampshire College, sees a dangerous future for America and its recent efforts to contain China since 2001. Professor Klare, author of *Blood and Oil: The Dangers and Consequences of America's Growing Dependency on Imported Petroleum*, believes that the events of 9/11 only delayed further planning by the first Bush administration (2001–2005) to continue its long-term efforts toward neutralizing China's influence in East Asia. However, Klare writes that the second Bush administration is once again focusing its attention upon China. He writes, "By the time the second Bush administration came into office, however, the pool of potential rivals had been narrowed in elite thinking to just one: the People's Republic of China. Only China, it was claimed, possessed the economic and military capacity to challenge the United States as an aspiring superpower; and so perpetuating U.S. global predominance meant containing Chinese power."[30]

Professor Klare declares the efforts to bring democracy to the Middle East may be the primary focus of current concerns within the White House, but "they do not govern key decisions regarding the allocation of long-term military resources. The truly commanding objective—the underlying basis for budgets and troop developments—is the containment of China . . . its paramount focus on China is risking a new Asian arms race with potentially catastrophic consequences."[31]

In contrast, it is interesting to analyze China's response to America's activities toward containing them. According to Klare, China is reaching out and providing extraordinary economic benefits to America's key allies: Australia, Japan, South Korea, and India. This savvy and far-sighted strategy has loosened up, to some degree, the rigidity of their support for U.S. objectives in Asia-Pacific. Ironically, it is also China's neighbors, several of whom support U.S. interests, who are inadvertently helping the Chinese to grow—economically and militarily.

In 2006, China's President Hu Jintao, shocked accepted protocol during his visit to the U.S. by visiting the headquarters of American corporate icons, Boeing and Microsoft, before visiting the White House. It was an effective stratagem to remind the American business community (and the U.S. Congress) that a lot of money is to be made by *doing* business with China.[32] In retrospect, this clever and nuanced 'twist' of China's foreign policy quite effectively promoted good ol' fashion corporate greed in the U.S. Thus, diminishing potential neo-conservative plans toward containing and threatening China's future as an Asian power, and its recognized territorial sovereignty.

Chalmers Johnson, professor emeritus at the University of California, San Diego, and former CIA analyst, wrote an interesting paper, "*No Longer the 'Lone' Superpower: Coming to Terms with China*", on the new reality facing America with the rise of China. Johnson, who is presently the Director of the Japan Policy Research Institute, believes if we base our analysis concerning the future of East Asia, during the 21st century, on what occurred in the 20th century, we might be in for a very troubling time.[33] According to Professor Johnson, "The major question for the twenty-first century is whether this fateful inability to adjust to changes in the global power-structure can be overcome."[34]

Johnson also indicates that the U.S. and Great Britain were not very conciliatory toward the rise of new powers during the 20th century—Germany, Japan and Russia—which he believes led to the following: two world wars, a 45-year Cold War, the Vietnam debacle and numerous clandestine involvements with wars of national liberation. The former CIA analyst points to arrogance and racism as being the primary foundational factors of American, European, and Japanese colonialism and imperialism.[35]

Perhaps, a new multi-polar global landscape will provide a different version of 'containment' for America and China. Johnson quotes *Time* magazine writer, Tony Karon, "All over the world, new bonds of trade and strategic

cooperation are being forged around the U.S. China has not only begun to dis-
place the U.S. as the dominant player in the Asia Pacific Economic Cooperation (APEC) . . . it is emerging as the major trading partner to some of Latin
America's largest economies."[36] China is a part of an emerging independent
marketplace in East Asia. In 2002, Yoichi Funabashi, a senior Japanese political commentator, stated, "The ratio of intra-regional trade (in East Asia) to
worldwide trade was 52% in 2002."[37]

After reading Professor Johnson's work on America coming to terms with
China, I came away thinking that two former methodologies of dealing with
a rising hegemonic power will not work with present-day China. First, military confrontation with the Chinese would end globalization as we know it,
because China is the economic locomotive for East Asia—where the fastest
growing economies exist in the world. Also, during the past decade, China
has purchased billions of dollars worth of U.S. Treasury bills financing our
over-consumption as a society, and American corporations have invested
billions into the Chinese economy. *All* would be lost if a war occurred between these two major powers. Secondly, the implementation of some kind
of containment policy will not work either. This places America's allies in an
untenable position—pick America or China. America, for many Asia-Pacific
nations, represents their security blanket against a rising China, or a resurgent
Japan. Though, all nations in Asia-Pacific trade with the U.S., there is no
doubt, in any anyone's mind, that it is the Chinese economy that is pulling
the economic wagon in the region.

Finally, I want to present a final perspective on U.S. activities and policies
in Asia. Lee Sustar, editor of the *Socialist Worker* newspaper, believes that
the U.S. is moving with undue haste during the past few years to consolidate
its vulnerable positions in Central Asia and the Pacific. Sustar interprets
Washington's overly-energetic behavior in Central Asia and the Pacific as a
result of its failing wars in Iraq and Afghanstan. The byproduct of America's
recent efforts in these two key regions is identified by Sustar as 'Little
NATO'—membership includes the U.S., Australia, Japan, Philippines, and
Thailand. Of course, the U.S. government and military told questioners that
their real reason for enhancing relations with the 'Little NATO' countries was
the 'war on terror'.[38]

In reality, these efforts were in concert with other efforts, according to
Sustar, to "conceal the real aim of the operation: to encircle China by hard-
wiring the military's regions to the Pentagon and positioning Special Forces
and 'counter-terrorism' units."[39] Later on in the article, the editor of the
Socialist Worker, points out that the Pentagon's 2006 *Quadrennial Defense
Review* identified China as the greatest threat to America's military suprem-
acy throughout the world, "Of the major and emerging powers, China has

the greatest potential to compete militarily with the United States and field disruptive military technologies that could over time offset traditional U.S. military advantages absent U.S. counter-strategies."[40]

The strain upon the U.S. military due to an unexpected high level of resistance in Iraq and Afghanistan have indeed taken its toll, but, according to Sustar, it has not deterred the U.S. government from its primary objective to pursue an encirclement strategy concerning the Middle Kingdom, "Containing China is U.S. imperialism's overarching—and highly dangerous—goal."[41]

Interestingly, even though Sustar is the editor of a leftist newspaper, and his reflections echo the sentiments of fellow travelers throughout the world, his perspectives very are similar to foreign policy titan and conservative Republican, Henry Kissinger. Both men are from distinctly different walks of life, politically, but both are equally dubious about the chances of success if the U.S. implements 'containment' as a strategy against China in the 21st century.

I want to present some final observations on America and its difficulties in Asia-Pacific during this period of historic transition. The U.S. could find itself very lonely if they mishandle the 'China Factor'. I have learned from living, researching, studying and working in this region for approximately a decade is that America is still greatly respected, and it remains a symbol of success to most Asians. However, as always, 'times are a changin' as the old Bob Dylan song goes, and America is experiencing a fundamental and seismic shift in its influence throughout Asia-Pacific—economically and militarily.

In this chapter, you have been exposed to different perspectives about what America should do or not do, concerning its future relations with China. War, or the implementation of 'soft containment', is not the right remedy, or a real choice, when evaluating the present geo-strategic challenges confronting America with concern to China's rise in Asia-Pacific.

Either path will lead the United States toward disastrous results: The first path (war) will lead to the potential destruction of regional financial institutions, and regional trade and security agreements established after WWII. The post-WWI era (1920-1939) is a prime example of how difficult it is to put the world back together after a global conflagration; The second path (containment) will potentially produce the political isolation of China—which may very well lead to the destruction of the established regional defense agreements amongst America's most ardent allies since the early 1950s.

Put bluntly, several U.S. allies (Australia, South Korea, and Japan) are increasingly dependent upon business contracts with the Chinese government to keep their national unemployment levels low, and their national economies productive and prosperous.

If our key allies in the region perceive America having *provoked* a military confrontation with China over a rather *dubious* issue (i.e. trade tariffs, copyright laws or currency manipulation), or a matter of *vital* interest to the Chinese (i.e. Taiwan, access to energy or a 'preventive' attack upon North Korea), America may very well find itself all alone in the biggest geographical backyard in the world—Asia-Pacific.

I believe the next ten to fifteen years will be extraordinarily important for the future prosperity and stability of the most dynamic and fastest growing region in the world. Some have already termed the 21st century—'The Pacific Century'. Can the 'roots of war' be avoided in the 21st century? I firmly believe it can, despite the factors of hegemony, history and politics being powerful forces which have often influenced and shaped human history. Perhaps, in the end, it will be this knowledge and the wisdom produced by it, that will save us from ourselves in this century.

NOTES

1. Tim Shorrock, "China's Elite Clearly Split over Foreign Policy", *Asia Times*, 15 February 2002.

2. William H. Overholt, *Asia, America, and the Transformation of Geopolitics* (New York: Cambridge University Press, 2008), pp. 224–225.

3. Henry Kissinger, *Does America Need a Foreign Policy? Toward a Diplomacy for the 21st Century* (New York: Simon & Schuster, 2001), pp. 145–149.

4. Ibid., p. 149.

5. Ibid., pp. 145–149.

6. Derek McDougall, *Asia Pacific in World Politics* (London: Lynne Rienner Publishers, 2007), p. 324.

7. John Mearsheimer, *The Tragedy of Great Power Politics* (New York: W.W. Norton & Company, 2001)

8. Zbigniew Brzezinski, *The Choice: Global Domination or Global Leadership* (New York: Basic Books, 2004), pp. 118–120.

9. Zbigniew Brzezinski and Brent Scowcroft (moderated by David Ignatius), *American and the World: Conversations on the Future of American Foreign Policy* (New York: Basic Books, 2008), p. 114.

10. Ibid., pp. 114, 119.

11. Paul Krugman, *The Return of Depression Economics and the Crisis of 2008* (New York: W. W. Norton & Company, 2009), p. 189-191.

12. Emad Mekay, "U.S. Warned on War Spending and Deficits", *www.zmag.org*, 1 October 2006.

13. Ibid.

14. Paul Kennedy, *The Rise and Fall of the Great Powers: Economic Change and Military Conflict from 1500 to 2000* (New York: Random House, 1987).

15. Joseph Nye, *Bound to Lead: The Changing Nature of American Power* (New York: Perseus Publishing, 1991).

Niall Ferguson, *The Cash Nexus: Money and Power in the Modern World, 1700-2000* (New York: Basic Books, 2001).

16. Jyoti Thottam, "Where the Good Jobs Are Going", *Time*, 28 July 2003. I pulled this article off the website: www.time.com.

17. Martin Crutsinger, "Factory Jobs: 3 Million Lost Since 2000", Associated Press, *USA Today*, 20 April 2007.

18. Frank Bentayou, "Ohio Job Loss Second Only To Michigan Since 2000", *The Plain Dealer*, 22 October 2008.

19. Richard C. Longworth, *Caught in the Middle: America's Heartland in the Age of Globalism* (New York: Bloomsbury USA, 2007)

20. Richard C. Longworth, "Can The Midwest Regain Its Economic Clout", *Chicago Tribune*, 6 January 2008.

21. Ibid.

22. Kathy Barks Hoffman, "Michigan Auto Jobs Continue to Disappear; Loss May Be Slowing", *Associated Press*, WSBT 22 (Michigan Television Station), 25 May 2008.

23. Ibid.

24. Kalamazoo Gazette, "Michigan Loses 34% of Auto Jobs, Still Leads Nation, *Michigan Business: International and Local Small Business News on Economics & Finance*, 8 October 2007.

25. Bernard Simon, "Toyota Overtakes GM As Top Carmaker", *Financial Times*, 21 January 2009.

26. Robert Morley, "The Death of American Manufacturing", *The Trumpet. Com*, February 2006. The subtitle of the article: "Globalization and Outsourcing Are Hammering Our Icons of Industry"

27. Niall Ferguson, *Colossus: The Price of America's Empire* (New York: Penguin Group, 2004).

28. Peter Baker and Susan Glasser, *Kremlin Rising: Vladimir Putin's Russia and The End of Revolution* (New York: Schribner's—A Lisa Drew Book, 2005); At an event at the bookstore called Politics and Prose, in Washington, DC, these two writers made it quite clear that Russian democracy is increasingly a sham.

29. Edited by Klaus Dodds and James D. Sidaway, *The Geographical Journal: Special Issue—Halford MacKinder and the 'Geographical Pivot of History'*, December 2004, Volume 170, Part 4, p. 298.

30. Michael T. Klare, "Containing China", _www.zmag.org_, 18 April 2006.

31. Ibid.

32. Ibid.

33. Chalmers Johnson, "No Longer the 'Lone' Superpower: Coming to Terms with China", *Japan Policy Research Institute*, March 2005, JPRI Working Paper No. 105.

34. Ibid.

35. Ibid.

36. Ibid.

37. Ibid.

38. Lee Sustar, "Containing China: The United States on the Asian Chessboard", *International Socialist Review*, July–August 2006.

39. Ibid.

40. Ibid.

41. Ibid.

Part III

THE 'ASIA-PACIFIC CENTURY'

Chapter Eight

Asia-Pacific Rising:
The Challenges, Dangers
and Prospects in the 21st Century

As the 21st century unfolds in Asia-Pacific, a new geopolitical language is emerging and its profundity may well define the future destiny of the region. The language itself is actually metaphorical terms representing the new attitudes and strategies amongst the major powers within this volatile area. George Orwell, the great English political satirist during the 20th century, possessed the linguistic gift of penetrating the literary artifice of manufactured political language that often represents a nation's concentrated and unending effort to propagandize, or 'spin', its citizenry's perception of reality. His classic work, *1984*, showed the disturbing, if not frightening, influence and power a government possesses in this regard, especially its *use* of language in *defining* that reality.

Thus, Orwell could truly appreciate and understand the nature of the new (and old) terminology being exercised today, and the inherent dangers it possesses with regard to defining the current situation existing within Asia-Pacific. Terms such as *'Area Denial'*, *'Hedging'*, *'Soft Containment'*, and *'Peaceful Rise'*, just to mention a few, are increasingly the recognized geopolitical identification terms used by national governments, regional analysts and policy experts, within their private and public domains, concerning the future development of this vital region.

Henceforth, this chapter will examine the emerging geopolitical challenges, issues and trends, and the geopolitical *'terms'* (i.e. strategies) that are now being presented as possible scenarios or solutions within the foreign policy community at-large. In essence, these new terms represent the present-day foundational language of those justifying or seeking regional influence and hegemonic power, if not absolute dominance, within Asia-Pacific during the 21st century.

THE RED DRAGON AWAKENS

The rise of China, and of Asia, will over the next decades, bring about a substantial reordering of the international system. The centre of gravity of world affairs is shifting from the Atlantic, where it was lodged for the past three centuries, to the Pacific. The most rapidly developing countries are located in Asia, with a growing means to vindicate their perception of the national interest[1]
Dr. Henry Kissinger, former U.S. Secretary of State (1973–1977)

The dramatic rise of China has certainly caught the attention of academics, global leaders, and journalists. *Financial Times* writer James Kynge, and author of critically acclaimed *China Shakes the World*, responded to a question from an individual who perceives China's rising stature as a threat to the western world, by stating, "China's rise is a big challenge, and a bigger potential challenge, to many people and countries in the West. But we should not despair, for a number of reasons, most of which are foreshadowed by the work of David Ricardo, the 18th century Scottish economist who described the principle of 'comparative advantage'. . . . China may dominate in manufacturing, it will continue to need the resources, energy and services that either cannot be supplied domestically or are better supplied from overseas."[2]

However, within the U.S. foreign policy and military establishments, it is China's emergence as a regional political and military power that has them increasingly concerned about the future development of Asia-Pacific in the 21st century. A plethora of articles, books, DVDs and reports are presently produced to analyze China's every action, decision or response to events within the region. These literary and media artifacts are now filling up shelves at various libraries within the U.S. government, think-tanks, colleges and universities, and foundations who have a vested interest in China and/or Asia. The Center for Strategic and International Studies and the Institute for International Economics published a work in 2006 that stated, "The direction that China and U.S.-China relations take will define the strategic future of the world for years to come. No relationship matters more in resolving the enduring challenges of our time . . . a rising China has an increasingly important impact on American prosperity and security, calling for some clear-eyed thinking and tough economic, political, and security choices."[3]

Eamonn Fingleton, author of *In The Jaws Of The Dragon*, believes the U.S. did not really understand the true dynamics of globalization and the devastating effect it would have on American society, and completely underestimated its affect upon Chinese society. In short, China has used the massive investments and technology provided by the West and used them to create an emerging export-driven financial juggernaut. Fingleton writes, "To Americans and Europeans, the most obvious aspect of this export-or-die strategy has been that Beijing has persuaded thousands of Western corporations to set up export-oriented subsidiaries on Chinese soil…Less obviously but almost equally important, Beijing has invested massively in providing exporters with a first-class infrastructure. . . The result is that the China-sourced content in Chinese exports has increased dramatically in the last decade—and with it the size of China's current account surpluses.[4]

According to Niall Ferguson, the Laurence A. Tisch Professor of History at Harvard University, author of the bestselling book, *The Ascent of Money*, that, in reality, America and China are now joint-partners in running the global economy in the first decade of the 21st century. Ferguson states, "Welcome to the wonderful dual country of 'Chimerica'—China plus America—which accounts for just over a tenth of the world's land surface, a quarter of its population, a third of its economic output and more than half of global economic growth in the past eight years."[5]

There is no doubt that quite a bit of serious thinking has occurred within the various government agencies, private foundations, non-profit organizations and corporate-sponsored think-tanks. Thus, it should not come as a surprise that a panoramic variety of viewpoints have emerged amongst and within these separate entities. Literally, these groups, and the experts and researchers within them, simply can not make up their minds on how to properly respond to China's emergence as a certified power in Asia-Pacific. The best example of this intellectual quandary and institutional indecisiveness was best presented by a former mid-level official in the Clinton administration, David Rothkopf, in his entertaining and insightful book, *Running the World*. Rothkopf, now a visiting scholar at the Carnegie Endowment for International Peace, mentions in his book that he surveyed almost 180 individuals at the institute, in 2005, on the matter of short and long-term U.S. foreign policy matters.

These individuals answered Rothkopf's multiple questions concerning American foreign policy, and the contentious issues and potential challengers to our global status today and in the near future. However, I will only focus on a few of the answers that Rothkopf and his research team obtained from those surveyed. These "experts" were asked twice a double-fold question: The first was which countries and/or entities are most likely to be important allies, friends, or otherwise important to the support of U.S. initiatives over the next five and the next twenty years? The second question was the flip side of the first question. Which countries and/or entities would most likely be America's potential adversaries, rivals, or challengers to our interests in the world over the next five years and the next twenty years? The answer given for ALL four categories: China.[6]

Though, China appears to be in everyone's equations concerning future 'great-power' scenarios, Bill Emmott, the former editor-in-chief of the

Economist, believes America and Europe are missing a much bigger development which is evolving right now in Asia. Emmott believes that the emerging competition between China, Japan and India for regional hegemony is intense and will be a far greater influencer than many geo-strategists think, he writes,

"Human affairs never have a sole driver or explanation, and it will be the same in Asia: The new power game between China, Japan and India is not going to shape everything that happens during the next few decades. But it is going to shape an increasing amount of what happens. Indeed, it is already doing so. Once you look at Asia through the prism of this balance-of power game, many things start to make more sense."[7]

In China, the foreign policy elite are equally split amongst themselves over the issue of how to respond to the preeminence of U.S. power within Asia-Pacific during the 21st century. Tim Shorrock, a writer for *Asia Times*, states "The country's government and intellectual elite are deeply spilt about how to deal with the world's only superpower . . ."[8] Shorrock interviewed Shi Yinhong, a professor of international relations at Renmin University, who is widely recognized for his work on China's internal debate concerning its role in the world. Professor Yinhong commented, "A rising China will be a somewhat uncertain and perplexed China, consistent and clear national strategies are still missing" from the national leadership. Thus, he further states that the country's foreign policy remains "inconsistent and fragmentary" which often reflects the "vicissitudes of immediate world events."[9]

According to China expert Bates Gill, the Freeman Chair in China Studies at the Center for Strategic and International Studies (CSIS), some Chinese scholars, government officials and military figures wish to continue the foreign policy principles established by former Chinese reformist leader Deng Xiaoping in the 1990s, such as China's intention to be a "responsible great power" and also that "China's peaceful rise" was the real agenda of the communist government. In fact, these particular security concepts, according to Gill, who prior to joining CSIS—was the former director of the Center for Northeast Asian Policy Studies at the Brookings Institution, find their intellectual roots within the Five Principles of Peaceful Coexistence which were established at the Bandung Conference in 1955.[10] Gill believes that China is presently, indeed, following the foreign policy precepts set down by former Chairman Deng, he writes, "Compared with past practices, China's diplomacy has indeed displayed a new face . . . from the 1980s to early this century is on the creation of an excellent environment for economic development, then the focus at present is to take a more active part in international affairs and play a role that a responsible power should on the basis of satisfying the security and development interest."[11]

Yet, there are Chinese scholars who remain very cautious with their analysis of China's 'peaceful rise'. For instance, Zhuang Liwei, a scholar from the Southeast Asia Research Institute at Jinan University in Guangdong Province, recognizes China's dramatic emergence but he is also aware of the country's inherent internal weaknesses,

> We can see a China in an awesome rising; at the same time, we should be well alert to the quality and costs of such rising. At present, China is getting ahead by its prosperity in material civilization, but the rise in damage to the environment and resources is creating a huge dilemma for the Chinese people. Meanwhile, the growth of China's GDP is overly dependent on foreign investment and budget expenditures, resulting in an extremely unbalanced economic structure.[12]

This immediate concern over internal factors undermining China's quest to regain its former prominence in Asian affairs, if not the world, is also echoed in Professor Susan Shirk's new work, *China: Fragile Superpower*. In *The Wall Street Journal*, a book review of Shirk's work revealed her serious concerns about China's 'rise' in the 21st century due to the government's deep-seated insecurities. She believes that China's profound insecurities about its restless citizenry and its increasing power and wealth are the real threats to Asia's future peace and stability, not its 'rise' as a regional power. Thus, the author observes, "preventing war with China is one of the most difficult foreign policy challenges our country faces."[13]

Professor Shirk, who teaches in the School of International Relations and Pacific Studies at the University of California—San Diego, observed that the Communist government has still not completely recovered from the Tiananmen Square uprising in 1989. She mentions in the article that the entire governmental apparatus almost collapsed upon itself during the student-led revolt against the government and its lack of accessibility. The government's calloused indifference toward the student protesters and their demands—more political freedom and participation in national affairs—only exacerbated the crisis; thus, putting an intense international spotlight upon China's domestic disorder, Shirk commented,

> In 1989, the Communist dynasty almost ended in its fortieth year. For more than six weeks, millions of students demonstrated for democracy in Beijing's Tiananmen Square and 132 other cities in every Chinese province. The Communist Party was spilt over how to deal with the demonstrations. And, the People's Republic just barely survived.[14]

Despite China's volatile domestic political situation and an enduring perception that their foreign policy remains a bit discombobulated and undefined at times, nevertheless, a new course of military action and development has emerged. It is a situation that is producing a heightening level of anxiety amongst its Asian neighbors, and new tensions particularly with the major powers situated in northeast Asia.

To give an example, China has slowly but steadily put together the makings of a potentially respectable blue-water naval force. Since the 1990s, the Chinese have developed, or purchased from Russia, submarines (conventional and nuclear-powered), destroyers (with supersonic anti-ship missiles) and frigates (home-grown air defense systems on them). Plus, there are persistent rumors that China is about to launch its first nuclear-powered ballistic missile submarines. The Beijing government has stated that this type of naval development is necessary to protect its future access to oil from the Middle East, gas from South-East Asia and the vital natural resources, primarily from Australia, which are absolutely necessary to ensure China's continued economic growth.

The U.S. government, however, finds China's geopolitical justification for the enlargement of its naval capabilities just a bit disingenuous because they believe its U.S. Navy has acted honorably in keeping the sea lanes open throughout Asia since the end of WWII.[15] As a consequence, *all* nations, including China, in the region have benefited from America's commitment to maintaining the freedom of the seas—everywhere. Therefore, the U.S. asks, skeptically, 'why the intense and sudden surge in naval (as well as the other military branches) development within China?'

This type of inquiry becomes more pertinent, not just due to China's growing naval prowess, but it is directly related to China's comprehensive and vast buildup of *all* its military capabilities. Thus, in 2007, the Office of the Secretary of Defense sent its Annual Report to Congress concerning the *"Military Power of the People's Republic of China"*. Its analysis, quantitatively and qualitatively, was quite stunning concerning the overall buildup and expenditures relating to the Chinese military. In the Executive Summary, the term 'Area Denial' was used by analysts to indicate China's intention to lessen, if not remove, America's military footprint in waters or regions vital to Chinese national security, particularly the Taiwan Straits. The term 'Area Denial' itself says it all. It is interpreted by U.S. geopolitical strategists, quite correctly, to mean that China would eventually like to see the U.S. military presence reduced to a minor role in regional security affairs.[16] However, I believe there will be a strong backlash amongst America's key allies, as well as amongst other concerned nations within the Pacific area, over China's prospective geopolitical agenda for the 21st century.

This significant departure from China's historic lack of a naval presence in the Asia-Pacific region appears to indicate, to many regional observers, that the Chinese now perceive America as a potential threat to their long-term economic development. Specifically, it is the U.S. Navy's control of the Malacca Straits through which approximately 80% of China's oil from the Middle East flows that has made the Chinese government increasingly uncomfortable.[17] It doesn't take a geopolitical genius to figure out that the Chinese leadership is unwilling to accept this degree of vulnerability from an economic or security standpoint. As a result, the Middle Kingdom has taken the historic step toward restoring its past maritime prowess.

China has not been able to project any type of real naval presence in East Asia, or anywhere else, since the 15th century and the dynamic travels of Ming dynasty Admiral Zheng He.[18] Admiral Zheng's exploits were magnificently described within Gavin Menzies's book, *1421*, that explored the idea that the Chinese admiral might have visited the North American continent approximately 90 years before Columbus. Menzies, a former British naval officer, after years of extensive research conducted at archival centers and museums throughout the world, does provide some very interesting evidence that has provoked a bit of a dust-up among historians.[19] Nevertheless, Michael Yahuda, professor of international relations at the London School of Economics, has written that the Chinese, historically and by nature, have not had overwhelming success in developing effective naval forces. Professor Yahuda writes, "Most of China's trouble (historically) came from powers that were strong at sea. For its decision-makers, there is a feeling that if China is to return to its true greatness, it has got to have a naval capacity."[20]

THE AMERICAN EMPIRE DIVIDED FROM WITHIN

The U.S. foreign policy establishment is gripped by indecision due to paralysis-through-analysis concerning its geopolitical response to China's dramatic rise in regional and global affairs. No doubt, there are indeed plenty of opinions, but they are mostly based upon, or contain within them, assumptions, attitudes, beliefs, a bit of paranoia, and fragments of racist untruths concerning China's history and future. Yet, there is significant evidence, thus far, that China has strongly promoted and utilized a cooperative and peaceful diplomatic course for itself with concern to the outside world, but especially in cultivating and developing new relationships with its Asian neighbors since the early 1990s. Its 'peaceful rise' has so far been given, to some degree, the benefit-of-the-doubt by its regional neighbors and by many American analysts.

There is also equally compelling evidence that China's somewhat benign foreign policy is due to the monumental challenges confronting the central government in Beijing. Much of their current domestic troubles (i.e. government corruption, environmental degradation, economic inequities, social unrest, unemployment, etc.) are related to their astronomical double-digit economic growth since 1980. Unfortunately, over 80% of the national growth has only occurred in the eastern portion of the nation—and primarily only in the cities. Literally, hundreds of millions in the eastern, central and western portions of China have not greatly benefited from this historic economic transformation.

Therefore, it is often mentioned by China-watchers that it is true that the nation's military buildup is quite real and geopolitically significant, but it is a *secondary* priority within the Chinese government due to the overwhelming challenges from within. The problems mentioned above are deeply troubling and extraordinarily dangerous for the current Communist Party and its political leadership. As demonstrated by Tiananmen uprising in 1989, the Chinese people hold the destiny of the nation in its hands. It is my belief that the Communist government will not use military force, again, against its own people because too many of the Chinese citizenry remember the carnage from the last engagement. Yet, the West *must* understand that if China collapses internally, the economic and geopolitical fallout will be massive, perhaps even endangering the future security and stability of the West, East, North, South, Middle East and all points in-between.

Therefore, in this section of the chapter, I will explore the wide spectrum of American opinions that exist within the foreign policy establishment. If we truly understand what is at stake—if we fail—then it becomes ever more imperative that the U.S. create a China policy that is based upon, and recognizes, both nations' national interests. Preserving regional and global security and stability, is not simply a cliché or overdone hyperbole. In a world that is increasingly interdependent, mishandling China and Asia-Pacific may very well lead to our own self-destruction. Hence, David Rothkopf's survey of the foreign policy experts and researchers at the Carnegie Endowment for International Peace is quite prescient in its exposure of an American intelligentsia that is confounded and stymied by its own interpretations, perceptions and shifting views related to what China *has* become and what it *will* be in the 21st century.

It is my own belief, that this fractured community of scholars has prevented the U.S. government, to a large degree, from creating a coherent and cohesive policy toward China. A number of critics have stated that what the U.S. foreign policy establishment needs is another George F. Kennan to emerge and create a unified and visionary post-Cold War, if not a post-9/11, global strategy. Kennan is often credited with being the primary architect of the 'containment' policy after WWII. In truth, though, 'containment' was often interpreted differently by various political factions, but, fundamentally, this geopolitical philosophy essentially represented the backbone of U.S. foreign policy for almost half a century. Former Secretary of State Henry Kissinger states unequivocally in his book, *Diplomacy,*

> (Kennan's) containment was an extraordinary theory—at once hardheaded and idealistic, profound in it assessment of Soviet motivations yet curiously abstract in its prescriptions. Thoroughly American in its utopianism, it assumed that the collapse of a totalitarian adversary could be achieved in an essentially benign way. Although this doctrine was formulated at the height of America's absolute power, it preached America's relative weakness.[21]

Needless to say, Kennan came as close as any single American, within his own generation, of creating a U.S. foreign policy that was primarily founded upon his own philosophy and vision to meet the challenges from America's primary post-WWII adversary—the Soviet Union. Today, it is believed that a similar philosophical and visionary global stratagem is greatly needed to address the dramatic rise of China and the multitude of possible implications for the West, particularly for the U.S.

In short, can we, yet again, create an instinctively, operational and rational geopolitical roadmap that can preserve America's vital interests and values without leading to a catastrophic conclusion in East Asia, and for the world? Where will the next geopolitical theory emerge from—perhaps, once again, from a gifted individual, or, maybe, from an institutional consensus? Equally important, will the current political environment allow such philosophy or vision to be refined and implemented properly? These are important questions that, unfortunately, are lacking answers at this time.

Thus, as expected, the current debate rages on amongst dedicated and serious-minded individuals seeking an appropriate, functional and respectful U.S. response to the looming and growing presence of China in the 21st century. The process itself is filled with vociferous and volatile exchanges within the American foreign policy establishment. As a result, it is very startling to witness former hard-nosed and uncompromising hawks from the Cold War era now fighting amongst themselves over the future direction of U.S. foreign policy in the 21st century—especially towards China and Asia. Simply put, the irrefutable fact remains that there is no acknowledged consensus concerning the presence of a philosophy, strategy or theory needed to meet the intense and varied challenges related to this contentious and vital geopolitical matter.

Perhaps, the most poignant and symbolic debate that is occurring within the U.S. foreign policy community is the one between Zbigniew Brzezinski and John Mearsheimer. Both men are greatly respected within the realm of U.S. foreign policy. Brzezinski was the key NSC adviser to former President Jimmy Carter from 1977 to 1981. Mearsheimer is a distinguished professor of international relations at the University of Chicago. Yet, their disagreement is a clear example of the deep policy and strategic chasm existing amongst U.S. analysts regarding China, and America's response to what many are calling 'The Pacific Century'.

In the January/February 2005 issue of *Foreign Policy* magazine, a debate between Professors Brzezinski and Mearsheimer entitled, "Clash of the Titans", was published which clearly indicates the tumultuous argument transpiring amongst America's elite experts with regard to China. Simply put, both men acknowledge the same factors, issues and trends associated with U.S.-China relations, China's rise (economically and militarily) and America's future status in Asia-Pacific. However, they simply interpret these major elements in a fundamentally different way.

Dr. Brzezinski believes that China is not presently inclined to challenge the U.S. militarily, but instead is very focused upon continued economic development and being accepted by the global community as an emerging global power. He believes that Mearsheimer's primary focus upon 'great power theory' is understandable and worthy, but theory is "essentially retrospective."[22] The former NSC adviser states, "When something happens that does not fit the theory, it gets revised. And I suspect that will happen in the U.S.-China relationship."[23] Finally, Brzezinski asks, "How can China push the United States out of East Asia?"[24] After mentioning the fact that if this occurred, Japan would almost certainly attempt to regain its former leadership role within the region, he finally observes, "Frankly, I doubt that China could push the United States out of Asia. But even if it could, I don't think it would want to live with the consequences: a powerful, nationalistic, and nuclear armed Japan."[25]

Professor Mearsheimer, however, in response, doesn't pull any punches on the matter of future U.S.-China relations, "China cannot rise peacefully, and if it continues its dramatic economic growth over the next few decades, the United States and China are likely to engage in an intense security competition with considerable potential for war."[26] He also believes that China's immediate neighbors, within the region, will assist America in containing the growing prowess of the Middle Kingdom. I am somewhat dubious of this assumption. Nevertheless, Mearsheimer is firm believer that an individual or nation requires a theory on understanding the behavior of a rising power and how the international community will react to its new prominence. He remains convinced that this theoretical approach will enable most rational-minded analysts to interpret the future actions of China, and Asia at-large, more accurately,

> To predict the future in Asia, one needs a theory that explains how rising powers are likely to act and how other states will react to them. My theory of interna-

tional politics says that the mightiest states attempt to establish hegemony in their own region while making sure that no rival great power dominates another region. The ultimate goal of every great power is to maximize its share of world power and eventually dominate the system.[27]

Hence, Brzezinski and Mearsheimer truly represent different "schools of thought" on present-day China and how the U.S. should perceive this 'rising' power in East Asia. Both schools have numerous advocates and representatives. The 'Brzezinski School', at least publicly, holds the upper hand at the moment in terms of debate and perception of what China means to the U.S. and its future status in East Asia. Judging from what I have heard on corporate television during the past few years, China represents the following:

1) A serious competitor for global manufacturing jobs, international investment and available natural resources; Also, it has increased its influence within Asia-Pacific;
2) A threat to global stability due to its terrifying environmental problems which are now slowly spilling over its borders and affecting the environments of other countries—including the United States.
3) A potential financial collapse due to its inability to handle the huge amounts of commerce, finance and trade, and massive government corruption. All of which could bring down the entire Asian-Pacific economy, and would probably represent the end of the ruling Communist Party as well; Thus, creating political and social chaos, and frightening instability, within a nation of 1.4 billion people.
4) The potential for a military conflagration with Taiwan, resulting in the geopolitical balance of power in Asia-Pacific being altered dramatically. Plus, the final outcome would not be a "slam-dunk"; In fact, you could count on it!

Despite these pressing realities and possible scenarios, the 'Brzezinski School' contends that China will continue to grow in significance and that their evolutionary process—for now- appears to be peaceful and productive for all concerned. Don't misunderstand this 'school of thought', China is certainly a country that needs to be reckoned and respected with the greatest degree of seriousness. Yet, as it stands today, there is no overwhelming evidence to initiate a fundamental re-thinking by Brzezinski and others about China's current status with the U.S., or with its neighbors throughout East Asia.

American politicians, scholars and noted China-watchers such as Henry Kissinger, David Shambaugh, Robert Sutter, G. John Ikenberry, and the Center for Strategic and International Studies are representative of those who agree, in principle, that China is not presently a direct military threat to the United States. Though, this could change in the near future. However, at this moment, they strongly believe these two hegemonic Pacific powers have far more in common, and at stake, represented by their mutual geopolitical interests, than the differences that are often focused upon by skeptical critics of U.S.-China relations and, especially China's future intentions concerning the Asia-Pacific region.

These sentiments, expressed by the distinguished China-watchers mentioned above, are echoed within the pages of Kishore Mahbubani's new book, *The New Asian Hemisphere*, concerning the influence that the U.S. has had on China since the 1970s. Mahbubani, dean and Professor in the Practice of Public Policy of the Lee Kuan Yew School of Public Policy at the National University of Singapore, writes ". . . just compare the state of Chinese society in 1972 with Chinese society in 2002. The Chinese civilization remained intact. But the approach of Chinese society to the rest of the world changed dramatically. Instead of threatening the world, China began to engage deeply. Half a million Chinese students have studied in American universities. Hundreds of thousands of Americans have visited China. By 2005, America had invested more than US$18.06 billion in China. Today, most Chinese people have one big dream: the American Dream. They want peace; their own homes, TVs, and washing machines; and to travel to Disneyland and study at Harvard. Without even trying to do so, America has completely transformed Chinese society."[28]

In 1971–1972, Dr. Henry Kissinger, then U.S. national security advisor and one of the primary architects, along with President Richard Nixon, designed and constructed a new American foreign policy paradigm specifically for the People's Republic of China. Kissinger and Nixon moved cautiously, but courageously, toward 'Opening China' and creating a new chapter in U.S.-China relations; even though it was considered politically controversial and, perhaps, even strategically dangerous by many conservatives within the American political establishment at the time. Upon hindsight, this dramatic and well-planned initiative is directly responsible for the present-day foundation for the reconfiguration of U.S. geopolitical relations within Asia-Pacific and with the most populous nation in the world—China. Thus far, it has proven to be an enormous success—for now.

NOTES

    1. Henry Kissinger, "China Shifts Centre of Gravity", *The Australian*, 13 June 2005.

2. James Kynge, "Ask the Expert", *Financial Times*, 15 May 2006. This was an online

3. C. Fred Bergsten, Bates Gill, Nicholas R. Lardy and Derek Mitchell, *China: The Balance Sheet—What the World Needs to Know Now About the Emerging Superpower* (New York: Public Affairs, 2006), p. 1.

4. Eamonn Fingleton, *In The Jaws Of The Dragon: America's Fate In The Coming Era of Chinese Hegemony* (New York: Thomas Dunne Books, 2008), pp. 284–285.

5. Niall Ferguson, *The Ascent of Money: A Financial History of The World* (New York: The Penguin Press, 2008), p. 335.

6. David Rothkopf, *Running The World: The Inside Story of the National Security Council and the Architects of American Power* (New York: Public Affairs, 2005), pp. 452–53.

7. Bill Emmott, *Rivals: How The Power Struggle Between China , India and Japan Will Shape Out Next Decade* (New York: Harcourt, Inc., 2008), p. 11.

8. Tim Shorrock, "China's Elite Clearly Spilt Over Foreign Policy", *Asia Times* online, 15 February 2002.

9. Ibid.

10. Bates Gill, *Rising Star: China's New Security Diplomacy* (Washington, DC: Brookings Institution Press, 2007), pp. 4–5.

11. Ibid., p. 203.

12. Zhuang Liwei, "Are We Prepared For a Peaceful Rise?", *Beijing Review*, January 2007.

13. Emily Parker, "Pursuing Power—Trying to Keep It", *The Wall Street Journal* online, book review of Susan Shirk's book, *China: Fragile Superpower*, 17 May 2007.

14. Ibid.

15. Mure Dickie and Stephen Fidler, "Dragon Fleet -- China Aims to End the U.S. Navy's Long Pacific Dominance", *Financial Times*, 12 June 2007, p. 9.

16. Office of the Secretary of Defense, *Annual Report To Congress: Military Power of the People's Republic of China—2007* (Executive Summary)

17. Dickie and Fidler, "Dragon Fleet", 12 June 2007, p. 9.

18. Ibid.

19. Gavin Menzies, 1421:

20. Dickie and Fidler, "Dragon Fleet", 12 June 2007. p. 9.

21. Henry Kissinger, *Diplomacy* (New York: Simon & Schuster, 1994), p. 471.

22. Zbigniew Brzezinski and John J. Mearsheimer, "Clash of the Titans", *Foreign Policy*, January/February 2005.

23. Ibid.

24. Ibid.

25. Ibid.

26. Ibid.

27. Ibid.

28. Kishore Mahbubani, *The New Asian Hemisphere: The Irresistible Shift Of Global Power To The East* (New York: Public Affairs, 2008), p. 274.

Bibliography

Akutsu, Hiroyasu. "A New Era for Japan-ROK Relations," *The Association of Japanese Institutes of Strategic Studies*, 14 March 2008.

Alford, Peter. "Japanese PM Faces a Mutiny," *The Australian*, 26 April 2008.

Auslin, Michael. "Caught between Giant Elephants," *The American* (A Magazine of Ideas), 11 December 2007.

Australia 2020 Summit, *Initial Summit Report*, April 2008.

Baker, Peter and Susan Glasser. *Kremlin Rising: Vladimir Putin's Russia and the End of Revolution* (New York: Scribner's—A Lisa Drew Book, 2005).

Bates, Gill. *Rising Star: China's New Security Diplomacy* (Washington, DC: Brookings Institution Press, 2007).

Beehner, Lionel. "The Rise of the Shanghai Cooperation Organization," *Council on Foreign Relations*, 12 June 2006.

Bello, Walden. "The Post-Washington Dissensus," *Foreign Policy in Focus*, 24 September 2007.

Bentayou, Frank. "Ohio Job Loss Second Only to Michigan since 2000," *The Plain Dealer*, 22 October 2008.

Berger, Suzanne. *How We Compete: What Companies around the World Are Doing to Make it Today's Global Economy* (New York: Currency—a division of Random House, 2005).

Bergsten, C. Fred, Charles Freeman, Nicholas R. Lardy and Derek J. Mitchell. *China's Rise: Challenges and Opportunities* (Washington, DC: Peterson Institute for International Economies, 2008).

Bergsten, C. Fred, et al. *China's Rise: Challenges and Opportunities* (Washington, DC: Peterson Institute for International Economics and the Center for Strategic and International Studies, 2008).

Bergsten, C. Freed, Bates Gill, Nicholas R. Lardy and Derek Mitchell. *China: The Balance Sheet—What the World Needs to Know Now About the Emerging Superpower* (New York: Public Affairs, 2006).

Bradsher, Keith. "China Seeking Auto Industry, Piece by Piece," *The New York Times*, 17 February 2006.

Brown, Lester R. "China is Replacing U.S. as World's Leading Consumer," *New Perspectives Quarterly*, Spring 2005.

Brown, Lester R. *Plan B 2.0: Rescuing a Planet under Stress and a Civilization in Trouble* (New York: W.W. Norton & Company, 2006).

Brzezinski, Zbigniew and Brenth Scowcroft (moderated by David Ignatius). *America and the World: Conversations on the Future of American Foreign Policy* (New York: Basic Books, 2008).

Brzezinski, Zbigniew and John J. Mearsheimer. "Clash of the Titans," Foreign Policy, January/February 2005.

Brzezinski, Zbigniew. *The Choice: Global Domination or Global Leadership* (New York: Basic Books, 2004).

Calder, Kent E. "China and Japan's Simmering Rivalry," *Foreign Affairs*, March/April 2006.

Callick, "Strong Ties with China Are Critical," *The Australian*, 17 March 2008.

Callick, Rowan. "China Close to Turning Point," *The Australian*, 2 August 2007.

Caryl, Christian and Akiko Kashiwagi. "This Nation Is an Island," *Newsweek* (International Edition), 12 May 2008.

Chaibong, Hahm. "The Two South Koreas: A House Divided," *The Washington Quarterly*, Summer 2005.

Cheong-mo, Yoo. "Lee Proposes Ministerial Talks with Japan, China Over Global Turmoil," *Yonhap News Agency*, 3 October 2008.

Cheong-mo, Yoo. "Lee, Hu Set New Milestone to South Korea-China Relations," *Yonhap News Agency*, 25 August 2008.

China Daily, "Japan Takes First Step in Revising Pacifist Charter," 15 May 2007.

Clark, Gregory. "No Rest for 'China Threat' Lobby," *Japan Times*, 7 January 2006.

Collier, Joe Guy. "Growth in China Gives GM a Boost," *Detroit Free Press*, 6 January 2006.

Crutsinger, Martin. "Factory Jobs: 3 Million Lost since 2000," Associated Press, *USA Today*, 20 April 2007.

Cumings, Bruce. "The World Shakes China," *The National Interest*, Spring 1996.

De Blij, Harm. *Why Geography Matters: Three Challenges Facing America* (New York: Oxford University Press, 2005).

Department of the U.S. Treasury/Federal Reserve Board, Major Foreign Holders of Treasury Securities, 16 September 2008.

Diamond, Jared. *Guns, Germs, and Steel: the Fates of Human Societies* (New York: W.W. Norton & Company, 2005).

Dickie, Mure and Stephen Fidler. "Dragon Fleet—China Aims to End the U.S. Navy's Long Pacific Dominance," *Financial Times*, 12 June 2007.

Dickie, Mure, Kathrin Hille and Demetri Sevastopulo. "Report Strikes Beijing Nerve at Politically Sensitive Time," *Financial Times*, 21 July 2005.

Dodds, Klaus and James D. Sidaway, eds. *The Geographical Journal: Special Issue—Halford MacKinder and the "Geographical Pivot of History,"* December 2004, Volume 170, Part 4.

Dumbaugh, Kerry. "China-U.S. Relations: Current Issues and Implications for U.S. Policy," *CRS Report for Congress*, Congressional Research Service—the Library of Congress, 20 January 2006.

Editorial, "China, the World's 4th Largest Economy?" *Asia Times*, 14 December 2005.

Editorial, "East Asia Community: Japan Should Work to Give Shape to Such a Bloc," *The Asahi Shimbun*, 21 November 2007, p. 25.

Editorial, "Security 'Key to Australia's Future,'" *The Australian*, 19 April 2008.

Editors, "Special Report: The Cold War in Asia—In Dangerous Waters," *The Economist*, 7 October 2006.

Emmott, Bill. Rivals: *How the Power Struggle Between China, India and Japan Will Shape Out Next Decade* (New York: Harcourt, Inc., 2008).

Ezrati, Milton. "On the Horizon: The Dawn of a New Sino-Japanese Rivalry," *Harvard International Review*, Volume 24 (1), Spring 2002.

Feffer, John. "The Paradox of East Asian Peace," *Foreign Policy in Focus*, 13 December 2007.

Ferguson, Niall. *Colossus: The Price of America's Empire* (New York: Penguin Group, 2004).

Ferguson, Niall. *The Ascent of Money: A Financial History of the World* (New York: The Penguin Press, 2008).

Ferguson, Niall. *The Cash Nexus: Money and Power in the Modern World, 1700-2000* (New York: Basic Books, 2001).

Fingleton, Eamonn. *In the Jaws of the Dragon: America's Fate in the Coming Era of Chinese Hegemony* (New York: Thomas Dunne Books, 2008).

Forney, Matthew. "Why China Loves to Hate Japan," *Time*, 10 December 2005.

Francis, Neil. "For an East Asian Union: Rethinking Asia's Cold War Alliances," *Global Catastrophe*, Volume 28 (3)—Fall 2006, Harvard International Review website.

Frost, Ellen. "Designing Asia: Chinese-Led Integration of East Asia Spurs an Economic Boom and Diminishes U.S. Role in the Region," *YaleGlobal*, 12 May 2008.

Fullilove, Michael. "Ban's Debut is Chance for Asia to Step in to Spotlight," *Financial Times*, 19 December 2006.

Glosserman, Brad and Katsu Furukawa. "A New U.S.-Japan Agenda," *Pacific Forum CSIS*, Volume 8, Number 4, Honolulu, Hawaii, March 2008.

Green, Michael. "The Role of Japan in Securing Stability in Asia," *The Center for National Policy*, 28 May 2008.

Green, Michael. *The Koreans: Who They Are, What They Want, Where Their Future Lies* (New York: St. Martin' Griffin, 2004).

Gyngell, Allan and Michael Wesley. "Regional Diplomacy Has New Impetus," *The Australian Financial Review*, 3 April 2008.

Haass, Richard N. "What to Do about China," *U.S. News and World Report*, 20 June 2005.

Heginbotham, Eric and Christopher P. Twomey. "America's Bismarckian Asia Policy," *Current History*, September 2005.

Hoffmann, Kathy Barks. "Michigan Auto Jobs Continue to Disappear; Loss May be Slowing," Associated Press, *WSBT* 23 (Michigan Television Station), 25 May 2008.

Hutton, Will. *The Writing on the Wall: Why We Must Embrace China as a Partner or Face It as an Enemy* (New York: Free Press, 2006).

Hyo-sik, Lee. "Economic Trouble Deepens," *The Korean Times*, 1 August 2008.

International Institute for Strategic Studies, "The Shangri-La Dialogue," *Asia Security Summit*, May–June 2008, Singapore.

Jeong-ju, Na. "Seoul Maps Out Countermeasures to Tokyo's Claim Over Dokdo," *The Korean Times*, 14 July 2008.

Jin, Ryu. "Asia Summit Augurs Power Struggle," *The Korea Times*, 14 December 2005.

Johnson, Chalmers. "No Longer the 'Lone' Superpower: Coming to Terms with China," *Japan Policy Research Institute*, March 2005, JPRI Working Paper No. 105.

Johnson, Chalmers. "Why the U.S.-Japan Security Treaty is in Trouble," *Pacific Rim Report*, February 2000.

Kalamazoo Gazette, "Michigan Loses 34% of Auto Jobs, Still Leads Nation," *Michigan Business: International and Local Small Business News on Economics & Finance*, 8 October 2007.

Kaplan, Robert D. "How We Would Fight China," *The Atlantic Monthly*, June 2005.

Kelly, Paul. *100 Years: The Australian Story* (New South Wales: Allen & Unwin, 2001).

Kennedy, Paul. *The Rise and Fall of the Great Powers: Economic Change and Military Conflict form 1500 to 2000* (New York: Random House, 1987).

Khanna, Parag. *The Second World: Empires and Influence in the New Global Order* (New York: Random House, 2008), p. 262.

Ki-Moon, Ban. "For Permanent Peace: Beyond the Nuclear Challenge and the Cold War," *Harvard International Review*, Summer 2006.

Kissinger, Henry, "The Three Revolutions," *The Washington Post*, 7 April 2008.

Kissinger, Henry. "China Shifts Centre of Gravity," *The Australian*, 13 June 2005.

Kissinger, Henry. *Diplomacy* (New York: Simon & Schuster, 1994).

Kissinger, Henry. *Does America Need a Foreign Policy? Toward a Diplomacy for the 21st Century* (New York: Simon & Schuster, 2001).

Kitazume, Takashi. "Changing World Asks More of Japan," *The Japan Times*, 24 November 2007.

Klare, Michael T. "Revving Up the China Threat," *The Nation*, 24 October 2005.

Krugman, Paul. *The Return of Depression Economics and the Crisis of 2008* (New York: W.W. Norton & Company, 2009).

Kurlantzick, Joshua. "Pax Asia-Pacifica? East Asian Integration and Its Implications for the United States," *The Washington Quarterly*, Summer 2007.

Kynge, James. "Ask the Expert," *Financial Times*, 15 May 2006.

Kynge, James. *China Shakes the World: A Titan's Rise and Troubled Future—and the Challenge for America* (Boston: Houghton Mifflin Company, 2006).

Kyodo News, "Seoul, Taipei Wanted Nukes on Okinawa: Return Islands to Japan but Stay Strong for Cold War, They Told U.S.," *The Japan Times*, 22 November 2007.

Kyodo News, "U.S. Envoys Involved in '60s Secret Nuke Arms Pact," *The Japan Times*, 12 November 2007.

Larimer, Tim. "National Colors," *Time*, 16 August 1999.

Liwei, Zhuang. "Are We Prepared for a Peaceful Rise?" *Beijing Review*, January 2007.

Longworth, Richard C. "Can the Midwest Regain its Economic Clout," *Chicago Tribune*, 6 January 2008.

Longworth, Richard C., *Caught in the Middle: America's Heartland in the Age of Globalization* (New York: Bloomsbury USA, 2007).

Lowry Institute for International Policy, "Australians Turn to the United States but Are Increasingly Wary of China: Lowry Poll 2008," 28 September 2008.

Mahan, Alfred Thayer. *The Influence of Sea Power upon History* (originally published in 1890).

Mahbubani, Kishore. *The New Asian Hemisphere: The Irresistible Shift of Global Power to the East* (New York: Public Affairs, 2008).

Mallet, Victor. "Japan's Best Chance to Strike a Deal with China," *Financial Times*, 28 September 2006.

McDonnell, John. "Special Relationships are Fraught," *The Australian*, 14 April 2008.

McDougall, Derek. *Asia Pacific in World Politics* (London: Lynne Reinner Publishers, 2007).

Mead, Walter Russell. *Power, Terror, Peace and War: America's Grand Strategy in a World at Risk* (New York: Vintage Books, 2004).

Mearsheimer, John. "The Rise of China Will not Be Peaceful at All," *The Australian*, 18 November 2005.

Mearsheimer, John. *The Tragedy of Great Power Politics* (New York: W.W. Norton & Company, 2001).

Mohamad, Mahathir bin. "Globalization: Challenges and Impact on Asia," *Recreating Asia: Visions for a New Century* (Singapore: John Wiley & Sons [Asia], 2002).

Morita, Akio and Shintaro Ishihara. *The Japan that Can Say No: Why Japan will be First among Equals* (New York: Simon & Schuster, 1991).

Murai, Tomohide. "SDF Peace Missions for Stable Japan-China Relations," *The Association of Japanese Institutes of Strategic Studies*, 20 February 2008.

Nanto, Dick. "East Asian Regional Architecture: New Economic and Security Arrangements and U.S. Policy," *CRS Report for Congress*, Congressional Research Service, 4 January 2008.

News Brief, "GM, Ford See Sales in China Jump," *The Detroit News*, 9 January 2007.

Nye, Joseph S. "Future of Japan-U.S. Alliance," *The Korea Times*, 12 May 2008.

Nye, Joseph S. *Soft Power: The Means to Succeed in World Politics* (New York: Public Affairs, 2004).

Nye, Joseph. *Bound to Lead: The Changing Nature of American Power* (New York: Perseus Publishing, 1991).

Oakes, Laurie, "Election that Changes Everything," *The Bulletin*, 4 December 2007.

Oberdorfer, Don. *The Two Koreas: A Contemporary History* (New York: Basic Books, 2001).

Office of the Secretary of Defense, "The Military Power of the People's Republic of China," *Annual Report to Congress*, 2005.

Office of the Secretary of Defense, *Annual Report to Congress: Military Power of the People's Republic of China—2007* (Executive Summary).

Onishi, Norimitsu. "Japan's Likely Next Premier in Hawkish Stand," *The New York Times*, 2 September 2006.

Overholt, William H. *Asia, America, and the Transformation of Geopolitics* (New York: Cambridge University Press, 2008).

Pilling, David and Mure Dickie. "Japan's New PM Pushes for Summit with China," *Financial Times*, 28 September 2006.

Rigol, Natalia. "A Game of Giants: The Future of Sino-U.S. Relations," *Harvard International Review*, Spring 2005.

Rothkopf, David. *Running the World: The Inside Story of the National Security Council and the Architects of American Power* (New York: Public Affairs, 2005).

Samuels, Richard J. *Securing Japan: Tokyo's Grand Strategy and the Future of East Asia* (Ithaca: Cornell University Press, 2007).

Shanahan, Dennis. "Move to Join Security Group," *The Australian*, 2 April 2008.

Shaplen, Jason T. and James Laney. "Washington's Eastern Sunset: The Decline of U.S. Power in Northeast Asia," *Foreign Affairs*, November/December 2007.

Shenkar, Oded. *The Chinese Century: The Rising Chinese Economy and Its Impact on the Global Economy, the Balance of Power, and Your Job* (Upper Saddle River, NJ: Wharton School Publishing, 2006).

Sheridan, Greg. "PM Makes Great Leap on China," *The Australian*, 12 April 2008.

Shorrock, Tim. "China's Elite Clearly Split over Foreign Policy," *Asia Times*, 15 February 2002.

Simon, Bernard. "Toyota Overtakes GM as Top Carmaker," *Financial Times*, 21 January 2009.

Skilling, David. "An Asia-Pacific Century?" *The New Zealand Institute*, 21 April 2006.

Smith, Patrick. *Japan: A Reinterpretation* (New York: Pantheon Books, 1997).

Snyder, Scott. "Inauguration of Lee Myung-bak: Grappling with Korea's Future Challenges, Brookings Northeast Asia Commentry, *Brookings Institute*, 27 February 2008.

Spence, Jonathan D. "The Once and Future China," *Foreign Policy*, January/February 2005.

Sustar, Lee. "Containing China: The United States on the Asian Chessboard," *International Socialist Review*, July–August 2006.

Takagi, Seichiro. "Japan-China Relations: How to Build a 'Strategic Relationship of Mutual Benefit,'" *The Japan Institute of International Affairs*, 13 February 2008.

Takagi, Seiichiro. "Japan-China Relations: How to Build a 'Strategic Relationship of Mutual Benefit,'" *The Association of Japanese Institutes of Strategic Studies*, 13 February 2008.

Tan, Seng and Ralf Emmers, editors. "An Agenda for the East Asia Summit," *Institute of Defence and Strategic Studies* (Singapore, November 2005), Executive Summary.

Terrill, Ross. *The New Chinese Empire: And What it Means for the United States* (Cambridge, MA: Perseus Books Group, 2003).

The Associated Press, "Australia Calls for Security Forum: Regional Link Sought for Northeast Asia," *International Herald Tribune*, 7 June 2007.

The Economist, "Another Grey Man Bites the Dust," 4 September 2008.

The Economist, "Keeping His Head Just Above Water," 2 August 2007.

Vaughn, Bruce, "U.S. Strategic and Defense Relationships in the Asia-Pacific Region," *CRS Report for Congress*, Congressional Research Service, 22 January 2007.

Vaughn, Bruce. "East Asian Summit: Issues for Congress," *CRS Report for Congress*, Congressional Research Service, 9 December 2005.

Vaughn, Bruce. "U.S. Strategic and Defense Relationships in the Asia-Pacific Regions" (Washington, DC: Congressional Research Service Report for Congress, 22 January 2007).

Vogel, Ezra. *The Four Little Dragons: The Spread of Industrialization in East Asia* (Cambridge: Harvard University Press, 1991).

Walters, Patrick. "Cuts will Weaken Our 'Soft Power,'" *The Australian*, 11 April 2008.

Walters, Patrick. "Defense Spending Jumps 10.6pc to $22 Billion," *The Australian*, 8 May 2007.

Walters, Patrick. "East Asia Summit 'No Threat,'" *The Australian*, 14 December 2005.

White, Hugh. "Beyond the Defense of Australia: Finding a New Balance in Australian Strategic Policy," *Lowry Institute for International Policy*, Lowry Institute Paper 16, 2006.

Wilson, Robert. "China Exports Take Aim at Austalia," *The Australian*, 29 March 2006.

Ying, Ding. "The Season for Regeneration," *Beijing Review*, 15 May 2008.

Yongsheng, Zhou. "Rising Sun? Japan Tries to Establish Itself on the International Stage with its Assertive Foreign Policy," *Beijing Review*, 1 February 2007.

Zakaria, Fareed. *The Post-American World* (New York: W.W. Norton & Company, 2008).

Zhaokui, Feng. "Clearing Away the Ice: China and Japan are on the Right Path to Developing a 'Culture of Trust,'" *Beijing Review*, 12 April 2007.

INTERVIEWS

Interview with Alexander Downer, Australian Foreign Minister, Canberra, ACT, 22 May 2006.

Interview with Australian Foreign Minister Alexander Downer, 22 May 2006.
Interview with Don Oberdorfer, 28 December 2006.
Interview with Dr. Wu Huaizhong, 20 May 2008, Chinese Academy of Social Sciences, Beijing, China.
Interview with Peer Abigail, Australian Strategic Policy Institute, Canberra, *Australia*, 22 May 2006.
Interview with Peter Abigail, former Australian Army General, Canberra, ACT, 22 May 2006.
Interview with Professor Zbigniew Brzezinski, 8 January 2007.
Interview with Zhang Yong, 20 May 2008, Chinese Academy of Social Sciences, Beijing, China.
Interview with Zhang Yuping, 25 April 2006.

LECTURE/SPEECHES

Merle Goldman Lecture at Alma College (Michigan), 16 October 2006.
Australian Prime Minister Kevin Rudd speech, "It's Time to Build an Asia-Pacific Community," The Asia Society Australasia Centre, Sydney, Australia, 4 June 2008.
Australian Prime Minister Kevin Rudd speech, The Asia Society Australasia Centre, Sydney, 4 June 2008, titled "It's Time to Build an Asia Pacific Community.
C. Fred Bergsten speech, "Embedding Pacific Asia in the Asia Pacific: The Global Impact of an East Asian Community, *Japan National Press Club*, 2 September 2005.
Dr. Han Seung-Soo, Prime Minister of the Republic of Korea, "Global Korea in the 21st Century," 50th Anniversary and the Asian Institute Inauguration," 26 September 2008.
David Shambaugh Lecture. "The Changing Nature of the Regional Systems in Asia-Pacific," *Chicago Council of Foreign Affairs*, 26 January 2006.
White, Hugh. "Conflict in Asia: Why War in Asia Remains Thinkable," speech given at the IISS-JIIA Conference in Tokyo, Japan, 3-4 June 2008.

ONLINE SOURCES

Achcar, Gilbert. "Accessing China," www.zmag.org, 25 June 2005.
Bello, Walden. "All Fall Down: Ten Years after the Asian Financial Crisis," www.zmag.org, 13 August 2007.
Kelly, Paul. "Time May Not be Ripe," *The Australian* Blog, 9 July 2008.
White, Hugh. "Rudd's Asia Plan Lacks Conviction," *The Lowry Institute* Blog, 16 June 2008.
http://blogs.theaustralian.news.com.au/paulkelly/index.php/theaustralian.

Katz, Richard and Peter Ennis. "What Next for Japan?" www.foreignaffairs.org, 1 August 2007.

Klare, Michael T. "Continuing China," www.zmag.org, 18 April 2006.

McCormick, Gavan. "Korea at 60," www.zmag.org, 8 September 2008.

Mekay, Emad. "U.S. Warned on War Spending and Deficits," www.zmag.org, 1 October 2006.

Miks, Jason. "New Optimism for Japan-South Korea Relations, but Sources of Tension Remain," www.worldpoliticsreview.com, 3 March 2008.

Morley, Robert. "The Death of American Manufacturing," *The Trumpet.Com*, February 2006 ("Globalization and Outsourcing Are Hammering Our Icons of Industry').

Parker, Emily. "Pursuing Power—Trying to Keep It," *The Wall Street Journal* online, book review of Susan Shirk's book, *China: Fragile Superpower*, 17 May 2007.

Sachdev, Ameet. "Trade, China and Steel," *Chicago Tribune*, August 2005 (www.danieldrezner.com).

Shorrock, Tim. "China's Elite Clearly Split over Foreign Policy," *Asia Times* online, 15 February 2002.

Tabuchi, Hiroko. "Japan's Parliament Passes Anti-Terror Bill to Revive Indian Ocean Mission," *Daily Yomiuri* Online, 11 January 2008.

The Yomiuri Shimbun, "Aso Elected LDP Head," *Daily Yomiuri Online*, 22 September 2008.

The Yomiuri Shimbun. "Fukuda May Admit Pledge Can't be Met/Apology for Broken Pension Promise Eyed," *Daily Yomiuri Online*, 18 December 2007.

The Yomiuri Shimbun. "Fukuda Triumphs in LDP Race/New Leader Eyes 'Revival' of Party after Winning 63% of Vote, *Daily Yomiuri Online*, 24 September 2007.

Thottam, Jyoti. "Where the Good Jobs are Going?" *Time*, 28 July 2003 (www.time.com).

About the Author

Dr. Randall Doyle, a Visiting Assistant Professor, teaches courses related to the following topics: East Asian History, Modern China, the Asia-Pacific Rim, and American Diplomatic History at Central Michigan University. He has taught, studied and/or lived in Asia, Australia, Europe and North America during his academic career. Professor Doyle has taught at Central Michigan University since 2005.

In 2008, Dr. Doyle was awarded a *Visiting Professorship* from Aichi University and the International Center for Chinese Studies (ICCS), in Nagoya, Japan. *ICCS* is the highest rated institute concerning Chinese Studies in Japan. And, in 2008, he was also awarded a *Research Fellowship* from the Institute of Japanese Studies within the Chinese Academy of Social Sciences (CASS) in Beijing, China. *CASS* is the top-rated think-tank in Asia.

In 2006 and 2007, Professor Doyle received *Teaching Fellowships* to lecture on American Diplomatic History and U.S. Government and Politics at North China University of Technology in Beijing, China. In 2007, he also received a *Research Fellowship* from the Bob Hawke Prime Ministerial Centre at the University of South Australia.

In 2007, Dr. Doyle also lectured on U.S Foreign Policy at International Christian University in Tokyo, Japan, and at the International Center for Chinese Studies (ICCS) at Aichi University in Nagoya, Japan.

Professor Doyle's current research and next book, *The Dragon's Destiny*, will focus upon the future path of China during the 21st century. The Middle Kingdom is currently facing serious challenges and emerging problems, domestically and internationally. Either one, or both realms, simultaneously, might very well undermine its unprecedented economic reforms and success since 1978. Nevertheless, China will indeed play a critical role in the affairs concerning the Asia-Pacific region and the world during the 21st century.

Dr. Doyle has published books and articles, as well as given lectures in the U.S., and at international conferences in Asia and Europe, on various topics related to Asia-Pacific, U.S.-China relations, U.S. Diplomatic History, and contemporary Australian and American History. He has received numerous research grants, development awards, and teaching fellowships, all of which have greatly assisted his teaching and scholarly work during his tenure at Central Michigan University. His first encounter with Asia, and U.S. foreign policy, occurred during his military service in the United States Navy (1976–1980). He was stationed overseas at U.S. Naval Communication Stations (Harold E. Holt) in Western Australia and on the U.S. territory island of Guam.